UNITED STATES

Los Angeles

30°N

Oahu

Hawaii

H A W A I I

15°N

North Pacific Ocean

0°

Kiritimati

Line Islands

Marquesas
Islands

F R E N C H   P O L Y N E S I A

COOK ISLANDS

RICAN
AMOA

Tuamotu Archipelago

Society Islands

Tahiti

15°S

Rarotonga

Austral Islands

Gambier Islands

Pitcairn
Islands

uth Pacific Ocean

30°S

Easter

THE PACIFIC ISLANDS

Prepared for the Center for Pacific Islands Studies
University of Hawaii at Manoa
by Manoa Mapworks, Inc.
Revised 1991.

W—E

155°W

140°W

125°W

110°W

Woven Gods

Pacific Islands Monograph Series, No. 12

WOVEN GODS

FEMALE CLOWNS AND POWER IN ROTUMA

Vilsoni Hereniko

Center for Pacific Islands Studies
School of Hawaiian, Asian, and Pacific Studies
University of Hawai'i
UNIVERSITY OF HAWAI'I PRESS
Honolulu

95 96 97 98 99 00   5 4 3 2 1

Library of Congress Cataloging-in-Publication Data
Hereniko, Vilsoni.
Woven gods : female clowns and power in Rotuma / Vilsoni Hereniko.
    p.   cm. —(Pacific islands monograph series ; no. 12)
Includes bibliographical references and index.
ISBN 0–8248–1655–2
1. Ethnology—Fiji—Rotuma Island.   2. Clowning—Social aspects—
Fiji—Rotuma Island.   3. Folklore—Fiji—Rotuma Island—
Performance.   4. Marriage customs and rites—Fiji—Rotuma Island.
    5. Rotuma Island (Fiji)—Social life and customs.   I. Title.
II. Series.
GN671.F5H47   1995
398'.099611—dc20   94–13120
                                    CIP

Cartography by Manoa Mapworks, Inc.
Honolulu, Hawai'i

Designed by Kenneth Miyamoto

For Alan and Jan

Editor's Note

Vilsoni Hereniko's *Woven Gods: Female Clowns and Power in Rotuma* is volume 12 in the Pacific Islands Monograph Series, and the author brings unique talents and perspectives to his work. Hereniko spent the first sixteen years of his life on the small Polynesian island of Rotuma, the northernmost island in Fiji. His first major foray into the larger world came when he left home to complete his secondary education at the venerable Queen Victoria School not far from Suva on Viti Levu. Next came an undergraduate education at the University of the South Pacific, and thereafter Hereniko returned to Queen Victoria School as a teacher of English and history. Graduate studies took Hereniko to England, where he earned his master's degree from the University of Newcastle upon Tyne in 1982. Once again he returned to an alma mater as a teacher, this time to the University of the South Pacific, where he taught Pacific literature and launched a career as a playwright. Hereniko took his doctorate in 1992 at the same institution, and this monograph is a much revised version of his dissertation. In 1991, Hereniko joined the faculty of the Center for Pacific Islands Studies at the University of Hawai'i.

In the volume at hand, Hereniko is an ethnographer with a keen eye on his own people, but his vision is not limited by the boundaries of traditional academic disciplines. His primary focus is on the function of clowning in Rotuman marriage ceremonies, but he is also concerned with the wider phenomena of ritual clowning in the comparative context of Polynesia. Hereniko explores the origins and history of Rotuman clowning, and while his analysis is informed by cultural anthropology, comparative folklore, and the literary arts, it is an innovative departure from traditional ethnography. Hereniko dares to merge objective inquiry with intuitive and subjective insights that are ultimately rooted in the Rotuman part of his own identity. He draws on his talents as a creative writer and, from the depths of his imagination, provides an origin myth for Rotuman clowning.

In many respects, Hereniko's work represents a coming to terms with several dimensions of his own background—as Rotuman, western academician, teacher, and playwright. *Woven Gods* is a refreshing alternative to more traditional forms of scholarship and, it may be hoped, will inspire other Pacific Islanders to draw on their experiences and perspectives to examine their own cultures and histories.

Since moving to Hawai'i, Hereniko has been instrumental in introducing the indigenous literature of the Pacific to readers in America. As a professor, he has reached a large number of students at several campuses of the University of Hawai'i and the larger community in the state of Hawai'i. In an effort to reach an even larger reading audience, particularly in North America, he has recently become the editor of Talanoa, a new series in the literature of the contemporary Pacific, published by the University of Hawai'i Press. He has edited several issues of the literary journal *Mana*, published by the South Pacific Creative Arts Society, and he has been a guest editor for the journal *Mānoa: A Pacific Journal of International Writing*. His play, *The Last Virgin in Paradise*, met with much critical acclaim in Honolulu in the spring of 1994.

ROBERT C. KISTE

Contents

Illustrations

Acknowledgments

Many colleagues, between 1986 and 1993, have contributed to this final product. Funding and the loan of equipment, as well as moral support from my relatives and friends, have all been essential during the process of writing and researching this book.

This project officially began in 1985, when I was a lecturer in the Literature and Language Department of the University of the South Pacific (USP). Between 1986 and 1989, USP provided support in a number of ways. University funds allowed me to visit Rotuma in 1987 and 1989 to do field work. In 1990, USP granted me training leave. I left for Hawai'i, where I spent the next twelve months, financed by a grant from the Center for Pacific Islands Studies (CPIS) at the University of Hawai'i and the Pacific Islands Development Program (PIDP) at the East-West Center. Dr Robert C. Kiste, director of CPIS, and Dr Sitiveni Halapua, director of PIDP, helped me enormously by leaving me alone to write, unhindered by and uninvolved in the day-to-day concerns of their respective programs. I am also grateful to Dr Kiste for his understanding, patience, and continuing interest in my work.

Professor Alan Howard and Ms Janet Rensel helped me by being involved, from the beginning to the end. I needed a computer in 1990 and they loaned me one. I needed quick and constant feedback on what I was writing; they provided it. Because they were there, always, it is fitting that this book be dedicated to them, and, in particular, to Alan Howard, whose research and numerous publications on Rotuma have inspired and informed this work.

Others whose comments on various drafts I found particularly helpful include Dr Geoffrey White, Mr John O'Carroll, Dr John Charlot, Professor Barbara Babcock, Dr Terence Wesley-Smith, Professor Ron Crocombe, Professor Andrew Arno, Professor William Mitchell, Dr James Ritchie, Professor Epeli Hau'ofa, Professor Subramani, Dr Kerry James, Reverend Brian Macdonald-Milne, Dr Caroline Sinavaiana, Dr Ron Witton, Mr Tom Farber, and Ms Linley Chapman.

An important source of strength for me in Hawai'i were the many friends who invited me to their homes and treated me with much aloha: Paddy and Mary O'Sullivan, Michael and Safaira Ogden, Len and Hazel Mason, Mark and Jane Sturton, Epi Enari, John Charlot, and Renée Heyum. I am grateful, too, for the friendship of East-West Center students—particularly those associated with the Pan-Pacific Club—which helped keep me sane and entertained.

This book is the culmination of thirty-eight years' experience of and thinking about Rotuman culture and its people. My early years of growing up in Rotuma have been a source of confidence and inspiration during the course of this project. Memories of a father who loved to tell his children myths and legends in the evenings before bedtime, of a mother who gave birth to eleven children and yet managed to remain sane through it all, of brothers and sisters who struggled to provide the best education possible for their youngest brother: all these constantly remind me how much I owe to my parents and brothers and sisters, all of whom allowed me considerable freedom to be an individual in my own right. This early training in how to temper freedom with responsibility has stood me in good stead all these years, even as I researched and wrote this book.

Other Rotumans who have inspired me include the late Wilson Inia and his wife, Ilisapeti Inia. Their daughter Betty Inia as well as Vafo'ou Jiare, Harieta Katafono, Vaivao Fatiaki, the many clowns on the island, and my sister Vamarasi and relatives, particularly those living in or associated with Mea village in Hapmak, Rotuma, have all contributed to this work.

And so did Aren Baoa and Peter Miles who helped me in 1989 to produce a seventeen-minute documentary of the *Rotuman hȧn mane'ȧk su* 'ritual clown' who played in the wedding discussed at length in chapter 4. Unfortunately, because of practical difficulties, this videotape is not part of this package, although I have always intended it to be an integral part of this ethnographic work, providing a different voice, one that emphasizes the performative aspect of clowning. Anyone interested may acquire a copy of the videotape by writing to the Director, Media Center, University of the South Pacific, PO Box 1168, Suva, Fiji.

It is not possible to name all of the individuals who helped me in the course of this project; to you, should you ever come across this volume in a library or bookshop, my sincere apologies. May you feel included among those to whom I owe so much. If I had fine mats to give away, each of you would receive one!

Woven Gods

1 Prologue:
Homeward Bound

> In order to do interdisciplinary work, it is not enough
> to take a "subject" (a theme) and to arrange two
> or three sciences around it. Interdisciplinary study
> consists in creating a new object, which belongs to
> no one.
>
> ROLAND BARTHES, *The Rustle of Language*

Rotuma is so small that sometimes a dot cannot represent it faithfully on a map. More often than not, it is missing from a map because the cartographer is unaware the place exists. Nonetheless, it is there in the Pacific Ocean, situated approximately 470 kilometers north of Fiji, at the crossroads of Micronesia, Melanesia, and Polynesia. About 12 kilometers long and at its widest 5 kilometers across, Rotuma currently has a population of approximately 2,500 people, living in seven districts, each of which consists of a number of villages. The scholarly consensus is that the original inhabitants came from either Melanesia or Micronesia, followed by Samoan and Tongan invasions about the beginning of the seventeenth century (Gardiner 1898; Eason 1951; Irava 1977a; Shutler and Evrard 1991). Christianity was introduced in 1839, and in 1878 Catholics and Methodists fought. Warfare culminated in cession to Britain in 1881; since then Rotuma has been administered as part of Fiji, although its culture and language are different. About one-third of the inhabitants are Catholics; two-thirds are Methodists.

Rotuma is still relatively isolated, although the building of a wharf in the 1970s and the opening of an airstrip in 1981 have made modern goods, equipment, and Euro-American ideas much more accessible to people living on the island, who today constitute only a quarter of all Rotumans. Copra used to be the main source of income, but since Hurricane Bebe struck in 1972, it has been surpassed by remittances from relatives living in Fiji, Australia, New Zealand, and the United States. Concrete houses, refrigerators, indoor toilets, motorbikes, and pickup trucks are now common, evi-

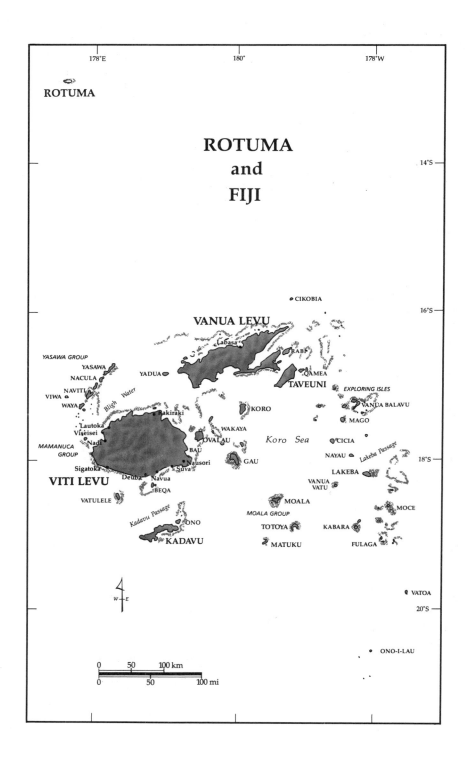

ROTUMA

ROTUMA
and
FIJI

178°E   180°   178°W

14°S

CIKOBIA

16°S

VANUA LEVU

Labasa

RABI

YASAWA GROUP
YASAWA
NACULA
YADUA
NAVITI
VIWA
WAYA

Bligh Water

QAMEA
TAVEUNI

EXPLORING ISLES
VANUA BALAVU
MAGO

KORO

Rakiraki
Lautoka
Viseisei
Nadi
MAMANUCA
GROUP

WAKAYA
OVALAU
BAU
Nausori
Suva

Koro Sea

CICIA
NAYAU

Lakeba Passage

GAU

18°S

Sigatoka
Deuba Navua
VITI LEVU
BEQA

VANUA
VATU

LAKEBA

VATULELE

Kadavu Passage
ONO

KADAVU

MOALA

MOALA GROUP
TOTOYA
MATUKU

KABARA

MOCE

FULAGA

N
W E

VATOA

20°S

0   50   100 km
0   50   100 mi

ONO-I-LAU

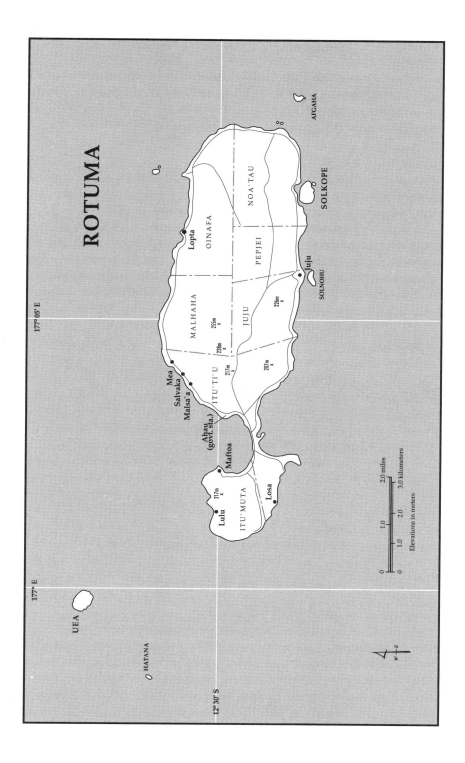

dences of a culture that has assimilated many ideas and influences from outside.[1]

Foreign goods and ideas that make their way to Rotuma are usually filtered through urban Fiji, where most Rotumans live. Frequent movement of people between Rotuma and Fiji means that the nature of life-crisis ceremonies on the island is determined to some extent by relatives in urban Fiji. The interplay of urban and rural influences, Christian and traditional beliefs, and Euro-American ideas and education for the past one hundred fifty years have resulted in an amalgam of customs and cultural traits that reflects the complexity of a society in transformation.

This transformation is most evident during Christmas season each year, when hundreds of Rotumans in Fiji and beyond return to the island to spend a few weeks with their relatives. In December 1992, I caught the *Wairua,* a cargo boat bound for Rotuma two days later. I was an individual among a large group of compatriots sometimes jokingly referred to as Rotuman "tourists." The *Wairua* was overloaded with some one hundred sixty passengers and cargo, making it difficult for everyone to find space on the deck to lie down comfortably. The last time I had been on such a boat was some twenty years before, when I made my first trip out of Rotuma into the big world of Fiji and beyond. I was only sixteen then. Now I'm approaching forty, assistant professor at the University of Hawai'i at Mānoa, and anxious about my ability to fit in with life on a small boat and Rotuma in general.

Since leaving Rotuma in 1970, I had been back several times (in 1981, 1987, and 1989), though only for a few weeks on each visit. On each of these visits, I had chosen to take the two-hour flight on Fiji Air. This time, I was catching the boat, partly because I could not get a plane seat during the Christmas season, but also because I wanted to relive the experience of being stranded on a small boat with fellow-Rotumans for two days and two nights. Two things happened during this trip that left a deep impression on me: the first made me unhappy, the second mitigated my distress and left me feeling at peace again by the end of the voyage.

Although I had asked my sister in Fiji to buy me a ticket for the deck, I learned on arriving from Hawai'i that whoever was in charge would sell me a ticket only for a room in the saloon. This was fine with me. I arrived at the boat two hours before it was supposed to leave and saw the man in charge of room allocation. He was most helpful and courteous: he showed me my cabin, and with the help of a brother and friends, we carried my suitcase and assortment of boxes onto the boat and into my room. After putting away my luggage, I went ashore to await the time when the boat would leave for Rotuma.

More and more people arrived at the wharf as the time of departure drew nearer and nearer. Passengers waited for their names to be called before they could board the boat. My name was the first. I climbed the wooden plank that led onto the boat and went straight to my cabin. Much to my surprise, I found my suitcase and boxes outside the room that had been allocated to me and beside a bed in the passageway where there was little privacy. As I stood there in dismay, the man who had assigned me the room appeared. This is a literal translation of what he said: "Don't be angry, but you will have to sleep on that bed [pointing] instead. I tried my best to stop what happened. The man who did this is more powerful than I, so I couldn't stop him. He wants his relatives inside your room. I told him that this is wrong, that this is not a boat that belongs to him and his kin. . . . I told him what I thought of his actions. I'm really sorry."

My anger dissipated when I saw how genuine this young man was, but nonetheless I told him that one of my bags was missing. He opened the room and we entered. Suitcases and boxes lined the walls. "Just look at these [pointing at the bags and the name tags]. It's people from Hapmak [which includes the village of Mea where I come from], your own people, who are doing this to you." I took my bag from the room and left, not wanting to know any more.

I was distressed that another Rotuman could be so callous to a compatriot. Although I did not particularly care to be in the room, as the air-conditioning had broken down and it was claustrophobic inside, this was not the point. Someone in a position of influence in Fiji had treated me badly, and I was hurt and disappointed that "my own people" would do this. I did not think this was typical Rotuman behavior at all. Or perhaps, I thought to myself, you have been out of touch. Welcome to the real world!

The second incident happened as I was lying in bed trying to sleep on the second night at sea, when I heard raucous laughter. I climbed up to the deck to find about thirty men and women singing popular Rotuman songs and kidding around. Someone would request that a song be sung—usually a silly song—and the others would laugh. The title of the song then became an excuse for all kinds of sexual innuendo and allusions. An example should suffice: A woman asked for the popular song "*Re se 'on mose ka hạsut surum*

'She dreamt that a horse came inside'." A man then responded: "*Re se 'on mose ka 'ait surum* 'She dreamt that a stick [*'ai* can mean different things: plant, tree, rod, etc.] came inside'." The men and some women burst into laughter. A different man then announced: "*Ma ia mamaf se ka 'on püs ta uf* 'And when she woke up, her vagina had been ripped apart'." At this, everyone burst into laughter again: everyone, that is, except a few women who seemed (or were they pretending?) offended. As I watched the kidding around and sang along with the group, I realized that a middle-aged woman dressed in a slightly eccentric manner (she wore short pants, make-up, and jewelry) was the catalyst. She was the one suggesting the titles of the silly songs, provoking the men to rise to the bait. She would then feign offense or deny any responsibility if someone accused her of initiating the outrageous joking that ensued. The group would then sing the song, and the general pattern would repeat itself. As I laughed and sang, I became aware that some of the jokes, for me, were shocking. But all this fooling around helped me forget the first incident, and by the time Rotuma appeared on the horizon, I was at peace again: with myself, and with the occupants of the room next door.

Like many Rotumans before and after me, I had left the island when I was sixteen to pursue a western education and career. Though my training, experience, and lifestyle may give the impression that I have forsaken my Rotuman heritage in favor of western ways of being and thinking, my early Rotuman upbringing remains an important window from which I view external reality. Sometimes I experience a struggle as my Rotuman self is challenged by and refuses to succumb to the pressures exerted by its Euro-American counterpart. Sometimes, my identity oscillates between these two positions, uncertain which to privilege or deemphasize. This tension was most evident when I arrived in Rotuma in 1987, with a film crew from the University of the South Pacific, to shoot a documentary of a *hàn mane'àk su*[2] 'woman who plays at the wedding' performing at a traditional wedding.

The use of technical equipment (tape recorders and cameras particularly) drew attention to me as an outsider. My physical appearance and ability to speak Rotuman, however, meant that I was acceptable as an insider. For instance, one Sunday morning we decided to film a choir competition. We arrived to find a group of men sitting outside the church building, waiting to go in. As the men watched, I held out a white board in front of the camera while the video producer adjusted his light meter. Then we attended to another matter. Laughter erupted. We turned around to find that two villagers were mimicking the scene they had just witnessed, burlesquing us. In all likelihood, these men found our actions strange and incomprehensible. Their laughter made me feel as though one part of myself was laughing at the other: specifically, my Rotuman self mocking my Euro-American self. This fleeting moment was like a flash of lightning in the dark, and, fortunately for me, illuminated a double exposure of myself that I had never been privy to before. What I saw was a man straddling two cultures (at least), neither one nor the other, but a hybrid. To accept this image is to accept difference, to accept one's identity, and to embrace a multicultural self. Further, this incident illuminated for me the role of clowning; for example, the way the clown's outrageous antics and bawdy language remind us of a part of ourselves we continually suppress in day-to-day interactions in order to appear respectable and acceptable to the majority.

In many instances, I felt torn between different subject positions: insider, outsider, or a synthesis of both? Should I remain betwixt and between? Is my role as researcher more precious to me than my identity as a Rotuman? As both insider and outsider, I had to carefully negotiate each encounter with other individuals of different social status; the bottom line for me was that if a decision had to be made as to whether my data or my relationship with other Rotumans was more important, the latter would prevail. This meant that the most comfortable approach for me as a researcher was to immerse myself in what people were doing. Later, I reflected on the events of the day, and their relevance to my research. Ironically, I found myself relying on white colonial accounts of Rotuma's history and culture to illuminate the trail that would lead to a better understanding of my Rotuman heritage. Gathering data this way meant that my heart and my head were both involved; my intuitions and instincts often providing me with clues as I sought to understand my experiences. This essentially subjective approach complemented the rational, scientific approach advocated by some sections of anthropology and other social sciences.

This "technique of participation that demands total involvement of our whole being" while doing fieldwork (Turnbull 1990, 51) is at odds with the western notion that knowledge should be split up into little compartments called disciplines. Anthropology, theater, literature, sociology, history—all fragments of the whole, a way of under-

standing culture that is alien to me. As a Rotuman, I am more comfortable with an integrated approach when attempting to understand Pacific societies, one that is holistic and embodies my personal
and cultural experience of reality. My topic is clowning; I want to
understand this phenomenon as fully as possible. To limit myself to
a single discipline is to limit my angle of vision. The result of such
an approach would be a study that is narrow and likely to be of little
use outside the confines of disciplines or university corridors. For
instance, what use would it be to me or Rotumans if I were to set out
to prove that clowning in Rotuma is theater and not some other
kind of genre by analyzing it in terms of its elements?

Another important issue is the question of objectivity and
whether it is possible or desirable in research of this nature.
Although the authorial voice in so-called objective ethnographies is
now regarded with suspicion, some traditions are hard to shake off;
the divide between the subjective and the objective or fiction and
nonfiction still exists in popular consciousness. In recent years, however, much debate and contention in anthropology has been concerned about the nature of culture, truth, and representation,
leading James Clifford, for example, to claim that ethnographic
texts are "constructed domains of truth, serious fictions" (1988, 10).
Many fiction writers will say this is what their work has been about all
along, and they should be forgiven if they are unimpressed by the
late arrival of the social scientist. Creative writers readily accept the
fictional and subjective nature of representation, unlike most social
scientists, who still cling to an academic style of writing that gives the
impression literary language has no stake on truth. This is unfortunate because fiction is the best medium for the expression of the
concrete as well as the abstract, the physical and intellectual as well
as the emotional. Fiction, like clowning, plays at being someone or
something else in a created and therefore different world. Through
implication and indirect means, broader patterns and parallels are
suggested, allowing the researcher to find clues that sometimes lead
to the discovery of further truths.[3] This "subtle interplay between
personal and disciplinary components" (Clifford 1988, 54) and the
blurring of boundaries between ethnography and fiction is welcome
indeed.

Similarly, I have many selves, all jostling for a space in this work.
There is a Rotuman self, a fiction-writing self, and an interpretive
"anthropological" self, at least. Do I deny certain parts of myself in
this scholarly study, or do I exploit my many selves to inform my

analysis? As a Rotuman engaged in a scholarly endeavor, which self should I privilege and why? These questions and tensions fuel the explorations in these pages as I attempt to harmonize these various and seemingly opposed selves. Fiction and nonfiction, subjective and objective accounts, intuition and dreams inform the findings in this book, and pose questions that are equally problematic for "western" scholarship. Let me elaborate.

Chapter 2 is a straightforward account of different contexts in which Rotuman clowning is manifest. It contains background information that exists in many scholarly works of this nature. Following is chapter 3, which is fictional, its purpose being to capture the emotional feel of a live performance, from the point of view of an observer watching from the audience, and from the inside of a clown's mind. These two fictional narratives are inspired by my own knowledge and experiences of Rotuman clowning at weddings; they attempt to capture emotional truths about clowning in Rotuma, something an "objective" account cannot convey.

Chapter 4 is an ethnographic account of the Rotuman social and cultural context in which clowning is embedded. Myths are analyzed to provide insight into the role of clowning and humor in relations between chiefs and commoners and between males and females. These two themes serve as a foil for the discussion of the social, cultural, and political contexts of clowning that follow.

Chapter 5 focuses on a specific Rotuman wedding to see how the themes of chapter 4 are played out on the days when the *hàn mane'àk su* performs—before, during, and after the wedding. Clowning is seen as an inversion of important Rotuman values, and the clown as playing multiple roles in the wedding context. The question of the origins of the institution of clowning, however, remains unanswered.

Chapter 6 begins with a created myth that explains the origin of the *hàn mane'àk su*. Significant elements in this myth are then identified and used to inform the mythological and cultural analyses in this chapter. The main interpretation in chapter 6, and the book as a whole, is that clowning in Rotuma was linked with the world of the dead, and the prestigious fine mats that Rotumans value so much were woven gods, with associations of *mana* 'potency'.

Chapter 7 sums up the main findings, and is followed by an epilogue that contrasts the preoccupations of the scholar with those of Rotuman men on the island, thereby raising more questions related to representation and identity.

The appendix contains a chapter that did not make it to the main body of this book. In an earlier draft, it came after Chapter 3. The material here is "factual," and attempts to summarize the works and views of different scholars who have written about clowning, primarily within the Pacific. I have avoided describing and interpreting in the main, partly because the Pacific data from which some of these accounts are extracted are very sketchy, but also because I wish to credit the work of scholars before me. Besides, as far as I am aware, this is the first time that what has been written on Polynesian clowning (mostly as side-references) has been gathered together in a single work and given a focus. Readers who want to know what has been written about clowning in the Pacific will find the appendix particularly useful. However, in spite of the academic nature of this exercise, my Rotuman self finds this chapter expendable in this book, and so I relegate it to an appendix.

To facilitate discussion in this book, clowning is used to refer to behavior that elicits overt signs of mirth or laughter from others. This behavior is usually absurd, broad, and exaggerated, and may or may not include speech. It is performed by either a man or a woman called a clown, although other terms such as *comedian, fool,* or *jester* may be used. These English words are inadequate as substitutes for their counterpart in Rotuman; I use them simply because they are widely accepted in the English language.

A playful and experimental streak also pervades this work: the interplay between my many selves and the many kinds of discourses, the privileging of creativity, my own voice, and the indigenous voices of Rotumans in what is supposedly a western discourse models the playful and potentially destabilizing nature of a clown's performance. Are these different ways of knowing in many Pacific cultures acceptable in "western" scholarship? If not, why not?

I have also chosen to reveal the thinking that goes on in my head (I use the present tense for these self-reflective moments) as I seek answers to crucial questions. I want readers to know why I have chosen to study clowning in this manner, and the steps that led me to the various interpretations in this book. For a work like this, I believe this approach is most appropriate. And I hope the explicit description of processes employed here—what Clifford calls "experiential, interpretive, dialogic, and polyphonic" (1988, 54)—will cause much reflection on issues that increasingly affect everyone engaged in some form of cultural representation.

Another reason for the self-reflective nature of this study is my desire to tell other Pacific Islanders interested in traveling the same road to take comfort in the knowledge that one of them has been on it before, and has left a map that they can use, modify, or discard as they choose. The cost of this map has been high, in financial as well as personal and emotional terms. I grew up in Rotuma until I was sixteen, then studied and lived in Fiji, England, and Hawai'i. The long and lonely journey thus far has been tortuous. Like most roads in the insular Pacific, potholes, stray animals, and fallen rocks appear when you least expect them, threatening to overturn your vehicle, and hospitalize you for the rest of your productive years. But having acquired a PhD (and missed falling into the gaping hole dug in the middle of the road by a horny dog), I feel a responsibility to share the experience. This is the least I can do, for I have benefited from the trail those before me have blazed.[4]

I hope this book will encourage Rotumans and other Pacific Islanders to empower themselves with their own cultural heritage. If there are non-Pacific islanders who find that this work strikes a chord with them, I hope they too will gain something. Through this study, I want to imply that reconciliation among our many selves is a must, for our own sakes and for the sake of future research.

When we deny our cultural heritage, we become disempowered and disconnected from indigenous sources of inspiration and knowledge. Therefore, let us search within, let us dig deep into our inner resources and those of our cultures, to discover how ancestral wisdom can inform our scholarly pursuits. This is a positive development, one that should stimulate debate on research methodology among those more comfortable with established Euro-American approaches to scholarship in the humanities and the social sciences.[5] I hope a dialogue will ensue.

Instead of being defensive, let us talk to each other; instead of an "*us* and *them*" mentality, let us explore the many different ways of knowing. Give my ancestors and their mythology as much credit as I give yours. Give my language—even if you cannot speak it—as much credit as I give yours. Give my rich cultural heritage with its storehouse of wisdom much respect, for this I give to yours.

Instead of shouting across the river, let us find a bridge on which we can meet. Let us have the option of crossing the river that threatens to separate us. Sometimes, let us be adventurous and cross over to the other side. Let us stand in the middle of this bridge, holding forth together. This is where the view is best.

2 Homemade Entertainment

To better understand a Rotuman, you should learn
how to play cards, the Rotuman way. Not so that you
can play to win, but so you can win when you play.
And remember, don't take yourself too seriously when
you lose. Instead, learn to laugh at yourself, even
when *you* are the chief.

ROTUMAN CLOWN

Rotumans refer to the Christmas period as *av mane'a* 'time to play'.
For about four to six weeks during December–January each year, *av
mane'a* is in force. In 1992–1993, for example, *av mane'a* began on
1 December and ended on 16 January. During the Christmas
season, the prevailing atmosphere is one of taking things easy.
Those who spend their time working are teased and reminded of
the importance of play; those who neglect to feed their pigs or to
tend their gardens have a ready excuse. If unforeseeable circumstances should interfere with the general merrymaking, *av mane'a*
may be extended, as in 1989, when the play season was lengthened
by two weeks. Too many deaths during the festive season—in this
case three—had interfered with people's play time.[1]

During *av mane'a,* a common practice is to go *fara.* To *fara* is to
ask; in this case, to ask (indirectly) for gifts. Young and old alike go
from house to house singing, dancing, and making merry, usually
at night. In return, the household or village being entertained
is expected to provide refreshments—watermelon, pineapple, or
something to drink. Today, talcum powder is sprinkled on the hair
or shoulders and pomade is rubbed on the hair of the performers.
If the hosts are impressed by the dancing and singing, the merrymakers may be held "hostage." Instead of moving on to the next
house or village, the dancers and singers are "forced" by custom to
remain and entertain the hosts, who not only feed them but also
join in the fun. Clowning and dancing become the social lubricant
that keeps guests and hosts entertained. The only way the group of
merrymakers can be released is for their relatives to visit the house

or village where the "hostages" are held and present their captors with food and mats. This social institution of *fara* offers a setting for considerable license.

In December 1989, the young people of Hapmak, where I was staying in Rotuma, approached me to teach them some dances for a *fara*.[2] During rehearsals I noticed a lot of sexual teasing. The village catechist often set the example by calling out to a young man who had just been circumcised,[3] *"Rue 'aklalậi la 'ou juậ heta se tukia"* 'Move carefully or you will hurt your oversized balls.' His comment was usually taken as a cue by others to tease the "victim" even more. Not only did the young girls laugh, they also added their own mock insults.

Members of the opposite sex mixed much more freely with each other than we did when I was growing up. On my last night on the island we hired a truck that took us around the island for half the night, singing and dancing at various districts.[4] On our return to Hapmak, we stayed up for the rest of the night, singing songs, dancing, and playing cards.[5]

Playing cards is so popular among Rotumans that one might be forgiven for thinking they invented it. When individuals get together and wonder how to amuse themselves, a game of cards is often called to the rescue. Men pair up against the women as if to try and prove their superiority. As these card games require little physical energy but depend largely on luck and mental agility (only for those who take the game seriously), anyone can play. Children learn to play by watching their parents or brothers and sisters as soon as they can hold a few cards. Sometimes, during the *av mane'a* season, a whole village may spend a day playing cards; if there is a visiting group, card-playing turns everyone into a clown of one kind or another. Raucous laughter, teasing, joking, dancing, drinking kava *(Piper methysticum),* eating, and general merrymaking become the norm as individuals enjoy a good time.

He' 'ese was a favorite card game on this particular night. To play this game, all cards are dealt out; in turn each person requests a certain card. Whoever has the card must then fulfill a demand, usually to do something outrageous or taboo. The actions requested and carried out, usually eagerly, were that

> The catechist kiss his wife, who was sleeping.
> A young man kiss another on the mouth.
> A girl kiss a boy, either on the mouth or on the cheek (several times).

A Rotuman woman kiss her Australian husband (who was fast asleep) and say "I love you, darling." Another woman kiss this Australian man. A man open his *haʻfạli* 'cotton wraparound' to reveal his underwear.

A young man take off his T-shirt and hand it over to the one who called his card. A wristwatch was similarly requested later in the game.

A married woman go and kiss the owner of the house—a retired school principal—who was dozing on a chair by the door.

A married woman kiss others on the mouth or be kissed by others.[6]

Several men and women stand up and dance—at different times.

A young girl stand up and declare "*Otou ʻuta hoi ʻe ʻuf*" meaning "My head is full of nits and lice."

Anyone who agrees to play *heʻ ʻese* is basically saying, "I agree to do anything, within reason, that anyone asks if I have the card that is called." The kind of act requested by each person is revealing of the individual's idea of what is taboo or ludicrous. Seven of the ten requests were related to sexual matters, including kissing, showing underwear, and declaring love. Dancing was the next most popular. Two requests to hand over personal items were made, and ridicule occurred once.[7] The game was chosen spontaneously, to amuse ourselves, its main attraction being that it provided an acceptable context for breaking the usual taboos of culture and religion. The game sets up new rules that "force" one to break the normal ones.[8]

That Rotumans associate the lifting of taboos with freedom to indulge in acts with a sexual orientation is not unique, for the literature on clowning has numerous examples of such practices in other cultures. Compared with the antics of the Apaches or the Pueblos, contemporary Rotuman behavior and ideas of sexual innuendo are mild. In Rotuma's cultural milieu, however, the kissing was a major departure from the norm.

It is curious that dancing should be viewed as ludicrous. Why should dancing feature prominently in the game of cards and in the clown's performances at weddings? As Rotumans still place a high premium on dancing, it is intriguing that it should be associated with the comic or ludicrous. Traditional Rotuman dancing is performed as a group, and the Rotuman sense of aesthetics requires conformity and exactness in movement, with one general pattern for male dancers, and another for female. When the sacred clown forces individuals to dance, they have to perform solo, without having learned a set of predetermined actions in advance. Not only do they have to improvise, but they must perform in full view of their relatives and friends. Being put on the spot explains the embarrassed laughter that usually accompanies such interactions. For the spectators, laughter is triggered by a feeling of relief—that someone else is the butt. Or perhaps it is sympathy with, or embarrassment for, the person singled out for ridicule. Individuals who are commanded to dance have to shed the rules of behavior society imposes from an early age—that they should not show off or draw attention to themselves. But they still have to come up with movements and actions to a song that is sometimes in a foreign language and therefore unfamiliar. For example, for old Rotuman men and women to have to gyrate to the lyrics of the once-popular Australian song "Nuclear Waste Is Coming Down" must have been a real challenge. To me it presented a ludicrous picture in the context of a supposedly traditional Rotuman wedding—the one described in detail in chapter 5.

After the card game, and during breakfast when I stood up to give a speech, someone poured hot water on the ground next to where I was standing.[9] When I sat down, I discovered that someone had pushed four small pancakes into my cup of tea. My questioning was met with loud giggles and denials from those nearby.

When it was daylight and time for everyone to leave, the leader of the Sunday-school group—a man in his forties whose job is to supervise the children during Sunday services to ensure that they are quiet—stood by the door. As the youths filed out, they threw their garlands over his head and arms and into the bucket he held at arm's length. The young ones enjoyed this moment of permitted disrespect to their leader: they threw their garlands around him with much enthusiasm, transforming him into a ridiculous-looking statue by the door.

Card games and other informal contexts are usually marked by a lot of teasing banter. Sometimes someone will reminisce about the stupidity or arrogance of their friends and neighbors. Others may then start telling jokes about their own foolishness. If they tease someone, most Rotumans expect to be teased back. Whether it is women net-fishing in the lagoon or men hacking away together in the taro plantation, you can hear them laughing—not quiet laughter, but huge belly laughs that can ride the wind and reach the ears of folks a long way off.

Another example of teasing: In early 1993 when I was in Rotuma, a young man who is mute and regarded as slightly crazy appeared

Women of Mea play cards while waiting for the plane from Fiji to arrive, 1987.

one dark night when I was playing cards with the neighbors. His unexpected appearance (he was regarded as an outsider because he was from another village) became a target of banter during the course of the evening. Both men and women teased him: "How come you came in the dark on your own? Aren't you afraid of the ghosts?" a woman asked him. Her husband replied: "Why should he? He's a ghost himself!" The young man did not have a partner for the game of cards, and was asked to go and get himself a dog to be his partner. The teasing continued throughout the evening until this "outsider" left, but not before he had helped himself to our pineapple.

Worth mentioning here is my surprise at the way in which my fellow players treated the disabled young man. My Euro-American self felt an element of cruelty in their interaction. Rather than treating the mute young man with special attention, people treated him with what I considered disrespect. My Rotuman self, however, wondered why it felt sorry for the young man and why it could no longer identify with the prevailing attitude of the group. Even clowning, in this circumstance, seemed out of place to me (see Rensel and Howard 1993).

Sometimes clowning occurs as a peripheral part of *maka* 'dance'.[10] In dance, complex emotions can be expressed. Rotuma's traditional dance, called *tautoga*, builds up to a crescendo. The pace of the dance is slow at first, with the dancers' movements relatively restrained, then it picks up, and the motions become more expansive and vigorous. Free expression may then follow. Since chaos would ensue if all dancers performed with gay abandon, the role of a clown figure is designated to someone. In the *tautoga* of old, the individual who pranced around was called *manman heta* 'the bird' (Jiare 1989). Today, a designated dance clown is no longer a part of the *tautoga*, although occasionally one sees a dancer break away from the group to perform as an individual who incites laughter. Exaggerated body movements, facial contortions, or suggestive sexual antics are standard techniques.[11] Such uninhibited behavior contrasts starkly with the structured nature of the rest of the *tautoga*. Members of the audience who are sufficiently excited may join in, and sometimes two groups of dancers are created—one orderly, the other disorderly.

At the 1989 Oinafa celebrations on the island commemorating the one hundred fiftieth anniversary of the arrival of the first missionaries, spectators sometimes joined the dancers or parodied their movements.[12] For example, some men danced like women, one jumped and shouted, another grabbed a pole of the temporary shelter to test its strength, yet another rolled his eyes, extended his arms, and moved his knees in scissors fashion. Women performed similar antics. Sometimes one or several of the performers stood up, yelped, and danced in a vigorous or exaggerated manner before the rest of the dancers stood up to perform. A reason given for such behavior was that clowning cheered up dancers who had to stand in the rain while waiting to perform, or had been kept waiting too long.[13]

Sometimes spectators shouted comments, usually in mock criticism. At the Oinafa celebrations just mentioned, when some women from the crowd walked up to present a group of dancers with lengths of cotton fabric—a Fijian way of showing appreciation—a man from the audience shouted "*Tä' ma kau makag raksa' ta ka leuof la 'ua'ua'akia*" 'That's the worst dance of all and yet you're rewarding them'. This mock insult received laughter.

A more extreme mock insult is exemplified in the next incident, which occurred at a Methodist Youth Fellowship event in August 1989: During a *mak Rarotonga* 'Rotuman version of Cook Island dancing', a man emerged from the crowd with two empty buckets, mock-danced up to a fat woman in the middle of the (single) line of

Students of Rotuma High School begin to perform a *tạutoga,* 1992. *(A. Buckley)*

The actions become expansive and vigorous as the *tạutoga* comes to a finale, 1992. *(A. Buckley)*

dancers, and put the buckets down in front of her (Howard 1989). He then put his finger in his mouth and pretended to throw up into the buckets, drawing hilarious laughter from the audience.

Another arena for clowning is the beach picnic. Sometimes a group of people prepare food, travel to a familiar spot, and camp for the day. Swimming, playing cards, singing, and eating are the favorite activities on this type of outing, and individuals known to be natural clowns are eagerly welcomed. In his 1989 field notes, Howard wrote of a beach picnic that was without fun until a woman was summoned and acted as a catalyst in getting people involved.

Some forms of play that were once popular are no longer practiced. One of the most popular was the *manea' hune'ele* 'beach games' the young people played on moonlit nights. Although boys and girls normally kept their distance from each other, the opposite happened during beach games. Touching, embracing, and teasing banter were allowed in this culturally acceptable frame for such behavior.

Isolation means that Rotumans, like rural people everywhere, must provide their own entertainment. Mispronounced English words, pompous fools, and incongruous behavior often become sources of entertainment. As women fish in the sea, or as men work in the garden, they mimic amusing incidents or persons. In Rotuma, the humorist who can provide homemade entertainment is a popular person. If she is an old woman, she may even be invited to play the role of ritual clown at a traditional wedding.[14] This ritual clown, called the *hàn mane'àk su* 'woman who plays at the wedding,' is the main focus of this study.

As the ritual clown, the *hàn mane'àk su* is usually asked to perform on the day before the wedding, when food for the wedding feast is being prepared, on the wedding day itself, and on a designated day after the wedding, when the couple are taken to the groom's home. The chosen clown is not just a performer, but also the supreme ruler of the wedding activities. Because she has this authority, the chiefs and other men become the target of her antics, and are ordered about like little children. This inversion of the social order causes much laughter among the wedding guests.

A wedding context provides the Rotuman clown with considerable license to do as she wishes. Implicit in this frame are boundaries that are flexible and amenable to being stretched or tested for their resilience. A skillful clown who has acquired a certain amount of confidence and reputation can be very daring in her technique or interaction with the chiefs and other men; a less confident clown tends to avoid the risk of offending the chiefs.

On the whole, there has been a marked decline in the importance of the *hàn maneʻàk su* in weddings over the years. Unlike the wedding of 1987 (described and discussed in detail in chapter 5), the clowns in subsequent weddings (two, three, and four, in order of occurrence; I refer to them later) were peripheral to the action. Instead of dominating the events of the day and making their presence felt, they kept a low profile. Although they made several half-hearted attempts to inject humor into their behavior or to force individuals to perform, their efforts were unimpressive and mild.

The *hàn maneʻàk su* who performed in wedding two in 1989 was more confident than clowns three and four. Her repertoire included:[15]

A man gave the clown the jawbone of a pig, to replace her missing front teeth. Handing her the jawbone, he said, "Here's your teeth." The clown laughed, then put the jawbone up to her mouth and pretended to open and close it like false teeth, much to the crowd's amusement.

The school bus came by on the road and the clown stopped it imperially, yelling at the driver before letting him go on.

The doctor on the island drove up in the medical department's vehicle and stopped in front of the clown. He got out, grabbed her arm, pulled her to the passenger's side, and pretended to push her in. She resisted and went into a mock-begging mode, falling to her knees and pleading to be left alone. The doctor relented, then got into the car and backed away toward his house, next to the wedding site.[16]

A white man playfully took the clown's stick and put it between his legs as a mock penis. The clown started measuring it by hand lengths.

During the party when the couple were taken to the groom's house *(naag ʻinoso),* several individuals occupied the couple's seat of mats and pretended to be the bridal pair.[17] In a few instances someone would pull the groom off the seat and put another man in his place; in others the bride was replaced in the same manner. When a certain chief sat on the seat he pretended to be the bride, fanning himself with the bride's fan, assuming a mock-demure demeanor, hiding his face behind the fan, and rolling his eyes upward.

A woman approached the white man and dragged him over to the bridal seat. While the two of them were sitting there, and she was mock-fondling him, the chief mentioned earlier appeared with a

The *hàn mane'àk su* flirts with the anthropologist Alan Howard. Wedding two, 1989. *(Jan Rensel)*

woman's purse. Pretending it was a Bible, he started to conduct a marriage ceremony. As soon as he finished, the clown went over, dragged the other woman away, sat down, wrapped her legs around the white man, pulled him to her bosom, and started humping him up and down. The man played along and exaggerated the humping motion. Someone threw a cloth over them. A moment later someone covered them with a mat, as if to provide them with privacy for performing intercourse. Some of the young girls looked shocked, most of the crowd went wild with laughter, then someone brought a large plastic bucket and set it next to the clown. With the man still in her embrace, she picked it up and put it over her head. A roar of laughter. After she took it off someone picked it up and, pretending it was full of water, proceeded to douse the clown and her partner.[18]

The clown lined up a group of people whose kinship group is known for having thin legs, lifted up their *ha'fali* 'cotton wrap-arounds' to expose their legs, and ridiculed them with their *te samuga* 'mock insult', *"Gat ke uaua ma sui"* 'Nothing but skin and bones'.

The clown's costume for wedding two consisted of a bright red dress, a skirt of green leaves around her waist, a fan and stick, sunglasses, flowers in her hair, cigarette, and red shoulder bag. Of all

Rotuma's most popular *hån mane'åk su* today. Wedding two, 1989. *(Jan Rensel)*

four clowns, this one (Rua) was the most imaginative in her costume; she is now regarded by many as the best *hàn maneʻàk su* now living on the island. Her dramatis persona was more marginalized than the others, with a strong hint of being a modern prostitute. Unlike clowns three and four, she immediately exploited her opportunities, a skill that is invaluable in this type of unscripted performance. Although her performance was greatly appreciated by the audience, she went too far, according to the bride's father, to whom she was closely related. As a result she was denied the customary gifts of food and (at least) a fine mat;[19] after the wedding she was avoided by the bride's parents, who reside in Fiji.[20]

The *hàn maneʻàk su* who performed in wedding three in 1989 seemed too old for the part.[21] Not once did she shout at someone or raise her voice. Her repertoire consisted mainly of picking individuals to dance, but these were relatively polite gestures. Once I saw her direct a man and a woman to sit on her chair so that they were almost on each other's lap; another time I saw her dancing very close to the ground. On the whole, it was a nondescript performance, although ironically, she gave a formal speech at the end of her performance and asked the chiefs' forgiveness in case she had offended them.

The *hàn maneʻàk su* who performed in wedding four in 1989 was more assertive than clown three (but less so than clowns one and two), although she was uncertain about her role. Before the arrival of the groom's procession, she was noisy and flamboyant. I saw her force a kiss on a man who was standing by the roadside. She was dressed more gaudily than the third clown—bright yellow dress with shell garlands around her neck and a flower behind her ear. However, as soon as the groom's party arrived, she withdrew and became very restrained; so much so, that someone asked if the wedding had a *hàn maneʻàk su*.[22] Perhaps the social and physical circumstances were not in her favor.

This wedding was between individuals from different districts. Invited to entertain was the Fiji Police Band, consisting of Fijian men.[23] As this was the Christmas season, many visitors had come from Fiji and a handful from beyond, making the composition of the assembled company less homogeneous than usual. The *ri hapa* 'temporary shelter' built for the occasion was in a cramped location by the roadside and had a low ceiling. Instead of the usual U-shape with an open arena, it was oblong. These factors, together with the amplified music of pop songs, country music, and Fijian popular tunes and the use of microphones for announcements, gave the wedding a cosmopolitan and modern atmosphere, by Rotuman standards. Furthermore, a Fiji Rotuman who arrived with the band assumed the role of master of ceremonies, stealing the clown's thunder.

In one instance, this man announced over the microphone that the next dance would be "the couple's dance." When the music came on, the *hàn mane'àk su* was the first to stand up and pick a partner. The Fiji Rotuman hurried over to her and told her to sit. The *hàn mane'àk su* obeyed. When interviewed, she said her instinctive reaction was to tell the Fiji Rotuman that as *hàn mane'àk su* she had supreme authority over him and everyone. But because her usurper had a high position in the Fiji government, she felt obliged to submit. That the clown did not assert her rights is significant; the incident illustrates her ambivalent position today and the power that urban Rotumans wield—deliberately or otherwise—over their rural counterparts on the island.

In this instance, confusion reigned because of an unfamiliar custom with a set of rules outside the parameters of the clown's understanding and experience. Also, was this wedding a religious and sacred ceremony in which the clown presided, or was it an arena for secular and political power play? Was the Fiji Rotuman showing off his knowledge of European custom? Why should the Fiji man's position in the Fiji government surpass the power of the ritual clown? After all, the chiefs were under the clown's rule at this time. If the clown had been more assertive right from the start, perhaps the rules that ought to have been operative would have been clearer. But since she was weak in the role, she was easily displaced from her customary status by an "outsider." Clearly, the conjunction of western and traditional ritual in Rotuman weddings is a potential source of friction.[24] Fortunately, Rotumans steeped in the culture are expert negotiators, capable of diffusing tension—even humbling themselves—for the sake of social harmony.

The *hàn mane'àk su* of the third wedding asked publicly for the chiefs' forgiveness; the fourth clown went to her minister privately at the end of the wedding to confess her "sin": she had danced holding a man in her arms. According to her, Methodism forbids such intimacy, but she was forced into this "sinful" act when a man approached her to dance. Her minister told her she did right as the *hàn mane'àk su,* and the clown was relieved to learn that she could keep her privileged position in the Methodist church.

The *hàn mane'àk su* in present-day Rotuma faces challenges to her role as supreme ruler of a wedding. When interviewed, clowns three and four said they were afraid of offending the chiefs.[25] As a result, their performances were non-events. The clown who performed in the 1987 wedding expressed fear of pushing the chiefs too far and being punished by the spirits; her idea of the boundaries of license, however, was much broader than those of the third and fourth clowns. The second clown played the role to the hilt, only to be rejected by her relatives for overstepping the boundaries. As these boundaries are unwritten, and therefore contestable, this role requires extreme sensitivity, and an ability to walk a very fine line between autonomy and collective responsibility.

Unlike the actor in a western play, the *hàn mane'àk su* has no lines to learn beforehand; instead, she relies for her theatrics on the active participation and cooperation of the spectators. She is alert to the possibilities for laughter inherent in each circumstance, and exploits it for humorous effect. Because the specific circumstances of each wedding are different, no two performances are the same. The role also demands agility of body and mind, and the woman who agrees to be the ritual clown takes a considerable risk, because so much is dependent on unknown factors. Working in her favor, fortunately, are women relatives of the bride and groom—whom I refer to as "funny women"—who also engage in spontaneous clowning during the wedding celebrations. Between them and the *hàn mane'àk su*, the wedding guests, theoretically, are kept entertained and happy.

As a child, I attended many weddings. I looked forward to the feast that marked the culmination of the wedding festivities, but even more to the clown's outrageous antics. She was a figure of fun that I always took for granted—until 1986, when I started researching indigenous theater forms. My reading of the same phenomenon in other societies made me realize that the institution of ritual clowning is an important aspect of Rotuman culture that is yet to be understood. To comprehend its significance is to better understand my culture, and, ultimately, myself.

Until now, ethnographers have either overlooked or paid scant attention to the institution of the *hàn mane'àk su*. This study fills a blank in the literature by showing the sacred origins of the clown and her central role in women's production of culturally prestigious fine mats and in the celebration of marriage. My interpretation is that the *hàn mane'àk su* is an agent of the power structure in Rotuman society. However, because of the playful nature of her role, she is potentially a subversive force. In this sense, Rotuman clowning is both conservative and progressive.

Fine white mats—which feature prominently during the liminal period in Rotuman weddings when the *hån mane'åk su* performs— were regarded in the past as woven gods imbued with supernatural powers. Both the fine mats and the *hån mane'åk su* were conduits through which social and divine power were manifest. In contemporary Rotuma, however, these religious beliefs remain in the realm of intuition or the unconscious, although fine white mats and the *hån mane'åk su* continue to play significant roles in Rotuman weddings.

3 The "Feel" of Clowning Around

> Oceania deserves more than an attempt at mundane fact; only the imagination in free flight can hope—if not to contain her—to grasp some of her shape, plumage, and pain.
>
> ALBERT WENDT, *"Towards a New Oceania"*

Evocation: The Day of the Wedding

The *hàn mane'àk su* points her stick at a man seated close by and orders him to dance with her. He does. At the end of the music, she returns to her chair and fans herself. She straightens her red flowered dress and tightens the grass skirt around her waist, then looks at the *tefui* 'garland' of sweet-smelling flowers around her neck and breathes in their fragrance. She surveys the assembled company, then, leaning on the stick in her right hand, pushes herself upright. The band boys sing another song. This time she dances by herself, shaking her hips to and fro and waving her arms wildly in the air. She rolls her eyes in self-admiration and the women close by giggle like schoolgirls. At the end of the song, she marches up and down the arena created by the U-shape of the temporary shelter. A dog wanders into the arena; she grabs a handful of sand from underfoot and aims it at the animal; tail between its legs, it flees, chased by the laughter of little girls sitting by their mothers.

Observing the *hàn mane'àk su* and her antics from the top of a pile of fine mats is the bride. Like the rest of her kin, she is awaiting the arrival of the groom's party. She appears cool and relaxed under the corrugated shelter built to provide shade from the sun, which is just beginning to get hot. The sound of small waves lapping on the beach is faintly heard: the lagoon is only fifty yards or so behind the bride. In front of the bride is the arena where most of the rituals and dancing will take place; beyond the arena is the main road that circles the island. Seated underneath the U-shaped shelter to the bride's left are the chiefs of her district. Scattered behind the chiefs and around the temporary shelter are her relatives.

At the extreme end of the shelter is the band that produces the music: four boys, two guitars, a drum, an electric keyboard, and two microphones. Right now they're singing "Nuclear Waste Is Coming Down!" A few of the young girls are dancing; the clown is busy arguing with a man who refuses to dance.

Hidden behind one of the wooden posts that holds up the temporary shelter, I scribble away, hoping to be spared the clown's idea of fun. I bend my head and write furiously in my notebook, having checked to see that my tape recorder is turned on and running. The laughter stops abruptly. Silence. The clown announces for all to hear: "Here they come! Get ready!"

The groom and his kin come into view. In single file, they walk toward the temporary shelter. The *hån mane'åk su* sits back on a chair by the band boys and fans herself vigorously. She watches as the groom climbs onto the pile of mats and sits by his bride. The women in the groom's party screen the front of the temporary shelter with pink and blue cotton fabric; the chiefs in the groom's party take their seats on the ground to the right of the bride. The band plays a popular Rotuman song. The clown jumps up from her chair and strides in the opposite direction.

The *hån mane'åk su* points her stick at a chief and orders him to stand up and dance. He obeys. The clown dances with him for a while then points her stick at a spot a few yards away. The chief shifts position. The sun lights up his face; he is now in the glaring sun. Shouting at this chief to remain where he is, the *hån mane'åk su* struts away. She points her stick at the mother of the groom and orders her to dance. While dancing, the *hån mane'åk su* shouts at another woman, telling her to shut up. Then she orders the chief standing in the sun to sit down and struts away to the opposite side of the arena.

Laughter follows the *hån mane'åk su*. The wedding guests, numbering about a thousand, are all seated under or around the temporary shelter. Most of them are now enjoying the clown's theatrics. Some talk to their neighbors; a few look uninterested; the chiefs look uneasy.

The bride and groom sit quietly, without talking or looking at each other. The bride wears a blue silk dress; her long black hair, combed and oiled, falls below her shoulders, almost to her waist. Every now and then she lifts the pandanus fan that rests on her lap

A *hàn maneʻàk su* performs, 1987. *(Alan Howard)*

and waves it in front of her face, causing a few wisps of hair to brush across her cheeks and mouth. Occasionally she stares at the multicolored feathers that border her fan, momentarily lost in thought. The groom wears an ill-fitting gray suit, tie, and shoes. Like the bride, he looks demure and distant.

The ritual clown wanders over to the band of young men with their electric guitars and keyboard. She shouts at them: "Hurry up with the music! We want to dance!" The young man with the guitar speaks into the microphone. "This song is dedicated to the *hàn maneʻàk su*. It's called *Ka ʻàqe ne takia gou se gaogao!*" ("You are leading me to an isolated spot.") Everyone laughs; the clown tells them off: "What are you laughing about? Shut your mouths, or I'll hit you with my stick. Don't you forget I am the boss!" More laughter, before the singing from the band drowns her out. She marches over to a middle-aged woman wearing a yellow dress who is still laughing, grabs her by the right hand and pulls her up. "Go! Over there! When I tell you to stop laughing, you stop!"

The woman in the yellow dress protests but to no avail. She stands up suddenly, lets out a yelp, shakes her hips in quick succession, and the women seated next to her scream with delight and slap each other's back. "Go and get Chief Koko!" a voice shouts above the music. The woman in yellow turns to survey the line of chiefs seated on the opposite side. She decides to be daring and walks over to Chief Koko. Chief Koko doesn't resist. Instead, he stands up, stretches his back, bends his knees, and moves them in and out, scissors style. More laughter. The woman in yellow acts surprised, stops dancing, and stares down at the chief's legs. The ritual clown walks over and orders her sidekick to sit down. She obeys, protesting all the while. The *hån mane'åk su* dances right up to the chief, turns her back to him, then seductively rubs her buttocks against his front. The crowd goes wild. The *hån mane'åk su* rolls her eyes as though in ecstasy.

Bending her knees to the level of the chief, the ritual clown starts to shake her hips, slowly to the left, slowly to the right, slowly to the left, slowly to the right, her arms raised above her head, the stick in her right hand pointing to the blue sky above. The chief accelerates the scissors-like movement of his knees: in and out, in and out, in and out. He gasps and pants: faster, faster, faster; they move around each other, their arms raised, erect; the tempo builds and builds; a woman shouts some comment; raucous laughter erupts; abruptly, the music stops. Everyone turns to look at the band boys, who turn to each other and laugh. The crowd groans; the *hån mane'åk su* shouts: "Afekhuga, if I come over there, I'll smash your guitar on your head! You know we having fun so why you spoil us, huh?" She moves over to the band boys to threaten them with her stick, after which she sits on her chair and fans herself vigorously.

A group of women carrying fine mats proceed to the front of the bride and groom to perform a ritual. As they do, several women from the groom's side force the men from the bride's side to dance. The men are slow to obey, so the *hån mane'åk su* stands up from her seat and strides in their direction. The men get up hurriedly when the clown threatens them with her stick. They look like little boys at school assembly. The clown shouts: "Dance, or I'll hit you with my stick!" The men move to the music as the clown shouts to the assembled company: "Hurry up with the next ritual! The sooner we finish the rituals, the sooner we can eat."

The clown waves her stick and orders a drink. A young girl rushes over with a tray of glasses. The clown takes a glass of cordial and gulps it down. Then she tells the girl at the top of her voice: "Keep away from the young men sitting under the banana trees. They're bad news. Pay more attention to the women and the children; make sure they have plenty to drink!"

The clown orders Chief Piko to dance. He says he's got a sore leg. Chief Ono says he has a headache. The clown stands staring at them, then falls flat on her face. Chief Piko and Chief Ono look uncomfortable; reluctantly they stand up. The clown dances around them for a while, holding a chief on either arm. She loses interest when she sees a drunken man rubbing himself against another woman. "Get away from here. Get lost!" the clown shouts. The man blinks at her, but she is not amused. She pushes the man with her stick. He staggers away to join the men under the banana trees.

Another man walks up to the clown, who is now sitting down on her chair, and gestures at her for a dance. The women sitting close by call out funny comments; the man is the clown's husband. She tells the women that her husband is the best dancer on the island; after all, he's from Rarotonga, she says. The women laugh. Then she says: "I told him that on this day, I'm a single woman. Now he's following me around. I don't know why!" The women shout comments back at her; someone asks to sleep with her husband. She tells her to get on with it.

Then she sees Arnold, my Australian friend. She runs toward him and pulls him to dance with her. He does, and she rolls her eyes and collapses on the ground. Everybody laughs; she's telling them she's in love. She stands up only to discover that the white man has collapsed on the ground too. More laughter. They fool around, twisting and gyrating to the music. She shouts: "I'm going to take this white man home with me!" A Rotuman man appears from the bride's side and pushes the white man away. The clown chases the Rotuman man away: "I don't want a black man! I want a white one!" She grabs the hand of the white man; they elope to the opposite side, followed by the black man. The crowd goes wild. The black man follows and the *hàn mane'àk su* and her lover flee again, hand in hand. They stand and dance for a while, brushing each other's side as they move up and down. The music ends abruptly. She grabs the white man by the back of the head and smacks a kiss on his mouth. The crowd goes crazy.

The *hàn mane'àk su* announces that the bridal party will now leave for the church ceremony. "There won't be any fooling around for a while!" she proclaims. As people stand up to walk to the church building, I see the clown walk toward the neighbor's house, probably to relieve herself.

Me, the Clown

It's my job to entertain the wedding guests. Why they need me to keep them happy I don't know. Maybe they like the idea of an old woman—a freak of nature?—making a fool of herself. Maybe it makes them feel superior, above it all, so to speak. I don't think they care about the real me. And I don't just mean me. I mean any *hàn mane'àk su*. I suppose I shouldn't expect too much from people.

This is my first time as *hàn mane'àk su*. When they first approached me I said no. But they kept coming, and I said yes in the end. Since then I haven't had a good night's sleep. I dream every night about what I have to do. I try to think of all sorts of funny things to say or do that will make people laugh.

Supposing people don't laugh? If they don't, then I am showing off; this is my biggest fear. Imagine telling jokes that no one finds funny. I try not to think about failure; it only makes me feel hopeless. If people don't find me funny, I'll never be asked to be *hàn mane'àk su* again. Instead, they'll think I only want to draw attention to myself.

I have to get it just right; this is not easy. Rotumans are a funny people. Not funny like a clown is funny, but funny because you never know where you are with them. They can say one thing and mean another. They might laugh at your jokes then go back home and tell their family you're a show-off. If you ask them for hints, you get surprised—they don't know any better than you!

Malumu isn't much help either. Everyone says she's the best *hàn mane'àk su* on the island. I suppose they expect me to perform like her. But this isn't fair. She's had more experience. Yet, I'm sure they'll compare me with her. That's why I went last night to see Siko. But the old clown won't tell me anything: "I really can't help you. Clowning is my God-given talent. Now you're asking me to give it to you?" Well, you can't say I didn't try.

Why didn't they ask Siko? Simple. If you want to know the truth, it's really because I'm related to the bride. You see, the *hàn mane'àk su* gets a reward at the end of the wedding. My relatives (who are the givers of this reward) think it best to keep it within the family. Cunning, isn't it? Taro, meat, corned beef, *fekei* (that's Rotuman pudding), and at least a fine mat will be mine. Not bad, eh? That's why I have to play my part and not let them down.

My mother, when she was alive, she was funny. I suppose that's why they think I can be funny too. They're right. . . . I know I can be funny, but it's so much easier when I don't think about it. When you have to do it because of custom, that's a different thing. You have no choice. This is what my children don't understand. There are seven of them, but not one of them wants me to be the *hàn mane'àk su* because I will make a fool of myself. They don't care about me, mind, it's what their friends will think! They say I will make them feel ashamed.

God! This sun is hot already, although it's still early in the morning. I've been trying to entertain these people since the first arrivals. Easier than I thought. All I need to do is say something rude about somebody's appearance and they laugh. Why this is so funny, I'm not certain, but it sure works. Maybe it's all to do with the situation. They expect a clown to be funny, and so they just laugh at everything I say, without really thinking about what they're laughing at. Or perhaps I'm just voicing their secret thoughts, the evil in them. Maybe they're using me. Funny, I've never thought about it this way before.

Think about this. A moment ago, there was this fat woman, with all her front teeth missing, who shouted at me: "Why are you always picking my husband to dance? Are you in love with him?" I shouted back: "Who wants a husband with a bald head?" I just said what came to my head at the time, but everyone cracked up. Why? Is it because I dared to voice out loud what they only think in their heads? By the way, the woman's name is Lele and the man's name is Atu. Atu has a weakness for young girls with all their teeth intact (my girl Ala included), and it's a well-known fact that Atu's appetite has caused many ugly scenes in his household. So when Lele complained to me, my response embarrassed both of them, her and her husband. Atu now realizes he's not as good-looking as he thinks; Lele now feels stupid for ever thinking that her husband is worth a second look. I'm second-guessing, of course, but this is what I have to do to be good at this job. Anyway, the crowd enjoyed the insult, even if the victims didn't.

And yet . . . when the wedding is over, I will lose all my power. I will resume just being plain Potopoto (this is my name). Lele and Atu will remain my neighbors of course. What if they bear a grudge against me? Well, I don't think they will, but supposing things get really bad? I might have to take a fine mat (or something) and ask their forgiveness. But I haven't got time to think about such things now. I must get up and dance. Who will I get next?

Everybody expects me to be up and dancing all the time. But how can I? This band is no good. Why do they have to hire this band, with their fancy guitars and loud music? Most of the time they sing English songs; I haven't a clue what the words mean. And I don't know how to move to the music either. How do you dance the disco style—is this what you call it? I'm self-conscious . . . must stop this feeling from taking over. Oh, there's Chief Fekfeke just arriving now. He snubbed me the other day when I saw him at the shop. I'll teach him something today.

"Hey, you with the big stomach, so big you're dragging it on the ground. Come here and dance." He's hesitating. "Yes, you, Chief Fekfeke. Over here. I want to see you shake that fat stomach. Best way to lose weight." Everyone's laughing now. He's obeying me. . . . I can't believe this. I thought he'd ignore me. Just goes to show you. If you're confident, you get what you want. He's keeping to the shade. . . . He's from Malhaha, so what else can you expect. "Over here, you with the fat stomach, so full of other people's chickens. Dance in the hot sun. God sends it today for you." I push him with my stick. He laughs and obeys me! I'm learning, eh?

These chiefs. Small chiefs they are, really, but they think they're big shots. The same with the district officer. He's just a kid, the same age as my son Mose. And yet the Fiji government sends him here to lord it over us; only yesterday he was running around naked. Who do they think we are? Who cares anyway? Today, they have to listen to me. I'm the king, that's the Rotuman custom. So glad there are still enough old people around who still know the custom. In the past some chiefs were forced to kneel in the hot sun or go without food the whole day. Should I be just as hard with these chiefs? Tempting, isn't it? After all, this may be my only chance.

Why do they stop the music now, just as I'm beginning to flirt with the district officer? I'm sure they're trying to give me a hard time. I'll show them who's in charge around here.

"Hurry up! Start the music!" Laughter erupts. They're laughing because I've switched to speaking English now. They think an old clown like myself doesn't know any English. Well, I know more than they think; anyway, let them have their fun today. Let them laugh at my accent. After all, I have to give the impression I don't mind if they laugh at me. And I must tell them off for laughing. That will make them laugh even more. If they won't listen, well, I might have to use this stick!

"My name is *not* Potopoto. My name is Princess Potopoto!" Laughter again. They really enjoy my brand of English. I suppose it's hard

The *hàn mane'àk su* forces the highest ranking official (district officer) on the island to dance in the hot sun. Wedding two, 1989. *(Jan Rensel)*

to imagine a princess wearing a red dress of cheap cotton, a grass skirt across the waist, a garland of flowers around the neck and carrying a stick in one hand. And so vulgar and loud! The perfect fool, eh? Never mind. . . . I can't keep thinking like this. I must play the part. . . .

*   *   *

Although these two accounts are fictional, they are different, underlining the discrepancy between what the participant-observer sees and what may be actually happening in the minds of the people the ethnographer is studying. The first account emphasizes the external world and what is observable behavior; the second, because of its private nature, focuses on the unseen world of competing emotions. This section also highlights the tension between personal autonomy on the part of the *hàn mane'àk su* and collective responsibility, an important element in clowning that is not readily apparent to an observer.

Ethnography of this nature should be supplemented with as many different kinds of "texts" as possible, including photographs and video footage. Only when there is an intertextual encounter of different accounts or perspectives of the same event can we come nearer to a better understanding of human behavior. The meaning of what we seek to understand "is as transitional as it is transitory: in between, in the interplay; in the interconnections, the disjunctions; at the intersections, the crossroads; in the journey, not the arrival" (Babcock 1984, 108). The chapters that follow explore the possibilities inherent in a dialogic and creative encounter between different but complementary forms of discourse.

4 Mythologizing Humor
and Clowning

> One of the best ways to understand a people is to
> know what makes them laugh. Laughter encompasses
> the limits of the soul. In humor life is redefined and
> accepted. Irony and satire provide much keener
> insights into a people's psyche and values than do
> years of research.
>
> VINE DELORIA, *Custer Died for Your Sins*

In my search for published information on ritual clowning on
Rotuma, I discover nothing. The only clues to its practice in the past
are in the unpublished accounts of Hocart and MacGregor and in
Alan Howard's field notes from the 1960s. And the elders in the
community, who have their special memories of the weddings of
friends and the performances of the *hån mane'åk su* on those occasions. Most important are the *hån mane'åk su*, whose responses to my
questions are given in the interviews that follow.[1]

Interview with Ta, Clown One

December 1987

I found Ta washing her clothes. She wore a bright flowery dress and
sat next to a standing water-pipe from which she occasionally
reached forward to turn on the faucet. Under the faucet was a tub
filled with soapy water and the day's washing. I sat cross-legged on
the sand opposite her, some distance away but within earshot. I kept
my tape-recorder by my side, ready to be turned on. After some pre-
liminary greetings and explanations about my visit, I turned on the
tape, and started asking questions. Ta continued to wash her clothes
as we talked.

The author (left) poses with the *hàn mane'àk su* of wedding one and her husband after he interviews her. *(Aren Baoa)*

VH: How many times have you been a *hàn mane'ak su?*

TA: Two times.

VH: Why were you chosen as the clown?

TA: They think I'm funny, that I can do it.

VH: How did they know you're funny?

TA: I say funny things.

VH: Weren't you scared of the crowd?

TA: No. At first I was scared, but not now.

VH: What is your function as the clown?

TA: I am in charge of everything related to the wedding. But I can't overstep my powers.

VH: I was told that in the past, the *hàn mane'àk su* was very authoritarian.

TA: Yes. Sometimes they hit people who disobey them.

VH: Have you hit anyone yet with your stick?

TA: No. It's true I am the boss, but I must keep to the rules. Otherwise I will suffer bad luck.

VH: You're afraid of that?

TA: Yes.

VH: How many clowns are there on the island at present?

TA: Two others, I'm the third.

VH: Have you heard of 'Ioane, the famous clown?

TA: Yes, she's dead.

VH: Why was she popular?

TA: She said funny things. Her English was very funny.

VH: What do Rotumans find funny?

TA: Funny antics such as twisting the body like a snake, what you wear, not minding stupid things people shout at you, and playing along with them.

VH: Who asked you to be the clown at this recent wedding?

TA: The bride's parents.

VH: You weren't afraid?

TA: At first I said no. Find someone else. But they insisted, so I accepted.

VH: There was another very funny woman. Who is she?

TA: Her name is Lulu. Her mother is a sister of the bride's father's father. That's why she was doing funny things.

VH: How were you thanked for your services?

TA: They gave me a fine mat and six other mats. And a basket of food. Pork, corned beef, real beef, and *fekei* 'Rotuman pudding'.

VH: Did you get a basket of food for each of the three days you performed?

TA: Yes, from the bride's relatives.

VH: What about your costumes?

TA: They made three different costumes for the three days. Three dresses and three *ha̦'fali* 'cotton wraparounds'. Oh, and the garland, the skirt of leaves, and the other accessories I was wearing. That means I had to make sure everyone was entertained.

VH: Your family didn't mind you looking stupid in front of every-
      body?

TA: Not my husband.

VH: What about your children?

TA: They didn't mind.

VH: How many children do you have?

TA: Six. Five males, one female.

VH: How many brothers and sisters do you have in your family?

TA: Nine of us. I'm fourth youngest.

VH: Were your parents funny people?

TA: My mother was. She wasn't a *hån mane'åk su,* but everyone
      knew she could be very funny.

VH: Is that why you're funny?

TA: (Laughs.)

VH: The other two clowns. Did any of their ancestors have a simi-
      lar reputation?

TA: That I don't know.

VH: Were you happy with your performance at the last wedding?

TA: I didn't think I was good, but other people told me I was very
      good.

VH: What made you think you weren't good?

TA: Oh, I just thought that people would be critical, but instead
      they praised me.

VH: Was your second time better than your first?

TA: Yes. The first time I was frightened, but this time I wasn't.

VH: Maybe you'll be famous in future.

TA: Next time I'll be the clown for your son's wedding.
      (Laughs.)

VH: I saw your husband dancing at the wedding. He seems a
      funny man too. Why can't the two of you entertain the crowd
      as a team?

TA: Only women do it.

VH: But at the *naag 'inoso* two days after the wedding there was a male clown who painted his face black with charcoal. Didn't you see him?

TA: I suppose men can do it. But I don't know of a man playing a key role in the past. The men can help, that's all.

VH: Why didn't you perform when the bride and groom were brought to the groom's house?

TA: My grandmother died.

VH: Why did you stay overnight and not return to your district until the following day?

TA: The bride's parents told me to stay. I didn't have to stay, but they asked me to. They said I could do with some rest.

VH: Another question about Lulu. She seemed to have a slightly different idea about how to be funny. What do you think?

TA: I have nothing to say. She was good.

VH: Because she was acting funny, it meant you could rest for a while; other people were watching her instead. Right?

TA: Yes.

VH: You didn't mind?

TA: No, it would have been much harder on my own.

VH: Did you sleep well on the nights of the performances?

TA: Very well. I was so exhausted. But I couldn't eat because I was too tired. Not until the wedding was over. I just drank water.

VH: What do you think the clowns wore in the olden days?

TA: I don't know if there were clowns in the olden days or not. I can only talk about what I remember. I remember a clown called Marseu and 'Ioane. Both of them used to beat people who disobeyed them.

VH: Why did they beat people? Was it because they were angry, or were they trying to be funny?

TA: Sometimes people refuse to dance. If they are not frightened of you they won't obey you. So you have to scare them. But I don't like to do that. (Pause.) The fishing net you gave me. I'd like to sell it, because I don't use a net for fishing. I use a speargun instead. I don't know how to use a net, but my husband wants to keep the net.

VH: I see. Apart from fishing, what else do you do?

TA: I cut copra, but fishing mainly.

VH: Are the other two clowns older than you?

TA: Yes.

VH: How old are you?

TA: I'm forty-five.

VH: And your oldest child?

TA: Over twenty-one.

VH: I was told that the funny woman I mentioned earlier (Lulu) is not a *hàn mane'àk su* because her children do not like the idea of their mother making a fool of herself in public.

TA: No, her children are afraid that she might do something that isn't good, such as opening up her dress in public, swearing, or beating the wedding guests. Did you see the way she was behaving at the wedding? Did you notice the time Paurino annoyed her? She picked up something to throw at him. If she had, the object could have hit one of the chiefs. When the bride's parents approached me to be the clown, I suggested her, but they said they were afraid she might do something offensive. I'm always wary of the chiefs. If I do something to offend them, I can suffer bad luck.

VH: You mean, if you break the rules, you will pay for it later in life?

TA: Oh yes. I was told that in the past, after some weddings, the clown had to formally seek forgiveness by performing certain ceremonies to people she had offended. I don't like that. I agreed to be the clown because I am related to the bride. The bride's parents said that if they asked a non-relative then the wedding gifts would go to an outsider. In my case, the gifts may not be as plentiful, but I will still have to be thanked. We jointly own land.

VH: Before your first appearance, did you rehearse in your mind what you would be doing?

TA: Oh yes, I do think about it. And I'm anxious. I cannot be sure how people will react. After the wedding, I feel so relieved. Before the wedding I think of nothing else. I dream about nothing else. My thoughts are on the wedding, and what I can do to make people laugh. Supposing people don't laugh. If they don't, then you're showing off.

VH: Sometimes I see you rolling your eyes while dancing. Why?

TA: In order to be funny. For example, when I was dancing with the white man, I collapsed on the ground thinking that people would find that funny. And they did, They liked it. And when I stood up, the white man had fallen on the ground too. That's even funnier, because the man is a foreigner and he has to copy you.

VH: Why did you fall on the ground like that?

TA: So that people will say, "Looks like she's in love with the white man." It's like flirting with the man. So when I collapsed, it looked like I was overcome by my feelings. (Laughs.) Where's the white couple? Have they gone back to Fiji?

VH: Yes.

Interview with Rua, Clown Two

February 1990

Rua is well known on the island for her clowning behavior during social gatherings and is regarded by many as the most fearless ritual clown in Rotuma. Two years after the interview, at Christmas 1992, I saw Rua in Rotuma clowning around during a *fara*.

I was unsuccessful in personally interviewing Rua, partly because she was staying with various relatives in different parts of Fiji and therefore difficult to track down. However, I had met her on a few occasions previously and she was aware of my interest in her work as a *hån mane'åk su*. At my request, my sister tape-recorded this interview for me.

I provided my sister with a list of questions to ask Rua. Instead of using these questions merely as a guide, she followed them to the letter, which explains the stilted interview that follows.

VH: Why is it that the clown is from the bride's side?

RUA: It means the bride's side is in charge of the wedding.

VH: How do you make people laugh?

RUA: I expose the *te sạmuga* 'mock insults' of the relatives of the bride and the groom in order to make people laugh.

VH: How do you choose what to wear?

RUA: It is the bride's kin who decide. They tend to choose bright colors to make you stand out in the crowd.

VH: How were you rewarded?

RUA: Baskets of food and mats.

VH: How old are you? How many weddings have you performed at?

RUA: Fifty-three. I have performed at two weddings already.

VH: Where do you think we got this custom from?

RUA: I think the custom is handed down to us from our ancestors. It's an old custom.

VH: What is the purpose of the *'at fara* 'a small basket carried by a member of the bride's kin on the day of the wedding and when the bride and groom are formally taken to the groom's home a day or two after the wedding'?

RUA: It means the wedding is a proper wedding, and that the bride is a virgin. Money is put inside it.

VH: As clown, were you allowed to do anything to the bride and groom?

RUA: Yes. It is possible to get them to move away from their seat.

VH: What was the source of your power?

RUA: My license to rule came from the bride's kin. They chose me and gave me permission.

VH: Why were you chosen to be clown?

RUA: I think because I enjoy being funny, and I'm not afraid.

VH: Were there times when you were afraid to force the chiefs to do anything?

RUA: Not if I was trying to humor them, or to make them laugh. But I am afraid to beat them, because I will suffer bad luck.

VH: Why did you carry a stick?

RUA: The stick helped me to get people to do what I wanted.

VH: Were there times when people got angry with you?

RUA: They pretended they were angry when I forced them. No, the wedding guests did not get angry with me. It was just pretense.

Interview with Folu, Clown Three

December 1989

When I found her house, Folu was dressed up to go to a village at the other side of the island. She was reluctant to talk when I asked if she could answer some questions for me. I sensed nervousness. After the usual greetings, I made reference to my interest in the role of the *hàn mane'àk su*, and my having interviewed Ta.

FOLU: Who is the woman at Lopta you said is a *hàn mane'àk su?*

VH: Ta.

FOLU: What did she say about clowning? You know, I don't know very well what clowning is all about. But the other woman who was with me, Pasimata, I think this is her second time and I think she knows a lot, so if you go to her, she will tell you everything. But that was my first time. They asked me because I was related to the bride's parents, both of them. If the clown isn't related [this is possible, if a suitable and willing relative cannot be found] and something goes wrong, it can be difficult to resolve. So because it was my first time, there were some things that I just couldn't do. So go to the other woman.

VH: Oh, all right, I will go.

FOLU: The only thing I know is that it's true about the chiefs and what I should do, but I am afraid of them. The only thing I can do is pick them to dance. But the relatives of the groom—it is permissible for me to get them to kneel. Or, if the women are slow, you can call out to them to hurry up. Or, when the food is brought to the arena you can tell people to cover up the food to protect them from the flies.

VH: So you were chosen because you were closely related to the bride's parents?

FOLU: Yes, to both of them. It means that they are not likely to be angry with me. If it's someone else, she might say, "Oh, things are not done according to custom." Because the clown is really in charge on the wedding day, she can do whatever she wants. But because I am related to both, it wasn't like that. According to custom, the clown has to have a share of food.

VH: So where did you eat during the feast?

FOLU: Because I'm related to the bride's parents, I just went and joined the others, although I should have had a special seat. They didn't really worry about me.

VH: Supposing you weren't related. Then?

FOLU: Then they would have had to give me my own share of food, or they would have come and served my food. I could actually have ordered them to serve me. But because I was related I just joined the others. If it were someone unrelated, she would have been angry. Also, I didn't have a proper basket of food at the end. They gave me just six tins of corned beef and that was all. When I went to the wedding, I took a fine mat, two Rotuman mats and two Fijian mats. But they returned to me only one fine mat and one Rotuman mat. See what I told you. It's because we are closely related. But if I weren't related, they would have had to return more than they were given. So that was why they asked me. So I just hoped that God would give me strength so I could be of use to my granddaughter (the bride).

VH: Did you want to accept when they came to ask you?

FOLU: I said, "It looks as though this is going to be a big wedding. Is it going to be a proper wedding?" And they said no, just the *'öf söp ta* 'symbolic cutting of hair ritual' and that's all.

VH: Why wasn't the *fạu ta* 'binding of the couple in fine mats ritual' performed?

FOLU: I didn't go on the day of the *naag 'inoso* 'the day when the bride and groom are formally taken to the groom's home', so I don't know whether they did it then or not.

VH: Is that when this ritual is supposed to be performed, I mean, not on the wedding day?

FOLU: They do it differently all the time, so I don't quite know which is the right way to do it. At the Fag'uta wedding, they did it on the wedding day. Maybe it's because of the distance, and they had to go by car.

VH: So you didn't go to the *naag 'inoso?*

FOLU: No, I didn't. It was the day the district chief's wife died, so the bride's mother said it didn't matter if I didn't go.

VH: What about the *fao te* 'day before the wedding'?

FOLU: No, I didn't go. I should have gone, but you know, if it were done according to custom, then they should have found me transport to take me there.

VH: Was there anything at the wedding that you weren't happy about?

FOLU: Everything was good. The only thing is that it wasn't a proper wedding. Not like the wedding at Fagʻuta.

VH: What's the difference? Apart from not performing the *fau ta* ritual.

FOLU: And the *fitʻāk te* 'display of fine mats' too.

VH: So why didn't they do the *fitʻāk te*?

FOLU: It means it's not a full-scale wedding.

VH: Do you think you'll be a *hân maneʻāk su* again?

FOLU: That depends on whether anyone wants me or not. (Laughs.)

VH: Did you enjoy the role?

FOLU: I like it, but I'm too old. It's a whole day affair, and I get tired. It's a tiring role, because once the music starts, you have to be up. You can't just sit down listening to the music.

VH: So who are the people in the band?

FOLU: They're relatives of the bride's mother.

VH: Once I saw you tell a man and a woman to sit on your seat? What was that about?

FOLU: I was trying to be funny. Making them look like a married couple. I did it because the woman said to me, "Go and get that man over there so he and I can sit together."

VH: Were there other people telling you what to do?

FOLU: The parents of the bride can tell me things to do. Things that will entertain the crowd.

VH: When you were sitting on your chair, were there people close by giving you ideas?

FOLU: Oh yes, sometimes they tell me to go and force some people to dance.

VH: Did someone tell you to come and pick me to dance?

FOLU: Yes. It was someone from Suva. He told me to pick you to dance. I had seen you earlier, but because you're wearing glasses. . . .

VH: I notice you kept picking the European man to dance.

FOLU: Yes, that man really likes to dance. Also, because he stays next to our house in Itu'muta.

VH: What about 'Ioane? What do you know about her?

FOLU: She was a very good dancer.

VH: Did she ever beat the chiefs?

FOLU: No, she never did.

VH: How did she die?

FOLU: She was married to a man from Losa. You know, I think. . . . Losa is not a good place, so if you live there, you should not just do what you want. But I heard that she didn't care. So I think the spirits of the place got her. For example, at Losa, if there are visitors and it's early evening, you can't wear red clothes and stroll around. But I think she felt that because times have changed and now we see the light, she ignored the rules of the place. My transport has come. I really must go.

VH: Thank you very much.

Interview with Häke, Clown Four

December 1989

After leaving Folu's house, I went looking for Häke. I found her weaving a mat inside her house. Her granddaughter sat close to her on the mat and every now and then demanded the old woman's attention by crying. The little girl's mother was doing some chores in the kitchen, but within earshot.

After I had introduced myself by telling the old woman my parents' names and where I came from, I explained the purpose of my visit. She was happy to talk, although her granddaughter was a little upset (perhaps by my presence) and interrupted our conversation several times. Häke wove her mat as she answered my questions. Intermittently she would stop and chastise her granddaughter.

VH: How many times have you been *hàn mane'àk su?*

HÄKE: Three times.

VH: Can you tell me what is expected of you as the clown?

HÄKE: The clown is the supreme ruler. Whatever she says, goes. But it's the groom's kin that we pay particular attention to.

VH: And you're from the bride's side?

HÄKE: Yes. They really wanted Kava to be the clown but she had gone to Fiji.

VH: Did you go to the *fao te?*

HÄKE: No, I didn't go. I was going to, but someone died.

VH: So what do you have to do as the clown?

HÄKE: You are the ruler on the day of the *fao te,* but only for the bride's kin. You have no right to boss the groom's kin around on the day before the wedding, because you are chosen from the bride's side.

VH: Were you happy with the last performance?

HÄKE: The only thing I was satisfied with is that I did not offend anyone. It is true you are the ruler, but with the chiefs, you should realize that they're different. Some clowns of the past who didn't pay heed to this suffered bad luck. Once they became the clown they just ignored the chiefs, or the district officer. The only way you could tell I was the clown at the last wedding was my different behavior from others, but I was really afraid of the chiefs.

VH: It seems to me that at the last wedding, there was a man who was making a lot of announcements, as though he were the ruler of the wedding . . . what do you think?

HÄKE: He came and told me a number of times to say this and to say that, and I said, "Well, you people in the band came to entertain the crowd, so there shouldn't be a time for you people to rest. If there is anything I don't like, I will tell you. Also, you're an important man and I don't want to be telling you things."

VH: During the couple's dance, when he came and told you to sit down . . . I felt that he was wrong, that you should have asserted your authority.

HÄKE: (Laughs.) Yes, I know. I know my role, but when he said it
        was the couple's dance . . . he had no right to tell me to sit
        down. But when he told me to sit down . . .

VH: I think you were too mild. If that were me, I probably would
        have hit him on the head.

HÄKE: Yes, if it were some other clown, she would have told him to
        shut up. I was the ruler. The couple first and I was second.
        But I just let it go, because I didn't want anyone to have hard
        feelings towards me on that day.

VH: Yes, when I went home, I thought . . . the way that man was
        carrying on, as though he were in charge of the wedding.

HÄKE: Yes, he doesn't know that on this day, the bride's kin are in
        charge. They (the groom's kin) have no control over any-
        thing. If he wanted to say anything, he should have asked
        me. I was the "mouth" of the wedding. When he came and
        told me to sit down, I almost answered back "The couple's
        dance is my dance. You have no right to tell me I can't
        dance." But if I had said that, people would tease me, saying
        that I was really humbling myself. (Laughs.) I don't want
        people to say after the wedding: "You know that *hàn mane'àk
        su* over there, she wants to be!"

VH: If it were a traditional band, would it have been more fun?

HÄKE: Yes, that band's music was more suitable for European-type
        dancing. It's hard to move to such music. You see, my posi-
        tion in the church does not allow me to dance holding
        another man. But I had to dance twice. I can't say I won't
        dance when the men come to ask me. What kind of clown is
        that? So at the end of the wedding, I went to the minister to
        ask forgiveness. I said: "I'm sorry but I've sinned." "Why?" he
        asked. "I danced twice at the wedding," I said. But he said:
        "Woman, that rule is not from Fiji. It's our own rule. If our
        ministers can dance when they go to parties in Fiji, why can't
        you, when you're the *hàn mane'àk su?* So whatever it is you
        want to do as clown, go ahead." I told him I was telling him
        in case someone questioned my integrity as a Christian.

VH: As the clown, which was your favorite wedding?

HÄKE: Not the last one. The last one was difficult. You know the
        Oinafa side is a difficult lot. They are chiefly-oriented. So it

wasn't fun for me. You see, my relatives told me to do what Rua did at the July wedding. She lined up the kin of the groom and laughed at their thin legs. I didn't tell them I wouldn't do it, but I thought to myself, I would never do such a thing. I don't like the idea of making fun of big chiefs. And for what purpose? You may be very happy during the wedding, but you must remember that your elevated status is only temporary, so it is better for you to just dance, but not do what Rua did. Over a period of time, if you keep doing such things, you will suffer bad luck.

VH: There are many women who could have been chosen. Why you?

HÄKE: There are two kinds of clowns. One, you have to be funny; two, you have to be very ugly, so that when you try to do funny things, they'll be even funnier. (Laughs.)

VH: What are the funny things you do to make people laugh?

HÄKE: You tease them, you say funny things. You flirt with the men. But you must make sure that you never get angry. Otherwise you either look stupid, or you look too high and mighty. If you get angry, people will say, "It's only a small thing, but because she wants to show us she's the boss, she gets angry easily." So you have to be very careful.

VH: What about the other side's *te sạmuga* 'mock insult'?

HÄKE: Oh yes. That was why I asked people to tell me the *te sạmuga* of the groom's father. They told me and I shouted it out at the wedding.

VH: Did your relatives thank you for being the clown?

HÄKE: I told them that because we were closely related, they didn't have to thank me. So at the end they gave me just a Fijian mat.

For my purpose, the responses of the four *hàn mane'ȧk su* to my questions were unilluminating, for there was little that I did not know already. In the absence of satisfactory oral or published accounts, I decide to examine Rotuman mythology, to search for narratives that have anything to do with humor, clowning, and laughter. I feel their occurrence or otherwise in mythology will provide an essential clue to the way in which I should examine clowning in a wedding context. It seems important that oral narratives inform my analysis of the ritual clown's performance, and that these two separate genres support and reinforce each other. This will give more weight to my analysis.

Reflections in Myth

Alan Howard's analysis of Rotuman mythology proved very helpful. I discovered that he had found mythology a valuable source for understanding a curious form of kingship on Rotuma in which the position of *sạu* 'king' was held by different districts for restricted periods of time. His analysis confirms my belief that there is a wealth of information on Rotuman culture and history buried in what are often regarded as stories for children, and therefore not worthy of scholarly analysis.

Howard writes: "It is my hope that the case [his analysis of the myths] will prove sufficiently compelling that others will be encouraged to explore the value of myth for unravelling historical mysteries" (1985, 40). As I have been baffled by the mysteries surrounding the institution of *hàn mane'àk su,* I turn to the myths for instruction. Taking Howard's working assumptions as a guide,[2] I analyze the myth of *Kirkirsasa* to see what it has to say about clowning and Rotuman society.

The Myth of Kirkirsasa *and Other Narratives*

The following analysis seeks answers to questions about the nature of Rotuman social organization, particularly relations that influence the clown's behavior in the wedding context: between chiefs and commoners; between males and females; and between kin groups. My discussion here is restricted to what is relevant to the institution of clowning and its place in the Rotuman polity.

The story of *Kirkirsasa* is the only narrative in Churchward's collection in which there is reference to a female who acts the role of clown in order to defeat the 'enemy', although humor is used to similar effect in other tales. I refer to other myths when appropriate. Churchward's collection of oral narratives is the best to date, and the only source that provides both a Rotuman version and a direct English translation. Moreover, the Rotuman versions are written down in the manner they were told to Churchward and appear to be faithful to the oral medium. I reproduce the English translation here in the form it appears in Churchward.[3]

Kirkirsasa is told primarily as a story for children, and may or may not have been based on actual events. In accordance with its didactic nature, the myth encapsulates Rotuman beliefs about cultural order, particularly the consequences of disobedience to authority, and of authority that is oppressive. Embedded are several kinds of tensions inherent in interpersonal relations, as well as the Rotuman view of ritual and laughter as essential ingredients in attaining potency.

Kirkirsasa

(1) There was a woman named *Kirkirsasa*. (2) This woman lived at *Tarkei* (a part of *Maftoa*), and both her armpits were completely covered with tattoo-marks,— (3) They were quite black with them.

(4) Now this woman had some maid-servants living with her, who used to wait on her at all times. (5) The clothes which these maids wore were just pandanus leaf skirts. (6) One day *Kirkirsasa* said to two of these maid-servants of hers, (7) "You two girls take our two sets of coconut-shell cups to *Faniua*, to get some sea-water [with which] to fill our green coconuts; (8) for we put the stoppers in them yesterday but have not yet filled them with salt water."

(9) To this the two maids replied, "All right, madam."

(10) So they turned round and took the two sets of cups, and went off with them. (11) They went on until they reached *Faniua*. But, instead of getting the sea-water (12) they just went for a stroll at the foot of the hill. (13) Presently they went round the point, (14) and went on a little way towards the small beach, (15) when suddenly they heard something snoring at the foot of the big rock above it. (16) And when they looked, they saw something lying there,— a great monster, (17) with his mouth as wide open as it could be, (18) and his teeth fiery-red like red-hot coals of coconut shells. (19) And when they saw what [this huge fellow] was like, (20) it came into their minds at once that it was only giants that were in the habit of behaving in this way. (21) So the two girls discussed the situation for a while, and then decided that they would pelt the monster's teeth [with stones]. (22) Accordingly, each of them proceeded to pick up a stone, (23) which they then threw at the teeth of the giant. (24) This they kept on doing until the giant awoke. (25) On waking, the giant sat up, (26) and the two girls ran. (27) The giant called out to them, (28) but the girls just

glanced round and ran on; (29) and, just as their leaf skirts flew out behind them, the giant got up and chased after them.

(30) Presently *Kirkirsasa* saw the two girls that had gone to fetch sea-water coming along out of breath, exhausted with running, (31) and she exclaimed, "What-ever has happened to you? Is it anything much?"

(32) "O madam," answered the two girls, (33) "it is the most awful thing we have seen in our lives."

(34) "So you have brought disaster upon us, have you?" responded the woman.

(35) "Don't be angry, madam," pleaded the girls; (36) "but a tremendous thing is about to come upon us. (37) We didn't do the work that we went to do, (38) but did something different instead. (39) We woke something up at the foot of the hill—a giant we believe it was, (40) and we think he is just about to appear now. (41) We were in front, and he was behind chasing us."

(42) "You are tiresome and cowardly," said *Kirkirsasa*. (43) However, just seat yourselves down there, (44) and if the giant comes he will eat you. (45) We people are forbidden to do anything to the giant. (46) But don't run away like this."

(47) Before long there was a great clattering noise, (48) and they all turned round, and in came the giant! (49) Sitting down, he at once exclaimed, (50) "Wait till I have rested, and then I'll have my vengeance on you, you [bad] children. (51) Who in the world told you to pelt my teeth with stones?"

(52) *Kirkirsasa,* however, approached the giant with the words: (53) "Good afternoon, sir! (54) And, if you should feel so inclined, just sit down and rest for a few moments, (55) while I dance to you. Wait till that is over, and then eat my two girls, (if you are really going to eat them) after that."

(56) "Dance away!" said the giant, "and let us have a look."

(57) So the woman stood in front of the giant, and began:

(58) "Slap the armpits before the king,
      With a ho! hi! hey!

(59) Raise arms, lower them, dance and sing,
      With a ho! hi! hey!"

(60) Thus *Kirkirsasa* sang her song, (61) dancing all the time. (62) As she danced, she lifted her arms out, first this way and then that way, (63) slapping her tattooed armpits, (64) and extending both arms at once, and jumping up and down,

(65) this way and that way, (66) and raising her arms to reveal her tattoo marks. (67) The giant almost went into a fit with laughing, (68) and whichever way the woman bent over, the giant bent over in the same direction.

(69) As soon as the woman stopped, the giant said, (70) "I say, the markings that I saw in your armpits, what did you do to make them like that?"

(71) "So you like them, do you?" said the woman.

(72) "Oh yes," replied the giant; "[so much so that] if you can make my armpits exactly like yours, then I will not eat these two maids of yours."

(73) To this the woman responded: "Oh, it will be quite easy for me to make your armpits resemble mine, if you really desire it."

(74) "Then will you be kind enough to do it?" said the giant, "so that I may not eat your two maids."

(75) So the woman then told her people to light up a fire-hole, (76) and then to tell her as soon as the stones were red hot; (77) and in the meantime she would talk with the giant.

(78) As soon as the stones were red hot, a man came and told *Kirkirsasa,* (79) who then said to the giant, "Now then! come along to have your armpits tattooed."

(80) So the giant went along, and the woman said, (81) "lie down here between these two posts, that we may tattoo your armpits."

(82) So the giant lay down, (83) and immediately the women-folk brought a roll of sennit, (84) surrounded the giant, and bound him to the posts [in the center of the house, making his legs and arms quite fast. (85) That done, the woman told [them] to fetch a red hot stone. (86) So one of the men brought a red hot stone and gave it to the woman, (87) and the woman inserted it into one of the giant's armpits. (88) Immediately the giant began to yell. (89) But the woman said, "Don't yell for nothing! you see, if you behave like this, the tattooing will not show properly."

(90) But the giant exclaimed: "By and by, when I get free, I will eat up the whole lot of you."

(91) To which the women replied: "But how will you get free? (92) When a person is bound fast, how shall he escape?"

(93) In the meantime each member of the company present [brought] a red hot stone, (94) and some inserted them into

the giant's armpits, others rubbed them on his stomach, while others rubbed them into his eyes and nose. (95) And so it went on until the giant was dead.

(96) As soon as the giant was dead, the woman began to scold her two maid-servants, (97) and to warn all her household, never to do such a thing as this again; (98) lest a big calamity should come upon them and they should not be able to contrive [a way of escape]. (99) True, they had got off this time, (100) but they must never do such a thing in future.

(101) The two maids, on their part, proceeded to apologize to *Kirkirsasa,* (102) confessing that it was all due to their disobedience.

Chief-Commoner Relations

In *Kirkirsasa,* there is a distinction between two sets of associations that form an integral part of the digital code—male: chief, sea; and female: commoner, land (Howard 1985, 52). The giant symbolizes males, chiefs, and kings. *Kirkirsasa,* which literally means "tattooed armpits," symbolizes females, commoners, and the land. As though to reinforce her affiliation, Kirkirsasa lives at Maftoa, in Itu'muta, the westernmost part of the island, which is associated with commoners (Howard 1985, 74). She is portrayed as advising her maid-servants to prepare Rotuma's traditional food (something that women do rather than men), *tähroro* 'a type of sauce made from fermented coconut flesh'. Being tattooed further reinforces Kirkirsasa's association with culture and domesticity, in contrast to the giant, who is not tattooed and therefore wild and uncultured.[4] However, although Kirkirsasa is a woman and not a chief, she has servants to whom she gives orders, and is therefore a mediator between chiefs and commoners. She is an anomaly in that armpits are not ordinarily tattooed. They are both inside (hidden) and outside (seen) the body; her domestication is therefore ambiguous.

The pelting of the monster's teeth with stones sets the stage for a theme of opposition. Contrasted with the females who are up and about with their daily chores is the male (chief, or oppressor) who lies asleep, snoring in broad daylight. Hard work is a much-admired quality amongst Rotumans; *mösrani* 'daytime sleeping' epitomizes laziness. The pelting of the monster's teeth denounces laziness, and perhaps gluttony, as symbolized by the giant's wide open mouth and the "red hot coals." The word for giant in the Rotuman version is *mam'asa,* which means "cruel" or "monster." The giant is therefore a symbol of oppression.

Mention of the girls' attire (in sentences 5 and 29) seems, on the surface, superfluous. However, the descriptions evoke sexual connotations, for if the girls wore nothing else underneath, and "their leaf skirts flew out behind them," then the giant certainly had an "eyeful" of the girls' bare buttocks. Here is an example of action that is open to different readings.

One of the most offensive ways of belittling a male is for a woman to bare her buttocks, and Rotuman readers or listeners will not miss the innuendo in the reference to flying skirts. But the symbolism is as sexually provocative as it is insulting; the giant's response, which is to chase the girls, is suitably ambiguous. Here we encounter the problem of a live art—storytelling—being represented in print. Meanings that are simultaneously conveyed and clarified through tone of voice, facial expression, or gesture are lost; interpretation therefore has to rely solely on the printed word.

The chase inverts the normal order of precedence, with the commoners in front and the "chief" behind. The two maidservants flee for safety into the arms of a female protector, highlighting the male-female opposition, and female (or commoners') solidarity against male (or chiefly) oppression. The responsibility that has now been shifted to Kirkirsasa is daunting; the irony in her question "Is it anything much?" inverts the enormity of the problem. Such indirect belittling of authority figures is revealing of the Rotuman sense of humor.

The girls' plea to Kirkirsasa, "Don't be angry," opens a window into the Rotuman view of anger. To be angry is to be out of control, an emotional state that Rotumans view as destructive to interpersonal relations and the community. In day-to-day interactions, Rotumans "generally precede utterances that might conceivably give offense by saying, *"se fek"* 'don't be angry'" (Howard 1990, 269). To be able to contain one's anger is a sign of strength; even better is to be able to humor one's opponent. To dance in the midst of adversity, however, is to display total control, for it is impossible to dance when frightened, particularly if confronted with a cannibal.

How does the giant represent chiefly oppression? To answer this question, one might begin with Howard's analysis of chieftainship on Rotuma, which claims that chiefs have a kingly aspect that is sanctioned by the divine and a populist aspect that is enhanced by notions of humility and social responsibility (Howard 1992, 111).

Further, the relationship between chiefs and commoners is one of complementarity, "with the people producing food (and other goods and services) for the benefit of the chiefs, who intercede with the gods, who provide abundance to the land" (Howard 1985, 68). But what happens when chiefs are lazy, yet overly demanding? Do commoners continue to tolerate such behavior, or do they subvert authority? The *Kirkirsasa* narrative suggests that in such circumstances, chiefs need to be constrained or overthrown.

Cultural etiquette is important and is underscored by Kirkirsasa's attitude to the giant. Her polite welcome is true to the norm, the implication being that the rules of etiquette (as opposed to the throwing of stones at the giant by the girls) have potency. In other words, the solution is found within the culture. Even the giant approves of cultural control when he says "Dance away!" Furthermore, the rubbing of hot stones on the giant's body is controlled, reminiscent of the tattooing process in which relatives gathered around and laid their hands on the person being tattooed. Tattooing was a sacred act; published accounts indicate that the process was exceedingly painful, and sometimes people died. Men who weren't tattooed were considered incompetent to marry (Allen 1895, no. 5). The rubbing of hot stones on the human body further echoes the rubbing motions of the Rotuman masseuse to bring about healing. *Sarao* 'massage', even today, is one of the "means by which Rotumans maintain an active relationship with their [dead] ancestors" (Howard 1979, 272).

The opposition of "cold" and "hot" is important, for the cold stones symbolize a natural and untamed state (an apt description for the giant), while the hot stones imply a domesticated and controlled condition. The stones, in their "raw" form, are "cooked" by fire until they are red hot; as they come into contact with the giant's body, heat is transferred to cook the skin and surrounding area. Correspondingly, the stones become less and less hot, until they finally resume their previous cold state. The transformation and oscillation from extreme cold to extreme heat is a metaphor for the period that Turner calls the liminal state in which the norms of daily life are suspended. During this liminal state, "almost anything goes: taboos are lifted, fantasies are enacted, the low are exalted and the mighty abased" (Victor Turner 1984, 21).

Rotumans believe that although chiefs and kings are persons, they have a divine aspect. The hot stones are therefore apt metaphors for liminal beings, and aptly suited as the antidote to neutralize the fiery red teeth of the giant. Paradoxically, since in Rotuman thought the hot stones represent commoners,[5] they—particularly those who can take on a liminal state, such as Kirkirsasa or the ritual clown—are responsible for domesticating chiefs and bringing them under control.

If chiefs are not constrained, they will become "cannibalistic," as symbolized by the giant's "I will eat up the whole lot of you." Ideally, they should reflect the will of the people, as implied in the giant's imitation of Kirkirsasa's dance gestures and his wish to be tattooed. This is possible only through domestic constraints, as emphasized by the reference to the house posts and the use of sennit fiber manufactured from natural products. The process of domestication requires a transformation that may be painful, captured eloquently in the giant's yelling (which is uncultured), in resistance to tattooing.

Finally, Kirkirsasa scolds her two maidservants for their disobedience, her rebuke serving as a warning to accord proper respect for authority, and the values of Rotuman society. The two maids apologize for their wrongdoing, and social equilibrium is restored. Kirkirsasa's protective and compassionate attitude is a role model for men, chiefs, kings, and all those in positions of authority.

A narrative titled *The First Kings in Rotuma* (Churchward 1937) presents another rebellion against a king, led by a woman named Hänfakiu.[6] The king in this narrative falls in love with Hänfakiu's brother's wife and takes her. The brother is helpless and looks to his sister for help. She responds, "Don't cry! it's all right! stay where you are, and I will accomplish what you desire. You are a man, and yet you cry like a child." She strangles herself, becomes a spirit, and leads an army of men in a rebellion against the king, who is defeated in battle.[7] Again, the female "domesticates" the king, and restores social equilibrium. In the myths, females feature as mediators; they also reinforce the view that "it is the people who are responsible for elevating the chiefs, for facilitating their sanctification" (Howard 1985, 62).

As a corpus of information, the oral narratives provide insight into the Rotuman view of complementarity between chiefs and commoners. Implicit is the idea that chiefs are in their positions by virtue of popular support. Such support has to be reciprocated in the way of fairness and compassion. When chiefs become too oppressive, their subjects are no longer bound by the norms of society. A popular rebellion becomes justified.

Male–Female Relations

Also implicit in the story of *Kirkirsasa* is the notion that females ruled the land. This notion is reinforced in another narrative titled *The Planting of This Rotuma,* in which the rulers are the eldest and youngest of three sisters and surpass their brother Raho in political power.[8] (The same political structuring is also found in the story of *Mafi and Lu,* which begins with two sisters living in the sky [see Churchward 1938a].) On his arrival on Rotuma, Raho (from Samoa) tied a green coconut leaf around a tree but was cheated by Tokaniua (from Tonga) who arrived later than Raho but tied a dry coconut leaf instead. In his fury, Raho decides to break up the land. Further along in this narrative, he takes a digging stick, goes to the western end of the island, drives it into the ground, and levers up the point, creating the islets off the coast of Rotuma.

The story continues: "But the woman who lived in the scrub, observing that the land was about to be spoiled by *Raho,* came running towards him and bowed at his feet, and besought him not to be angry and not to spoil the land. . . ." When the female twins (of Raho's sister), who had gone to Tonga to bring back *kava* for Raho, learnt of Raho's disgraceful behavior, they sent the *kava* to "the queen of Faguta [district]" instead. Not only is there reversal in this instance, but the assumption that the female was first: the queen, like the woman who lived in the scrub, had been there all the time.

Curiously, the political office called *mua,* which Churchward defined as "chief ranking next to the *sạu* (king) in olden times," also means "to be or go in front or before or first—either in place or time or in order of merit" (Churchward 1940a, 268). According to a French priest, Father Trouillet, the *mua* appeared to be more associated with spiritual power.[9] Wood, writing in 1875 (20), commented that the *mua* was more important than the king, and "described as being like the woman, while the Sou [*Sạu*] was like the man." Both the *sạu* and the *mua* were crucial to the performance of the ritual cycle every six months, when there was a grand gathering, the conch shells were blown, and the various names of fruits and vegetables on the island were called out, in order to secure good crops. Rioting and feasting followed (Wood 1875, 22). Why is the office of *mua* (likened to the female), which means first, actually second to that of the *sạu* (male)? Is this male usurpation? Why are both essential for the efficacy of the rites of fertility?[10] The obvious answer is that females are symbolic of the land and therefore *mua* 'first', and both female and male substances are essential for reproduction. The combined offices therefore symbolized humankind, and the cosmic world, reproducing itself.

Both male and female are essential for regeneration, as symbolized by the complementary but different roles they play in Rotuman society. Men are in charge of muscular or dirty manual labor, including gardening in the bush, fishing in the deep sea, and cooking food in the earthen oven. Women do general light work that is relatively clean: cooking inside the house, looking after the children, fishing inside the lagoon, and weaving mats. The traditional dance called *tạutoga* in which men and women perform together in a *hafa* (half the dancers male, the other half female), symbolizes this code distinction between men and women. The movements for the women are restrained and circumscribed, the men's expansive and vigorous. Sometimes men jump around in a circle within their side of the dancing space, so that what the viewer sees is a juxtaposition of (relative) stasis and movement. The actions may be different, but both are essential for the unity of the dance. Similarly, the roles men and women play in real life may be different, but complementary. Both are interdependent, and cooperation is therefore imperative. Cooperative effort among the populace is also essential in the domestication of chiefs, as symbolized by the division of labor in lines 93–95 of *Kirkirsasa*. Individuals concentrate on "domesticating" different parts of the giant: the armpit (or sexual organs), stomach (gluttony or greed), eyes (sight), nose (sense of smell), and others. At weddings, the complementarity of the roles is clearly delineated: the men arrive with the heavy foodstuffs (cooked pigs, taro, cows), while the women carry the mats.

The relationship between the sexes is best illustrated in the story of *'Äeatos*—discussed in more detail in the next chapter—in which brother and sister are inseparable (Churchward 1938b). In this story, the sister stays around the home and prepares food and *kava* for her brother, who travels out to sea fishing. One day she waits for her brother to return, only to be heartbroken when she sees him carried up to the sky. She weeps and rubs her heel into the ground until she has made a small well, large enough to hold her tears. Her brother, when he finally manages to return to earth, rushes to embrace his sister, who crumbles into dust at his touch. Too lonely without him, she had died of grief, while still in a sitting posture.

The narrative of *'Äeatos* defines the domain of operation for the sexes: the female is confined to the home and its immediate surroundings, while the male wanders farther afield into wilder and more dangerous territories. Like Samoan males, Rotuman men are associated with wresting from hostile environments the energy and nourishment necessary for sustaining human growth. On the other hand, the female is more concerned with maintaining received order, sanitation, and cleanliness (see Shore 1977, 416). Both depend on each other. What happens then in a situation where males spend their days sleeping, as exemplified by the giant in *Kirkirsasa?*

In "Lalatäväke and Lilitäväke"[11] is another example of male oppression (Churchward 1939a). Lalatavake and Lilitavake are two sisters. The younger one, Lilitavake, marries the prince Tinrau and goes to live with him in the king's house.[12] But after the celebrations, the king says to his son, "I want to eat your wife." Before this happens, however, the elder sister arrives in the form of a bird and takes her sister's place, having hung up her feathers in a basket and covered her sister with a fine mat. The prince, who does not realize he is talking to a different sister, arrives just before the time appointed for the killing and starts weeping. "But the girl [elder sister], on speaking to the man [prince], laughed. 'What are you crying for?' she asked; 'surely your father cannot really want to eat me!'" The elder sister then puts her feathers on again and flies out of the curved end of the house, followed by her younger sister who is now transformed into a tropic bird and joins her in the air. In mythology, anything is possible, and females can acquire wings. But how does the female cope with a husband's tyranny in real life? Or, how do Rotumans deal with relations that are problematic and prone to conflict?

In Rotuma, there are few opportunities to see overt conflict. In my sixteen years of growing up on the island, not once did I witness a fist fight. This does not mean Rotumans never lose control. Rather, in situations where there is disagreement, Rotumans resort to nonphysical ways of mediation first. At the family or kin level, shame and ridicule are common ways of making people conform, or recognize that they have erred. In addition, many tensions are sublimated into play. In this safe arena, potential conflict is dissipated, even displaced. Sometimes tensions are veiled as mock insults, which may be accepted without losing face.

Teasing—known as *te sạmuga*—is a social institution on Rotuma. A *te sạmuga* is a mock insult that is identified with one's ancestors. Each kin group has a *te sạmuga,* the most well known of which is "biscuit planters." Although any Rotuman in Fiji may be teased as a biscuit planter by Fijians, it is strictly the *te sạmuga* of only a certain kin group who, according to the joke, planted biscuits thinking that they grew on trees. In *te sạmuga* is a gold mine of jokes that are not only humorous, but instructive about the early period of contact with Europeans.

A *te sạmuga* mock insult draws attention to differences and tensions between individuals or kin, and serves to belittle those not of the same ancestral stock. At the same time, it affirms solidarity with a particular group. It reminds individuals of their ignorance or (inherited) stupidity and prevents them from having inflated opinions of themselves. Anger, jealousy, arrogance, resentment, and their many permutations may be veiled in the form of *te sạmuga,* which is broad enough and ambiguous enough to encompass a range of intentions. As custom dictates that the party being called by their *te sạmuga* cannot take offense, it is particularly valuable as an indirect way of communicating ambivalence. In a wedding context, therefore, it is common for the ritual clown to announce the *te sạmuga* of the groom's side in an attempt to diffuse tension through laughter. Ritual clowning is one of the most effective ways of mediating tension.

*　　*　　*

My analysis of mythology supports the view that humor is an essential aspect of Rotuman culture; the practice of ritual clowning at weddings is therefore clowning par excellence. In the wedding context, humor is elevated to the status of a socioreligious institution. Logically then, all the pragmatic functions that humor serves in mythology and in other social contexts should also be present in the institution of ritual clowning at weddings.

Except for one main difference: Although clowning at other social occasions is spontaneous, it is not in traditional weddings because the *hàn mane'àk su* is formally chosen. In the wedding context, she becomes the supreme ruler, with customary license to instigate laughter and castigate those in positions of authority in any way she fancies. Why so? The answer lies in the value Rotumans place on humor, and its role in mediating conflict between disparate elements in society.

Howard is correct in noting several avenues for resolving conflict in Rotuma: punishment by the spirits (usually in the form of curses from the lips of chiefs); avoidance of each other; mediation by the chiefs between disputants in their domains; apologies (in private or in public); and law enforcement by the government of Fiji (Howard 1990). However, he omits an important avenue for conflict management (perhaps because it is covert and masquerades as laughter): the role of play or humor in conflict mediation, particularly the institution of ritual clowning embodied in the *hàn mane'àk su.*

With insights from mythology and the social contexts in which clowning occurs, my next step is to analyze data relevant to a specific wedding, then explicate the role and place of the *hàn mane'àk su* in Rotuman society at large.

5 *Woman on Top: Why Not?*

> Comedy [is a] playful speculation on what was, is, or
> might be; a remark on the indignity of any closed
> system.
>
> BARBARA BABCOCK, *"Arrange Me into Disorder"*

Prelude to a Wedding

Traditional Rotuman culture has always had a strict code of conduct
regarding premarital sex for girls, as reflected in its emphasis on
virginity for the bride.[1] The arrival of Christianity, with its own list
of prohibitions, further reinforced beliefs in the value of chastity
before marriage. Because marriages in the past were arranged, it
was possible for couples not to have met in secret until the wedding
day. A girl's virginity was seen as important in terms of securing a
husband, and it was in the interest of her kin to protect her from
male seduction. It was also customary for husbands to go to live at
the homes of their wives, and a girl who remained chaste had better
chances of attracting a husband than one who had a reputation for
being promiscuous. A virgin was an asset to her entire village and
kin. A young girl was forbidden to wander alone at night or to spend
time with a man on her own. One who was unfortunate enough to
become pregnant without a husband brought shame on herself and
her relatives. Boys, however, were allowed to be sexually active; they
could wander until all hours of the morning (see Howard n.d.).
Here was a double-standard in Rotuman socialization of young
people.

Marriage brings the period of youth, with all its associated privileges, to an abrupt end. Soon after the wedding, a newly married
couple, are expected to be productive members of the community.[2]
They are no longer called *haharagi* 'young'; instead they are *mamfua*
'old', implying that they have entered a new phase in life (adult-

65

hood), with family responsibilities. A wedding is a public announcement of this change in status for the couple.

There are three kinds of marriage (Malo 1975, 12). The "ideal marriage" is arranged between families and involves a series of gift exchanges that culminate in a full-scale wedding as befits a virgin bride. The other two kinds are smaller affairs either because the young man has taken the matter into his own hands and gone to stay with the young woman, or because the woman has run away with her preferred spouse. Both of these are tainted with shame, and the ceremonies are brief and usually confined to the immediate families of the couple.

Since the 1980s, many variations on these three types have emerged: More and more couples now choose their partners, although their parents may act as though the match were arranged. Today less shame is attached to non-arranged marriages and pregnant brides; such weddings are not necessarily confined to the immediate families, as was customary. Instead, all kin of the bride and the groom may be called on to share the burden of hosting a wedding.

Kin Groups: Kạinaga and Sal Hapa

Rotuman social organization is based on the concept of kạinaga 'relatives'.[3] Rotumans inherit privileges from both parents, and each person is regarded as having eight kạinaga, corresponding to each of their great-grandparents (see also Howard 1990). Because of the heavy burden of a full-scale traditional wedding, all kin belonging to the bride and groom are usually informed about the wedding, the implication being that they should assist. They are expected to contribute mats, food, and labor, with the implicit understanding that a reciprocal opportunity will occur sooner or later. Today, Rotumans believe that the more money you have, the more likely will your relatives be to recognize you or offer their help in life-crisis ceremonies. As money is now an integral part of life on the island, relatives are conscious of the costs of a full-scale traditional wedding, and such weddings are now rare. When they do occur, not all relatives may want to be involved. The burden to the immediate families can be great, and resentment may arise toward those unwilling or unable to assist.

Implicit in relations between kin are tensions associated with status. Each kin group is concerned about its status in the community and will ensure that in life-crisis ceremonies such as weddings or funerals its reputation and standing are consolidated, if not enhanced. Individuals will go out of their way, sometimes at great cost, to ensure a lavish display of food and mats at a traditional wedding. Those who attend weddings do so as members of a *kainaga*. No one goes as an individual, for one must have a *sal hapa* 'route' that links up with the *kainaga* of either the bride or groom.

The groom's kin are called the *kau fa* (*fa* meaning male), and the bride's kin *kau hani* (*hani* meaning female). But the word *kau* does not mean just "kin, sort, class, number or similar things," but also "to take sides with, to befriend; to second or support" (Churchward 1940a, 239). In a wedding, there is cooperation between members of the same kin group, and covert competition with other kin groups. Each kin group vies to create a better impression than the other, although none would admit that this is one of the main motives behind the weaving of fine mats and the assemblage of root crops and animals that take place months before a wedding. If the imbalance is marked when fine mats are exchanged between the two kin groups at the end of the wedding, it may appear that one group has benefited more than the other. Resentments may arise, but since airing them publicly would cause discord, they are usually whispered about and sublimated in play, in the context of ritual clowning.

In Rotuma, a person marries into another kin group and acquires new obligations, as well as a wife or husband. In cases where the kin of either side feel they have little to gain from an alliance with the other, tensions are likely to be covert, but nonetheless real. Like male–female relations, kin relations are marked by complementarity, as symbolized by the union of bride and groom, who are different in temperament (and gender) yet expected to live together in harmony. In relations of complementarity, conflict is not supposed to exist, yet it does, kept beneath the surface, rumbling like boiling lava in search of a vent to escape (see Shore 1977).

The Role of Chiefs

At the time of European discovery in 1791, Rotuma was divided into seven districts, each headed by a *gagaj 'es itu'u* 'district chief' (Howard 1986). Each district was composed of a number of villages, consisting of several households headed by a village chief. Three positions were pan-Rotuman in scope: the *fakpure*, the *sau*, and the *mua.* The *fakpure*, who was head of one of the districts, was convener and presiding officer of the council of district chiefs, and one of his responsibilities was to appoint the *sạu* 'king' (Howard 1985, 40–41). The *sạu*'s role was to be an object of veneration at the end of every six months, when the ritual cycle to maintain fertility of the land and the people was performed. Little has been written about the office of the *mua*, except in relation to his involvement in the ritual cycle. However, Gardiner claimed that the term of office for the *sạu* was six months (one Rotuman ritual cycle) although an extension was usually allowed if he could provide great masses of food to justify his position (Gardiner, 41).

Once chosen, the *sạu* moved out to live in another district (see Howard 1985, 67). It became the responsibility of his newly adopted district to feed and care for him. A *sạu* who was lazy and gluttonous became a burden to the people, and resentment grew as people became more and more aware of his lack of *mana* 'potency' and his failure to reciprocate in exchange for the burden of looking after him. Writing in 1875, Wood described the *sạu*'s duty, and the *mua*'s, as consisting "in being fed, night and day, in fact, systematically fattened." He added:

> Three times every night he was roused to eat, and pigs were killed everyday for him, the chiefs and old men eating with him: such waste and extravagance, indeed, was practised, that the tribe in which the [*sạu* and the] Mooa [sic] resided was generally short of provisions. (Wood 1875, 21)

In contemporary Rotuma, the office of *sạu* has been abandoned. Instead, chiefs with responsibility toward their subjects at the district level hold the highest political positions. Unlike Samoa and Tonga, where the chiefs still wield considerable political influence, Rotuman chiefs have little. Their function is mainly ceremonial. They are viewed with much ambivalence by many of their subjects, who see them as enjoying certain privileges (such as eating the best foods at ceremonies) without having the means (or inclination) to reciprocate. Today, the traditional chiefs sometimes have to compete with allegiances toward others who are more affluent in European terms.

Prior to a wedding, the parents of the bride and the groom separately seek the blessings of their district chief. Once the *hån mane'åk su* has been identified, she informs her district chief, who has to sanction her designated role as "ruler" of the wedding festivities. Though the two district chiefs involved and village-level subchiefs of these two districts usually attend the weddings of their subjects, they have no formal power to influence the proceedings. At the end of the wedding, however, each chief is thanked by those who sought their blessings prior to the wedding, usually with a *koua* 'offering of cooked foods and meat' and a fine mat.

The period leading up to the wedding requires consultation among everyone involved, but particularly between relatives of the bride and groom, if the proceedings are to run smoothly. It is a period when the bonds of kinship are tested. Aspirations of close relatives are usually high, but may not be matched by what they, or their relatives, are prepared to sacrifice in order to enhance their status. It is rare indeed not to hear criticisms of relatives who are seen as too mean, too lazy, too greedy, or too insensitive. Criticisms are often leveled at other kin whose ideas on specific details may not correspond with the wishes of members of the other party, or whose chosen bride or groom may not be seen as the "equal" of the other. Tensions are inevitable as the wedding draws near, but because of the need to present a united front before the other kin group and society at large, such "rumblings" remain half-suppressed and tend to surface primarily in the realm of *hagäe* 'slander' or 'backbiting'. People are mindful of the importance of maintaining harmonious relations, partly because everyone is in some way or other con-nected—if not related—and partly because the island is so small and people have to interact with each other frequently. After all, where can they escape? Ritual clowning at weddings provides a safety valve.

A Specific Wedding

Wedding one, in which Ta was the *hån mane'åk su,* was between a young man in paid employment and a woman from well-to-do par-ents. Though material wealth was not the dominant factor in the match, it is worth pointing out that today, a man or woman in paid employment is regarded as an attractive spouse. Likewise, a bride from a fairly wealthy family, or who has a regular paid job, is regarded as a sensible choice.[4] By today's standards, this was a big wedding in terms of mats, food, and the number of people who attended. Although Rotumans described this wedding as *su re fak su* 'a proper wedding' some elements were European in origin;[5] the wedding is best described by Adrienne Kaeppler's term "evolved tra-ditional" (1989, 236).

The video crew[6] of three and I stayed in Mea, my home village and the groom's as well. On the day before the wedding, the men and women of Mea gathered together and prepared food and other materials for the next day. However, because my main interest was the clown, the video crew and I left at six o'clock that morning for the bride's village, where her relatives, including the clown, were gathered. While the video crew filmed her, I observed the clown's behavior and the nature of her interaction with other people. We did the same on the wedding day. When the couple was brought to Mea two days after the wedding, the clown did not perform because a close relative had died.

In the past, the main consideration for the choice of clown was skill; today, relatedness to the bride's parents is the main factor. One reason for this shift could be that growing acquisitiveness among Rotumans motivates relatives of the bride to seek to keep the rewards of fine mats customarily given to the clown at the end of the wedding within their kin group. Secondly, a close relative is easier to influence; she can be told frankly where the boundaries of license lie. If she oversteps the boundary of privileged expression—as defined by those who selected her—she can be denied the customary rewards without fear of retaliation.

A typical setting for wedding celebrations on Rotuma, and the one that was adopted for this wedding, is illustrated on p. 71. The seating arrangement symbolizes the union of two kin groups through marriage; the oppositional arrangement of the kin groups symbolizes the tensions inherent in marriage.

The Day before the Wedding

The day before the wedding is called *fao te* 'the day of food preparation'.[7] Male relatives of the bride began arriving at the bride's home at daybreak, bringing with them live animals, bananas, bundles of taro, yams, and other root crops. Women relatives arrived bearing fine mats and mats of less importance.[8] The women stayed inside or near the house for most of the day; the men cleaned around the temporary shelter erected a few days earlier for the wedding guests. The men also made enormous earthen ovens to cook the food for the following day and let them smolder overnight, to be opened on the wedding morn.

The clown wore a bright blue dress with an overskirt of leaves tied around her waist and carried a four-foot stick given to her by a male

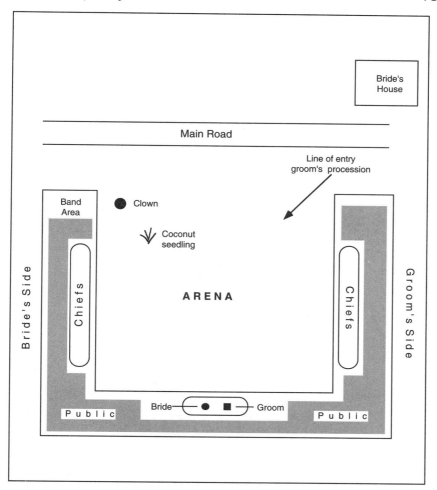

Layout of the wedding site, wedding one. (By *Alan Howard*)

relative.[9] She wore no make-up; apart from the overskirt and the stick she looked very much like the rest of the women. During the early morning the clown moved around the house supervising the work of the women, welcoming relatives, and coordinating the order of events for this day. Toward midday she moved to the arena, where women and children who had nothing to do were gathered. The band hired to play at the wedding was already in place tuning their instruments. The clown walked in and sat on a chair next to the band—the only other people seated on chairs—and started to hurry them up. Then she shouted at certain individuals in the

The *hàn mane'àk su* who performed for wedding one, 1987. *(Aren Baoa)*

crowd, threatening to force them to dance. Sometimes she teased people about their appearance.

Seeing me seated with my tape recorder, note book, and pen, the clown announced in a loud voice that she and I would be the first to dance when the music started. A woman close by responded on my behalf, telling the clown she ought to be kind to me on this day. I was from the groom's side, the clown answered, so what was I doing there? She announced that relatives of the groom would suffer when they arrived on the following day. When the music started, she pointed her stick at me. I got up and we danced.

The rest of the day proceeded in similar fashion, with the clown ordering people about or directing them to attend to certain chores. At lunch time, the guests were offered a meal, after which they dispersed. The clown's behavior on this day was like a dress rehearsal for the wedding day. During the food preparations at the bride's house, the groom's relatives were gathered at his home engaged in similar activities; however, they were not entertained by a clown.

The Day of the Wedding

The clown wore a bright red dress with a yellow grass skirt around her waist; where it ended, the white cotton material she wore under her dress was visible. Red flowers adorned her hair, which was pulled back from her face and tied in a bun. She carried a stick in her right hand and a fan in her left; occasionally she pulled out a handkerchief to wipe the perspiration from her face.

About seven thirty in the morning, the bride, her relatives, and the chiefs of her district took their seats underneath and around the temporary shelter to await the arrival of the groom's party, scheduled for nine o'clock. As people sat waiting the band played some songs and the clown tried to stimulate activity among the spectators. Occasionally she succeeded in forcing someone to dance with her in the arena.

The band hired for this wedding consisted of a group of men whose equipment included an electronic keyboard, several electric guitars, and loudspeakers. They sang mainly popular songs composed by overseas musicians (from Fiji, New Zealand, or America, especially); as a concession to the assembled company, they occasionally sang a Rotuman song to a pop tune. Youths and adults alike danced in disco style.

As soon as the groom's party appeared on the main road, the singing and dancing ceased and the bride's party took their places under the temporary shelter.[10] As they came close, the groom's procession crouched low to the ground as a mark of respect. At the front of the procession were the groom, his best man, and their chaperone—a woman skilled in Rotuman oratory—who was invited as the groom's spokesperson to request entry to the arena.[11] The chief's representative, called the *'asu* 'the one who eats the wedding feast', was next.[12] Behind them were women carrying fine mats, followed by more women laden with mats of lesser importance, yards of colorful fabric, and the couple's *mosega* 'bed' consisting of a mosquito net, a small basket called the *'at fara*, pillows, and bedclothes. The chiefs from the groom's side were next; at the rear were men carrying kava root, *fono* 'baskets of cooked food' (pork and beef that had been cooked overnight in the earthen ovens), *fekei* 'Rotuman puddings', and *te mafa* 'fruits'. At the very end of the procession were men carrying cooked taro called *utu*, which symbolized the groom coming home from his garden after a day's work.[13]

After a favorable response by an orator from the bride's side, the groom's party stood up and approached the center of the arena. The groom took his seat to the right of the bride, on top of the fine mats where she sat. The chiefs from the groom's district sat on the ground to the groom's right, facing the chiefs of the bride's side. After placing their mats in front of the couple, the women relatives of the groom screened the shelter with their colorful fabric[14]—in the past fine mats would have been used—to signal the beginning of the ritual clowning, the period Turner (1984, 22) called "liminality," the suspension of daily reality. The men followed with their food offerings, which they placed behind the mats in front of the couple, after which they proceeded to greet the bridal couple. The band played a lively tune and the merrymaking began. Those not directly involved in the rituals danced or fooled around, led by the clown, who was not directly involved in any of the rituals; instead, she hurried people up or hurled mock insults at them.

After the groom's party had joined the bride's, a number of rituals were performed: first the *paag ri* 'screening of the temporary shelter', then the *'öf söp ta* 'the symbolic cutting of hair of both bride and groom', followed by the *fit'ak te* 'a public display of fine mats', the *fạu ta* 'the wrapping of fine mats—separately—around the bride and groom', and the carrying of each of them on the shoulders of young men to the front of the chiefs seated at the groom's side of the temporary shelter.[15] Clowning continued during the enactment of the rituals. At about twelve thirty in the afternoon, the festivities culminated in a wedding feast, which signaled the end of the formal proceedings. Soon after the feast, the wedding guests started to walk back to their various homes.

Two Days after the Wedding

The bride and groom remained at the bride's home until two days after the wedding, when it was time for the ceremony called *naag 'inoso* 'to pass on the couple'. The bride and groom are sent to the groom's home for the first time, then sent back to the bride's home. On the second day, they and the bride's relatives were taken on a bus to the groom's home for the appropriate rituals and festivities. As is the custom, the relatives of the bride arrived on this occasion with a *koua* 'cooked food and meat used as an offering', *mosega* 'bed' for the couple to sleep on, and presents of mats. The *mosega,* provided by the bride's side this time, consisted of a pile of mats, a mosquito net, and two pillows. These were accompanied by the small basket—*'at fara*—that the bride's kin had brought on the wedding day, containing a piece of cloth that the bride was supposed to use after the sexual act to provide evidence of virginity. These days, when virginity tests are no longer practiced and money may be placed inside it instead, the basket is brought along for its symbolic meaning.

The clown did not perform on this day because of a death in her family; instead, two *haian re malumu* 'funny women' and a man provided the entertainment. The funny man appeared wearing a skirt of leaves and a blackened face. He ogled the girls and pranced around trying to scare the children. Accompanying him was a funny woman from the bride's side and another from the groom's side.[16]

The merrymaking culminated in feasting, after which the relatives of the bride returned to their homes in the early evening. The *hàn mane'àk su,* who had come dressed like any other woman, stayed behind with another woman relative to spend the night at the groom's house. In the morning, the clown, the bride and groom, and the female relative were taken back to the bride's home accompanied by the groom's relatives and a *koua.* The groom's relatives returned soon afterward and then dispersed to their homes. The return of the bride and groom marked the end of the clown's public responsibilities.

Discussion

If the men make the decisions, make the speeches, and strut around as chiefs in real life, then a traditional wedding redresses the imbalance. The spheres of operation, of dominance, for men and women are demarcated. However, Rotuman women do not feel the need to compete with men in day-to-day living; they are too busy keeping the machinery of life in the home functioning smoothly to strut around as chiefs. Unlike men, who are fascinated by power play—as symbolized by the fight for supremacy between Raho and Tokaniua over the land (see chapter 6)—women are more interested in stability, order, and spiritual matters (see also Shore 1989, 163). In the sanctioned arena of play, women make known to men that they, too, are capable of being chiefs. The hierarchy that culture has imposed is arbitrary and could be overturned unless women willingly support it.

Like Kirkirsasa (chapter 6), the clown is an anomaly, a powerful and mysterious figure that invites analysis. To understand her existence in a wedding context, and the messages she communicates by her actions, is to gain valuable insight into what makes Rotuman society tick, and tick so well. As an enigma, the clown's message is difficult to unravel. Does she really mean what she is saying, or is she just joking? Is she speaking in role, or is she speaking as a relative of the bride? Her communication may be direct—so direct that we laugh when we hear her. She relates in a way we do not experience at any other time, a way that is novel. For example, we are usually polite when we ask people to dance. We don't point a stick at a chief's face and say, "You, get up!" Her behavior may be inconsistent: sometimes she says one thing, but her body language says another. Such behavior is subject to multiple readings; her performance is "an exercise in understanding, a planned confusion created in order to be clarified" (Levin 1966, 128).

Rotuman clowning communicates through inversion. Values of humility, respect, and restraint—cornerstones of Rotuman society that are essential for the maintenance of social harmony—are inverted, and like the chiefs, replaced by their antithesis. Paradoxically, the clown's violation of Rotuman values reinforces them at the same time. For example, by dethroning the chiefs, she draws attention to who they are. By being arrogant, she reminds us of humility.

The clown's behavior, and that of other funny women who join her, provides another view of the structure of social relations, unhinging the foundations of the common patriarchal view and the norms instituted by culture and religion. Though suspension of the rules of daily life is only temporary, it has the potential to effect changes in the wider arena of daily interaction when the social drama is over. To turn the familiar world upside down is like standing on one's head to view the sky. The scene from the bottom up is unusual, often revealing, but we cannot walk around on our heads for too long; it is impossible. Yet, we have seen the view from the other side and are afterward more reflective about alternative ways of seeing. Should we decide that a different view of reality is more appealing, the necessary action for change rests with us. Although clowning and comedy "remind us of the existence of the rule" (Eco 1984, 6), they also remind us that such rules do not exist without support. The rules are rules as long as we obey them. Clowning has the potential to effect change; whether it does is another matter.

Although the *hàn mane'àk su*'s performance appears to be extemporaneous, certain implicitly obligatory kinds of behavior are nonetheless influential. The clown, together with other women from the bride's side, is expected to force the men of the groom's side to submit to her bidding, whatever it may be. On this day, women are given special recognition to compensate for their submissive status in normal everyday life.

At weddings, relations of complementarity that are conflictprone—between chief and commoner, between male and female, and between kin groups—are inverted and reexamined. The wedding context, like plays of the western world, provides a frame in which forces that are potentially threatening to the well-being of its members can be acted out and diffused, displaced, or resolved in a safe arena. Clowning, in the safe context of a wedding, is an act of communication, from females to males, from commoners to chiefs, and from the bride's kin to the groom's kin. The nature of the communication is from the bottom up, from the most oppressed, to the oppressor. Again, inversion (in this case, of the everyday hierarchy) is the pattern. What then are the messages?

Humility in Chief–Commoner Relations

The female clown causes much amusement by behaving like a chief, even one who embodies power in its most oppressive form. In a society where the chiefs are men, role and status reversal invite laughter, particularly when authority is displayed in its extreme form. Yet, such inversion is for a purpose. The wedding context offers an opportunity for chiefs to feel what it means to be ordered about. The clown saves the chiefs from being too pompous, from ever forgetting that although they may have divine sanctification for their positions, they are still mere mortals who depend on their fel-

At the wedding feast, the chiefs (men) are served their food on raised wooden tables by the women. Wedding two, 1989. *(Jan Rensel)*

low beings for their privileged status. A Rotuman wedding is an arena in which the chiefs and men learn humility.

Chiefs and ordinary men who are ordered about experience how it feels to submit. In Rotuma, as in other parts of Polynesia, the group is all important. Personal interest should not supersede community interest. For Rotuman society to function harmoniously, submission to authority is necessary. The clown therefore displaces the chief and assumes his power in its inverse, extreme form. If everyone in the community can submit to a clown, then submission to the powerful, supposedly the chiefs, should be second nature. For the chiefs, particularly, humility will prevent them from behaving like gods who walk the earth.

The actions of the clown reinforce the value of humility in an inverse way. For example, in this wedding the clown broke a number of Rotuman behavioral norms with the following actions:

> Holding a chief by the waist and directing his movements while they danced.
>
> Ordering the chiefs and the district officer dancing in the shade to move into the sunshine.
>
> Refusing to agree to a suggestion that the chiefs drink kava before lunch.[17]

Saying she was taking the district chief from the groom's side home at the end of the wedding.
Ordering two chiefs to stand in the hot sun.
Commanding the crowd to call her Princess Sakura.[18]

In one way or another, the clown was asserting her prerogative as supreme ruler of the wedding. During this period of free play, the world was turned upside down; the weak became strong, and the strong were forced to submit. Victor Turner noted that this phase is "about the doffing of masks, the stripping of statuses, the renunciation of roles, the demolishing of structures" (1984, 26). The higher the status of the clown's target, the louder the laughter. The clown and the old women sitting close to her took great delight in conspiring to get their own back. Once or twice the clown was annoyed at the reluctance of some chiefs to obey her orders to dance, and women close by were quick to remind her of her powers and to offer advice. Their coaxing was a challenge that the clown always took up. In one difficult case, she even went down on her knees in mock deference. When inversion did not work, she tried exaggerated politeness. The reluctant chief obliged in the end. By humbling herself, the clown focused attention on the chiefs' stubbornness, if not arrogance. Her message was: "Look, I can force you to obey me, I can even hit you with my stick, but I won't. Instead, I'll go down on my knees to beg you, sir." This of course is only one interpretation, for a clown's actions are always open to different readings.

The word *mane'ạki,* from which *mane'ȧk* is derived, means "to spoil, damage, injure; to waste; to desecrate, violate, profane; to break (a promise or a commandment); to upset the peace or well being of." The word *mane'a,* which is the meaning modern Rotumans associate with the word *mane'ȧk,* means "to play, to indulge in any form of recreation or relaxation" (Churchward 1940a, 259). Both meanings are embedded in the term *mane'ȧk,* although the play element is more apparent in the clown's antics today. The idea of the clown as spoiling or desecrating the wedding suggests a much more powerful and dangerous role.

In 1989, for example, I screened the videotape *The* Hàn Mane'ȧk Su *at a Rotuman Wedding* (which is about wedding one) at the University of the South Pacific in Suva, Fiji. After the seminar that followed, Vaivao Fatiaki (a Rotuman man living in Suva) pulled me to the side and said that the term *hàn mane'ȧk su* does not mean just to play or entertain, but also to *re mane'ȧk* 'to spoil'. According to him, the clown of the past often beat people up, was violent and abusive. She also destroyed food and implements brought by the groom's side. There is no evidence of such destruction in weddings today, although mock antagonism is still evident in a traditional wedding. What then was the clown supposed to be spoiling? Was she mimicking chiefly destruction? Was she reenacting the ancient myth of the founding of Rotuma? Was she playing the part of Raho, or *hanit te ma'us,* the "wild woman" who tried to prevent destruction of the land? Or did she perhaps embody both characters in her dramatis persona? Or was she playing the chief?

The influence of the "spirit-woman" or "woman who lived in the scrub" on Rotuman social behavior and thinking is under-researched, but worthy of further discussion. The word *ma'us* could mean either "scrub," as translated by Churchward, or "to be sexually stimulated or aroused." Rotumans believe that *hanit te ma'us* resides at the far western end of the island, which reinforces the earlier interpretation of females representing the common people. In mythology *hanit te ma'us* is a symbol of the land, combining domesticity and supernatural powers (Howard 1985, 56). When destruction of the land was threatened, she was the one who stepped in and mediated between two warring males, Raho and Tokaniua.

A similar but inverted pattern occurs in the wedding when the chiefs of the two kin groups sit facing each other as the clown runs around, carrying a stick and destroying the social hierarchy of society. Is this a symbolic destruction of the land, a reminder of how the island was threatened because of a battle between two warring chiefs? Does the scene at the wedding hark back to this ancient myth, the best-known of all Rotuman myths? Is the *hån mane'åk su* reminding the chiefs of the destructive nature of power, and of the saving grace of mediation and humility? Clearly, the clown's behavior is open to many interpretations, not all of which are obvious. But for Rotumans for whom mythology and reality are fused, the clown's destructive behavior may remind them of Raho's destruction of the land and the intervention of *hanit te ma'us.*

Restraint in Male–Female Relations

As Rotuman marriages were arranged in the past, the mock antagonisms of women toward men may stem from resentment that they were given away by their male kin, not only for childbearing, but for economic or political purposes as well. The clown leads the women who align themselves against the authority of men and elders, lamenting the absence of romantic love as a basis for marriage.[19] Today, most couples marry for love, and men and women play more equal roles, although chiefs are still males. As Rotuman society becomes more "democratic," and the power of chiefs erodes further, perhaps there will be less need for a clown. This may be one reason why the clowns of today are not as powerful, for there may be less need for a strong inversion by way of compensation for women's status in daily life. Marriages, for example, are no longer arranged without the bride and groom's consent, and women nowadays have a much greater say in whom they want to marry.

In Rotuman society, usually the man initiates. He is expected, however, to be polite in his approaches to a woman, winning her cooperation through gentle coaxing. Admittedly, this is not always the case. The clown and her funny women provide men with an opportunity to experience what it is like when men lose control, and treat women abominably. On rare occasions, women are sometimes shouted at, or forced against their will. Society expects women, young girls particularly, to be constrained and restrained, in contrast to men, who wander more freely, day and night. Old women who have borne many children and who weave the fine mats are probably the most oppressed, for their work is often taken for granted. Domestic and mundane responsibilities are usually left in their hands. Men, in contrast, make decisions that affect the whole of society, often without consultation. The reverse happens at weddings; women are afforded a chance to rule, if only temporarily.

In wedding one, for example, funny women from the bride's side bossed the men from the groom's side. One of them grabbed a young man and hit him on the head with her fist. She also threw a handful of sand at another man's face.[20] The aggressive manner in which this funny woman behaved, as well as the *hån mane'åk su's* commands and lack of manners, exemplify the opposite of the controlled behavior that is the norm in Rotuman culture in interactions between men and women.

The *hån mane'åk su* was accompanied in her performance by several old women, secure in their roles as wives and mothers. A woman from the groom's side challenged men from the bride's side to a karate duel, and the acceptance of this challenge caused much hilarity.[21] The karate duel consisted of exaggerated arm-swinging movements and manly posturing. There was no actual body contact, despite the flailing arms and kicking feet. In this instance, contrary behavior was the cause of laughter. The uneven match between the sexes depicted conflict that is unacceptable to Rotumans, and unthinkable. For the bride and groom watching, as well as the assembled company, the drama being enacted before them was "spiritual shock therapy...a playful speculation of what was, is, or might be" (Babcock 1984, 103). It was a symbolic representation of disharmony and the unleashing of chaotic emotion, which is destructive to family, kin, and group. Indeed, the threat to peaceful island life that was caused by a would-be king's attempt at power (Howard 1992) and inspired this karate duel, was evidence enough of the futility and dangers inherent in conflict, whether it be a man against the majority of society, or a domestic quarrel between man and wife. Capturing it in play allows Rotumans to laugh at a real story of conflict—of which kind is up to the spectator—that is not a laughing matter.

As the clown is female but behaves as male, both male and female attributes are indirectly communicated. The conjunction in the one individual of male aggressiveness and female lack of control, for example, results in chaos. The model that the clown holds up for scrutiny must be rejected. Through inversion, the clown affirms the complementary but different natures of the sexes. Also, since her rule results in chaos, the possibility of women taking over the reins of power outside the context of play is not taken seriously.

Unrestrained behavior, and in particular, sexual license, is anathema to Rotumans; it leads to quarrels that disrupt the peace. Yet the clown and her funny women violated taboos on provocative sexual behavior. Through gestures, rolling eyes, mock faints, and erotic idiom, they improvised sexual innuendoes that delighted spectators. Watching the clown and her funny women provided vicarious gratification. Even the chiefs joined in, acknowledging and sanctioning the clown's flagrant disregard of important taboos. By laughing, they were affirming their rightful positions in the play context.

The value of controlled sexuality is best realized in the high premium placed on virginity for the bride. A virgin bride embodies restraint in its extreme form: the bride's alter ego, the clown, celebrates such an accomplishment. A wedding without a virgin is a wedding without a clown. By her unbridled sexual license, the clown exalts the status of the virgin bride and the containment of her sexuality.

Rotumans often refer to an elevation in status as *Sik iạ se rere* 'to lift up someone on high', which is exactly what one of the rituals does. After being bound in fine mats, both bride and groom are lifted up and carried on the shoulders of young men, a symbolic statement of the value of sexual restraint. If everyone simply behaved according to the moods of the moment and the dictates of their sexual appetites, group harmony would be impossible. Perhaps the most difficult to control is the sexual urge. Being in control of this sphere of life on Rotuma is being in control of other desires that are more easily met. It is the ultimate test.

The clown achieved much laughter by violating the value of restraint. Such lack of control relates particularly to sexual matters. Forcing a man, or getting other women to do her bidding, reflects back to the men aggressive behavior that may threaten the institution of female virginity. If there is to be a virgin bride, and by association a clown, then male restraint is imperative. But although the clown's message is primarily for men, the multivocal nature of the clown's behavior speaks to everyone. When the clown acts jealous, or a funny woman flirts with a man, women are also reminded of society's expectations that they be restrained in speech, manner, and dress. The clown's violation of the norm may evoke past instances of conflict in the community that was caused by lack of control.

In wedding one, for example, the clown inverted the value of restraint (in terms of aggressiveness and sexuality) by:

Hurrying the band whenever it was slow to play.

Threatening to beat up several men who refused to obey her orders to stand up and dance.

Forcing two men who earlier had refused to dance to stand up and dance.

Running her stick across the corrugated iron ceiling and shouting threateningly at the top of her voice, like a drunk.

Ordering a drunken man to leave the arena.[22]

Poking a man in the ribs and forcing him to dance.

Scolding the band boys for stopping the singing too soon after she had picked a man to dance.

Admonishing and swearing at the band boys who jokingly said she "smelled of shit."[23]

Saying she had fallen in love with the Australian video man.

Dancing flirtatiously with the Australian video man.

Pretending to be jealous when her husband danced with a young girl.

Refusing to allow another woman to dance with a young man with whom she was dancing.

Ordering three women to pick three men to dance.

Forcing the white Australian man who was videotaping to dance.[24]

Saying of her husband when she saw him, "I told him to stay home today, and I have no idea what he's doing here."

Forcing the same man to dance a second time; the man's wife shouted, "Why are you always picking my husband? Are you in love with him?" to which the clown replied, "Your husband is bald. Who would want him?"

Picking a young man to dance, rolling her eyes, then doing a mock faint on the ground. She did the same with the Australian, implying she was in love.

The clown's suggestive sexual antics were highly amusing to the audience, almost as though the clown's silliness and the actions of the funny women released their own tensions and repressed feelings. What was usually taboo in public was now flaunted for everyone to see. Grabbing a chief by the waist, a funny woman guided him over a coconut seedling that was in the arena so that its leaves brushed against the inside of their thighs as they strode over it. "Making love to a coconut seedling" was replayed a few times; the audience loved it. Mock sexual activity delighted the audience; it brought out into the open what could only be entertained in the mind. What was unacceptable in real life was now sublimated in play.

Respect between Kin Groups

In attempting to explain why Rotuman marriages are "bride-directed," Malo wrote that this is because a woman is regarded as weak and in need of protection. The bridegroom's side therefore listens and obeys the wishes of the bride and her relatives (Malo 1975, 28). Yet to be host of a large celebration is to assume a heavier responsibility, as anyone who has organized even an evening party can testify. If being the weaker sex is really the reason, why does the bride assume the heavier responsibility? And why should the bride's relatives choose a female clown to rule over the ceremonies and display mock antagonism toward the groom's relatives?

Contrary to Malo's claim, I believe the wedding ceremony reaffirms female precedence, as encoded in mythology. Though Malo interprets the presentation of the *utu* 'cooked taro' by the groom's side on the wedding day correctly—"that the bridegroom is symbolically coming home"—he does not recognize this as the reason why traditional Rotuman weddings are "bride-directed."[25]

When dealing with sensitive matters that are potential sources of conflict, Rotumans usually take great care in the way they mediate. Usually, the communication is indirect and couched in pleasantries, if not humor. Indirect communication is a mark of respect for the other party's feelings, of not wanting to hurt. To be direct and abrasive is to display a lack of refinement, good sense, and good taste. By inverting the customary way in which Rotumans mediate conflict—that is, by being blunt and direct—the clown takes a risk. Her antics may be interpreted at face value as the truth spoken in jest. When this happens, schism occurs, and the play frame of licensed behavior is shattered. In this wedding, however, good sense prevailed, and the clown's seemingly hostile commands and insults were taken in good spirit. Like an audience at the theater, those attending the wedding are safe and secure in the comfort of their seats, even as the actors that they watch are being ridiculed or parodied. The audience receives vicarious pleasure in observing communication that is the inverse of indirect communication through pleasantries. The use of humor to diffuse tension is essential if real conflict is to be avoided. Everyone laughing together, whether at themselves or others, also reinforces group solidarity.

The clown's mediating role through the display of mock disrespect was illustrated in this wedding in several ways:

> She forced me to dance because I was related to the groom.
>
> When the young men from the groom's side were carrying the bride on their shoulders and it seemed that the bride was going to fall, the clown shouted, "Why is it that all the men from the groom's side are weak and ugly!"
>
> She was heard to shout threatening or rude comments to the relatives of the groom. For example, when a funny woman from the groom's side went over to challenge a man from the bride's side to a karate duel, she shouted to her in an aggressive manner, "Hurry up, and choose your partner quickly!" Some funny women from the groom's side displayed similar behavior to the clown's in relation to the bride's relatives.
>
> She acted as though the funny women from the bride's side were her allies; not once did she admonish them for their behavior.

Potential conflict between kin sides could arise from other factors. Sometimes the parents or relatives of the bride and groom may not agree with the choice of partner, the kind of wedding planned, or the venue. The parents of the bridal couple may feel ambivalent about losing control over a loved one, whether the pair will get along, even whether they have anything to gain in the new alliance. Because of the extensive work preparing the wedding feast—which should be so plentiful that the guests can eat as much as they want and still be able to take leftovers home—weaving mats, and worrying if there will be enough fine mats and food, close relatives of the couple are easily upset by criticism, intended or imagined. Matters trivial to outsiders take on an incredible significance, as illustrated by the following incident.

Before midday on the day of the wedding, the bride and groom were taken in a small truck to the church for a Christian ceremony. At the appropriate moment, the groom was asked to lift his bride's veil. This he did, but he did not kiss the bride. Further along in the ceremony, the bride's father stood up to seek an explanation. "Is it because my daughter is black?" he asked. "I know some people say my daughter is as black as stone; if the groom loves my daughter, why didn't he kiss her?" Silence. Startled to hear such direct communication, the congregation recognized impending conflict. The seconds ticked away as the ominous question hung in the air, waiting for an answer. The groom's father stood up, looked around, and began: "Your daughter is beautiful. Of course my son loves her. I apologize. It is our fault. Perhaps it is ignorance of the ways of the white man that my son did not behave appropriately." Though brief, the groom's father's attempt at reparation was moving, and his voice full of emotion. At the end of his apology, the groom's father bent down and kissed the bride. A hymn was sung and the ceremony continued.

This unpleasant incident in church was the only time there was an overt expression that all was not well. Significantly, the incident happened in a religious context in which the clown was absent. Why should such a seemingly petty omission be taken as an offense? This incident suggested that there were indeed underlying tensions that had not been diffused or resolved. It underscored the value of the play frame, and the importance of the clown as mediator. If she had said what the bride's father had said within the play frame, it would have made people laugh, just as her insult that the groom's relatives were weak and ugly was accepted in good humor and spectators laughed. But the same or a similar comment outside the play frame would have invited conflict, as happened in church. In the play frame, the bride's father's question would have caused laughter, and been left unanswered. Outside play, it hung in the air, ominously. In a ceremony that was supposed to highlight the unity of the couple, and, by implication, the kin groups, disunity reared its ugly head. Why?

Sometimes scholars view European culture as an imposition on the way of life of island people, as though the Islanders are passive players in the acculturation process. This is not always true: too often Polynesians eagerly adopt European ways without really understanding the symbolism or meaning behind the rituals or ceremonies they enact. Sometimes they co-opt the meanings of symbols and transfer them to Rotuman objects or things. For instance, sometimes decisions are made freely, without outside pressure, to wear all the costly regalia of a white dress, veil, and high heels for the bride; a dark suit, tie, and shoes for the groom; and similar fancy trappings for the bridesmaid and the best man. Important questions are not asked: For what purpose? Can we afford the expense? Do we know what we are doing here? Is this a traditional wedding or a European one? If it is to be a fusion of two cultures, how can misunderstanding be avoided? What are the rules that operate here?

The schism that occurred in church was caused by a confusion of context and meaning. According to Rotuman custom, it was inappropriate to kiss the bride, least of all in church, in front of one's parents and one's minister. It is the kind of act that a Rotuman lad associates with the white man. All his training has instilled in him the value of restraint, particularly in public. No Rotuman man on the island ever kisses his wife in public. Kissing is regarded as a filthy habit, humorously referred to as *haiʻaag alel* 'tongues fighting'. Husband and wife rarely walk together, or sit together at social gatherings. A public display of intimate affection excludes others, communicating, "We are the only ones who matter here." Its rightful place is within the play frame in which many couples are involved—beach games, and *av maneʻa* particularly. Although the groom and his bride may be dressed in urban style, they are still rural folk.[26] They look European, but they feel Rotuman. Whose rules operate then? Ambiguity may be the norm in play, but not in a real-life situation that demands an unprecedented action.

At the end of the church service, the dancing and the performance of other Rotuman rituals continued. A deliberate attempt by close relatives of the bride and groom to reconcile their differences was evident. They were seen dancing holding each other, as though to say to the assembled company, "All is well again." The clown, who did not attend the wedding service, was unaware of the church incident. Having rested during the intermission, she resumed her duties, instigating laughter, diffusing tension, and mediating potential conflict.[27]

What Is a *Hàn Mane'àk Su*?

In her inversion of societal norms of humility, restraint, and respect, the *hàn mane'àk su* played different roles. These roles varied depending on her relationship to the kin groups involved, her age, and her abilities. For example, a clown who was under fifty and closely related to the bride was chosen for wedding one. This may help to explain why she was much more involved with the proceedings than two of the clowns who featured in the 1989 weddings referred to in chapter 4. They were either too old for the part, not confident enough, or both.

In present-day Rotuma, the clown's role is unclear. It is assumed that the community and the clown know what her role at a wedding is supposed to be. Unfortunately, this is no longer the case. No one on the island appears well informed about correct protocol, or holds the custom as sacrosanct anymore. My observations of Rotuman weddings, however, suggest that the roles played by a *hàn mane'àk su* at a traditional wedding include those of entertainer and catalyst, mediator, cultural symbol, master of ceremonies, and liminal being.

Entertainer and Catalyst

An important function of the *hàn mane'àk su* in contemporary Rotuma is that of chief entertainer. It is her responsibility to ensure that the wedding guests have a good time. Laughter is music to her ears, for assessment of her success or failure at the end of the wedding celebrations depends mainly on her ability to create laughter.

Although today most weddings on the island no longer feature a traditional mass dance, *tautoga,* or *manman heta* who prances about, the ritual clown still runs around trying to get people to stand up and dance.[28] Without her, the majority of the chiefs and the men are likely to remain spectators. This was evident on the day before the wedding when the clown had to visit the toilet. No one stood up to dance while she was away, prompting an old man to ask out loud where the clown was. Then he sat on the vacant chair and said, "All right, I will be the clown."

The *hån mane'åk su*'s success as a catalyst depends to some extent on audience reception and cooperation. Unfortunately for the Rotuman clown, increasing contact with Fiji and the rest of the world means that young people today understand less about the significance of her role. Young chiefs, or the district officer representing the Fiji government, for example, may not feel as bound by custom as their predecessors. Accordingly, the clown is wary about overstepping her powers. Rotumans claim that today's clowns are not as dangerous as their predecessors, who were known to beat people up or prohibit them from eating. My observations on the island in 1989 bear testimony to a growing uncertainty about the clown's role in weddings.

Mediator

People in relationships that are structurally predisposed to conflict but lack overt institutions for mediation, sometimes resort to indirect channels of communication. Games (including card and beach games), sports (such as volleyball), teasing relationships, rituals of reversal (e.g., Children's Sunday), *av mane'a,* and *fara* are all latent control institutions on Rotuma; however, they are not generally recognized as contexts for resolving tensions in society. The traditional Rotuman wedding—the most complex and elaborate of these latent institutions for conflict management—may also be seen as a context in which contradictory and conflicting forces in the social system are continually being worked out (Shore 1977, 306, 307). The institution of *hån mane'åk su* in the play frame of a wedding is invaluable. It provides a safe vent for subsurface rumblings; tensions are diffused, displaced, redefined, and may even be resolved in ways that are socially acceptable. Writing in 1970, Howard was accurate in his bold assertion that Rotuman culture is founded on the basic premise that "social life should be harmonious and free of conflict" (1970a, 108).

Cultural Symbol

Implicit in the choice of a wedding clown is that she must have considerable knowledge of Rotuman culture. The clown who featured at the wedding in which Ta was the *hån mane'åk su,* for example, was asked by the bride's family to be one of two female instructors for the bride in matters of Rotuman etiquette. (This was the purpose of her staying behind overnight at the groom's house when bride and groom were taken there.[29]) In the past, the women who stayed behind were given household chores to do—making *tāhroro* 'fermented coconut sauce' particularly—and were never left idle (Jiare, pers. comm., 1989). They also played a central role in the virginity tests that were important then. Today, their role is restricted to preparing the couple's bed of mats and sleeping close to them at night.

Considerable skill on the part of the clown is required to keep people entertained throughout the day. She has to get it "just right" and should be funny without drawing attention to herself personally. In Clark's words, the clown is an impersonator; the moment she identifies with the fire (the licentious thing that she holds in her hands, psychologically) she is no longer funny, because "that fine, delightful sense of balance and mastery is lost" (quoted in Crumrine 1969, 14). Though the clown is expected to act as an extremely arrogant chief, she must also be the humble commoner who knows her place in society. Even as she embodies extreme individualism (which is antithetical to Rotuman thinking), she must remember collectivism.

A *hän mane'äk su* is a people's clown, chosen to provide a service to society, not to further her own self-image. Though the clown's rule is supreme, she is expected to be able to laugh at herself. For example, when the clown shouted in English "Come on, music!" or said she wanted to be called Princess Sakura, people laughed at her English, knowing very well that she could barely speak English. She was poking fun at her lack of western education by jokingly elevating her status through the use of a "superior" language. By putting herself down, she was making others feel superior. (Paradoxically, other Rotumans attribute this to the clown's sensitivity to others, and the clown's status is therefore enhanced.) This added to the audience's appreciation of her performance, for it displayed acute cultural sophistication.

Generosity is an important Rotuman value that a clown also embodies. She gives unstintingly of herself; at this wedding, the clown was up and dancing nearly all the time. There were only one or two songs she did not dance to on the wedding day, and then only because another funny woman had temporarily deflected people's attention from her.

The *hän mane'äk su* is also referred to as *iạ ta pure* 'the one who rules'. That the chiefs should be displaced and replaced by a clown is in itself a social commentary on the Rotuman view of chiefs. An implicit message is that culture is artificial and arbitrary. Its structure is human-made, and a chief could just as easily have been a woman, even an old woman clown.

The ritual clown, in the context of a traditional wedding, embodies the Rotuman conception of a person as a "many-faceted gem."[30] She is humorous, yet serious in intent. She is capable of emphasizing one identity and playing down another, or choosing to remain "betwixt and between" and have the best of both options. She is an actor, playing different roles depending on the demands of the moment, refusing to be wholly one or the other. She is inconsistent, with many sides to herself. She is Rotuman.

Master of Ceremonies

The clown is expected to act as master of ceremonies, particularly on the wedding day, when there are numerous rituals to be performed in a specific order. For example, in the 1987 wedding, the *hån mane'åk su* was heard to warn participants to organize themselves and in some cases she hastened the process by shouting comments such as "Hurry up! The sooner you finish the sooner we can eat." In this instance, the clown seemed to be speaking aloud for everyone else, as certain rituals had to be performed before the midday feast. A successful wedding is marked by an ostentatious display of wealth in the form of food and mats, and the highlight of any wedding on Rotuma is the feast. As soon as it is over, the wedding guests start dispersing. With no clown to hurry people, the rituals might drag on unnecessarily long.

The clown acted as master of ceremonies in a number of other ways as well. For instance, on the day before the wedding, she welcomed relatives to the bride's house by pecking old women lightly on the cheek or by shouting out words of welcome to the others. During the course of the festivities on the wedding day, she often ordered certain members of the audience to shout out formal words of appreciation (either to the band or the dancers); these individuals always obliged.

Liminal Being

The presence of a clown in the sacred frame of a religious ceremony suggests a metaphysical dimension that is absent from the performances of present-day clowns. Her oddity of dress, her complete dis-

Wedding festivities always culminate in a huge feast. Wedding two, 1989.
(Jan Rensel)

regard for earthly authority, her antisocial behavior and mocking
laughter, her inversion of values that Rotumans hold dear—all these
are antithetical to Rotuman culture. She has no manners, yet everyone submits to her foolish antics. Why?

The clown in this wedding, for example, dressed as a female but
behaved like a male. Another clown in a 1989 wedding wore a bright

red dress, sunglasses, and a shoulder bag. Was she dressed as a prostitute, or was she a modern version of a Rotuman ghost?[31] Or was she, perhaps, a caricature of the modern Rotuman woman? Add to this a phallic symbol in the form of a stick in her hand and she becomes ambiguous, if not confusingly seductive. Clowns of the past who blackened their features and wore men's clothing confused their dramatis personae even more, suggesting a link with the world of ancestral spirits that is not readily apparent in the performances of their present-day counterparts.

The liminal nature of the clown, and her role as cultural icon, have been eroded over the years. It is probable that today's clowns are but pale shadows of their earlier sisters, and that today's traditional weddings are diluted versions of a grander past. I suspect that the clown in earlier times did more than communicate messages of social and cultural import, or mediate between conflicting forces in the community. This notion is confirmed in a letter from Harieta Katafono, a Rotuman educator who is much respected in the Rotuman community. In response to a draft of this chapter, she wrote: "I think many Rotumans have a vague feeling that there is a deeper, and perhaps, spiritual significance to the clowning at weddings, but that for the most part, such feelings remain vague and sometimes regarded as fanciful because we, the present day Rotumans, are, in the main, not given to thinking much about our own culture." Then she added: "Perhaps we are too busy learning about and adapting to other cultures? However, you seem to be the exception to the rule."

I may be the exception, but I'm still none the wiser. What is the *hån mane'åk su*'s link with the spirits? This one remaining question begs an answer. I search for an origin myth, one that will explain how it all began, but find nothing. I interview elders in the community, but find their explanations unsatisfactory. I am stuck. Far in the distance I hear the clown's mocking laughter.

Interview with Rotuma's Historian

December 1990

I decide to interview the historian on the island.

Vafo'ou Jiare is employed as a historian by the Rotuma Council. He is not a formally qualified historian in the western sense, although he has worked for the Fiji government as an adviser on cultural matters for many years. His main responsibility in Rotuma is to write down the myths and legends of the island, its oral traditions, and its customs. He is one of a very few people in Rotuma who is keenly interested in the past.

Vafo'ou is also the best storyteller I know. His command of the Rotuman language is unique, with an uncanny ability to remember minute details of names, places, people, and historical events, rendering his narratives a credibility and touch of authenticity that is impressive. Cynics, however, have been heard to say that Vafo'ou has a lively imagination, implying that he makes things up and that a lot of his stories are not true.

When I first questioned Vafo'ou about the *hàn mane'àk su* and its origins, he was hesitant in his responses, as though he had not given much thought to this social institution prior to our conversation. (These hesitations are not obvious in the printed interview.) Other Rotumans on the island also gave me the same impression: that ritual clowning at weddings was simply taken for granted, until I raised it to the level of discussion. Vafo'ou, unlike many other Rotumans, felt obliged to provide a reasoned explanation. Although it is not one that I have adopted, it is nonetheless worthy of attention.[32]

VH: Where do you think the custom of having a *hàn mane'àk su* at weddings came from?

VJ: It began when Ma'afu from Tonga came to Rotuma. Then his daughter taught the people this custom. I say this because I don't have any information about this custom prior to this time. Also, look at what happens at weddings, the way the clowns treat the chiefs. It is not consistent with the way we treat our chiefs, which means it is an introduced custom. If it were our custom, then our ancestors would have made sure that our chiefs were respected; in the past, people really respected the chiefs.

VH: Did you say it was the daughter of Ma'afu?

VJ: Yes, the daughter whom he brought with him to Rotuma. She married Varomua' [a chief].

VH: So was it when the brother of Varomua' married that the first clown featured?

VJ: Well, there is no information I have that proves that. It was some years later that there is mention of a clown at weddings. I don't know when exactly it started, but it must have been some years after Ma'afu's daughter arrived on the island.

VH: Where did you get your information from?

VJ: From *tem ta* 'chanted poetry'. There is this chant that mentions a wedding at Hapmafạu, and someone strutting around during the ceremonies who was in charge of everything, and was even above the king. And whatever this person said had to be obeyed. It doesn't mention that it was a *hàn mane'àk su,* but whatever this person said, it had to be obeyed.

VH: When we talked last, you told me something about Manao and Nofaga's wedding. Can you repeat what you said then?

VJ: Yes, during the period of the *naag 'inoso,* the clown for this wedding, whose name was 'Akanisi, came and took my hand. Then she made me stand in front of the people, and then she said, "People of this island, breakfast tomorrow morning will be provided by my grandchild, this man here." So I had to go to Muaror's shop to buy all the things for breakfast. And when it was over, they brought me fine mats and other kinds of mats, a big roll of cloth, and baskets of food. Just think about how important a custom it was then. The clown just couldn't treat people anyhow without compensating them at the end. If she made someone kneel in the hot sun, then she had to thank that person when the wedding was over. When the clown forced someone to do something outrageous, relatives of the bride observed and remembered the individuals who had been treated badly. If the clown threw water on someone, then that person had to be provided with dry clothes—a shirt and a *hạ'fạli* 'cotton wraparound'. This is a very special custom. And it was taboo for anyone to do anything disrespectful toward the clown.

VH: Do you know of any other similar incidents?

VJ: Yes, lots. There was this wedding at Itu'muta, when I was a little boy. The clown forced all the chiefs to kneel. And when the wedding was over, each of the chiefs received a fine mat and another mat as compensation.

VH: Did you go to see the recent weddings?

VJ: No, I didn't go, but these days it's all for entertainment's sake. Times have changed. Nowadays, it depends on the wealth of the owners of the wedding. And the clown tends to do what will please the owners of the wedding, which means it's often just getting people to dance, and therefore there is no compensation. In the past, I think the owners of the wedding wanted the clown to really play the role to the hilt so that they could generously give away their wealth. But nowadays, people are not so keen to do this; instead of giving away gifts, they want the gifts to be brought to them. It is no longer like before. In the past, the clown institution was a custom, now it is not. It is only for the entertainment of the guests.

VH: When I asked some of the clowns at recent weddings why they were so mild toward the chiefs, they said they were frightened of them.

VJ: In the past, the chiefs followed the custom. But look at what is happening on this island today. For example, in the past, if there was a chief sitting here, then people kept their distance. Nowadays, if the chief doesn't move, someone will trip over him. So the clowns of today are not so sure where they stand. They might do something that will make the chiefs angry. But because it was a custom in the past, the chiefs had to follow it, so the clowns felt protected and were not frightened. But these days, if the clown does something that the chief doesn't like, the chief may end up telling her off, or saying something that doesn't sound good to the ears.

VH: What about 'Ioane? What was she like?

VJ: She was number one. The only thing was, when she started to be a popular *hàn mane'àk su*, this custom was beginning to erode in significance, around 1960 to 1970. The emphasis was shifting toward entertainment. Not like when Akanisi was the clown.

VH: When was that?

VJ: Around the 1950s I think, because I was not married then.

VH: There was also the custom of cutting the foreheads of the young men from the groom's side. Any comments?

VJ: That was a dangerous custom. It was performed when the bride was believed to be a virgin. So they cut their foreheads to let the blood out to show that they were the first to shed

Rotuma's famous clown of the 1960s and 1970s. *(Alan Howard)*

their blood, even before the groom had deflowered the bride.

VH: Do you think it was to compensate for the blood that the bride was going to shed?

VJ: You know, sometimes this custom caused problems. Sometimes the young men had shed their blood, but it turned out the bride was not a virgin ("an old woman"). Then . . . it could easily turn out violent.

VH: So when does the virginity test take place? On the first night, or some time later?

VJ: It was different in the past. For the days of the wedding celebrations, there was no sleeping. During the *naag 'inoso* period, the mother of the bride carried with her a basket, the *'at fara*. Inside was a bivalve shell *('ås he)*, some oil, and a piece of bark cloth *(uạh het)*.

VH: What is the bark cloth?

VJ: It's like the *kuta* (a type of soft mat) of the Fijian people. It was made from *hạu* or *väsväs*.

VH: So who owns this basket?

VJ: It's the mother of the bride.

VH: The bride's mother?

VJ: No, the groom's mother. This basket is put on the bed after it has been prepared.

VH: Is this basket put on the bed of the couple on the first night when they sleep at the bride's place?

VJ: Yes, it follows them when they go from place to place. When the women of the groom's side prepare the bed *(mosega)* on the first night, they put the basket on the bed, a way of saying they would like to find out whether the bride was a virgin or whether she had already slept with other men.

VH: Is this basket taken to the groom's place a few days later?

VJ: Yes, they keep taking it with them because they don't know when the couple will consummate the marriage. Once the marriage has been consummated and the women discover blood on the bark cloth, there is extreme happiness. Early in the morning, the earthen ovens will be lit, and if the pigs have their backsides facing the temporary shelter where the chiefs are seated, then everyone knows that the bride is an "old woman."

VH: So where does this happen?

VJ: At the groom's place.

VH: We don't display the bark cloth?

VJ: No, we turn the pigs around. But if the heads of the pigs are facing the chiefs, then a big celebration will follow, because it means the bride is a virgin.

VH: So who are the women who stay behind at the groom's place during the *naag 'inoso?*

VJ: They are very close relatives of the bride. Usually it's women who are related to both bride and groom, so that things will be easy. Otherwise, if the women are only related to the bride, then they just sit at the back door of the house. They can only enter and exit from that door. They sit there so that it will be easy for them to move around. They do the work for the bride; these are women who are there to work, not women to be waited upon.

VH: Does the clown stay as one of the women?

VJ: Sometimes the groom's kin invite the clown to entertain at their place during the *naag 'inoso.* But usually she doesn't stay; she goes back with the rest.

VH: Also, there was a water ceremony in the past. Any comments?

VJ: Yes. Yes, they lie in the water together. But this ritual only happens if the bride is a virgin. But things have changed these days. Some people say, "Look, that bride is not a virgin," and then someone else retorts, "So what! Is the groom a virgin?"

VH: So when does this water ceremony take place?

VJ: As far as I know, during the period of the *naag 'inoso,* the couple simply oil their bodies. As soon as the marriage has been consummated and the bride is a virgin, then they go to the sea where the washing ceremony takes place. They can do it publicly because there is no shame involved.

VH: You said there was a bivalve shell in the basket. What was that for?

VJ: For collecting the blood. The oil is for her wounds. She bleeds in a similar way to being cut, so the oil is to soothe her wounds. The bark cloth is for wiping herself, then she puts it on top of the shell.

VH: So where are the women on the night of the destruction of virginity?

VJ: Inside the house. They sleep right next to the couple.

VH: Why?

VJ: They want to listen to whatever is happening, so they hang around. That is why, in some cases, although the period of the *naag 'inoso* is over, the couple still haven't been able to consummate the marriage. But you know, it is usually the women from the groom's side who are anxious to know. The first night was spent at the bride's house and sometimes it was impossible to do anything.

VH: What was the *'at fara* made of?

VJ: From the bark of the *hau* tree. You know, we once had a meeting, and the chiefs were very angry with me. I told them that the *'at fara* should not be taken at the front of the procession. I asked them if they knew that the basket was the thing that smelled of "shit" *(te la huag pötö' heta)*. They were angry, but I told them that it should be carried at the back of the procession. It was not intended to be shown off.

VH: Someone told me that at the groom's place at night, women try to get inside the couple's mosquito net.

VJ: Yes, that is our custom. That is play. The sisters of the bride pretend to spoil the groom's chances of a sexual encounter with their sister. That is a chiefly custom, and the groom can't chase the women. It happens on the first night at the bride's house. If the sisters of the bride know that the bride is a virgin, then they will prefer the consummation to take place at the groom's house. So they try to spoil his chances. But if the sisters know that the bride is not a virgin, then they are not likely to stop the groom finding out on her home ground, for the shame is less.

VH: Does the same happen at the groom's place?

VJ: No, only at the bride's.

VH: What about the pillow?

VJ: It was a wooden pillow, provided by the groom's side, as part of the *mosega*. The mosquito net was a kind of curtain for privacy, made of *'uha* 'a type of bark cloth'.

VH: What about the *mosega*?

VJ: There are two *mosega*. The one provided by the groom's kin stays at the bride's; the bride's stays at the groom's house. A case of reciprocity.

VH: I read somewhere that the groom was given a knife as he left to stay with his new wife. Is this true?

VJ: The knife is a recent introduction. But what happens is that sometimes the parents of the bride want to test the groom. For example, they may grate coconuts [to prepare a meal], a lot of them, and just before the groom starts to squeeze out the juice, they open the earthen oven, so that the man will have to move really fast to catch up. Some men fail this test. That is why we have a saying that if you are a man who is going to marry outside your village, then you will have to be strong.

VH: You mean to live at the woman's place?

VJ: Yes.

VH: Do the parents behave this way because they are not too keen on the groom?

VJ: No. It's our custom. Sometimes, if the parents of the bride are strong people, or have a "warrior" temperament, then they will test the man.

VH: And if the man fails?

VJ: Sometimes, if the man cannot cope, he just leaves and goes back to his home.

VH: And the wife. If she turns out to be not a virgin, can the man chase her out?

VJ: It's been done. Sometimes they [the groom's relatives] prepare a cooked offering and then take her back. You see, it was the parents who decided on the marriage, so if something went wrong, it was the parents' responsibility. In the past, it was a marriage of parents.

VH: The screening of the temporary shelter. Did they use fine mats in the past?

VJ: The *paag ri* ritual? That is a screen. In the past they did not use cotton material. And it wasn't just the front, it was all around the temporary shelter.

VH: What is the purpose of this ritual?

VJ: That was the work of the mother of the groom being displayed, for the benefit of the bride and the general public.

VH: Why do you think the couple are seated on fine mats?

VJ: I think it is because we want to elevate them, to raise their status. They are the two biggest "chiefs" on this day for every-

one. But I have not thought about this before, so I don't
know why they are raised on mats.

VH: The stick the clown carries. What was it made of?

VJ: I don't know. I haven't investigated that. But it was a long
stick in the past, longer than the clown herself. And it was
decorated. Now any old stick will do.

VH: Did we have a "bird" *(mạnmạn heta)* of the dance before?

VJ: Yes, even the traditional dance *tạutoga* had a "bird." Sometimes, before the rows at the back make their way to the
front, this person will have already danced his way through
the middle to the front. At other times, while the dancers
are seated, he walks around and tells people what to do.

VH: Why has this practice [*mạnmạn heta*] stopped?

VJ: Because times change, times are different. People of today
don't like to do it this way. For example, in the past, when
people danced, when the dancers stretched out their arms,
their eyes followed them, and there was a story the dancers
were telling you. But today, the arms stretch this way while
the eyes wander another way, and there is nothing they are
telling you. Each generation wants to do things according to
their wishes, and so custom erodes. Now we dance, just for
entertainment.

Although I find some of Vafo'ou's comments and observations on
Rotuman weddings and clowning illuminating, his view that the *hån
mane'åk su* institution derived from Tonga is unsatisfactory to me.
What shall I do? Should I create an origin myth? I remember
Nietzsche's advice that *play* is an essential prerequisite to dealing
with great tasks (1969, 65). My forebears believed in this philosophy
as well, hence the many myths that try to explain the origins of certain phenomena, or certain physical peculiarities in nature. If they
were in my position, they would surely come up with a mythological
explanation. So what is stopping me? Why shouldn't I allow my
fiction self to bail me out of this impasse? I realize that my main
obstacle is fear. Fear of being unconventional. Fear of challenging
the hallowed traditions of western academia.

6 Fine Mats and Spirits

Mystics, radical philosophers, and theologians have long regarded laughter as a higher form of consciousness, a way of confronting the higher realities on which the whole of existence rests.

HARVEY COX, *The Feast of Fools*

My anthropological self says, "Academic writing is not the same as creative writing. Follow the tradition of scholarship." But my Rotuman and fiction selves think otherwise, and so I decide to create a new myth, to explain how the Rotuman *hån mane'åk su* came to be. It is the kind of explanation my father, who used to tell me all kinds of stories at bedtime, would have told me. Thinking that in recreating this Rotuman tradition I might discover something I did not know before, I fished out this myth from my imagination.[1]

A New Myth: "When Gods Meet"

As the first rays of the sun appeared above the eastern horizon, a group of weary canoe paddlers beached at a tiny island in the middle of the Pacific Ocean. Exhausted from their long journey, they barely managed to drag their canoes above the shoreline. When they had rested, they wandered inland, where they saw fruit trees of different kinds growing wild. Coconut trees were everywhere. At sunset when they went to bathe in the lagoon, they found it teeming with fish. Counting themselves lucky, they decided to settle down on this island. Over the years their numbers grew. Life was relatively easy in their new home, and they had ample reason to be happy.

Twelve years later a hurricane struck. The wind and rain tore apart their thatched huts and dumped them in the sea. The yams that had been carefully cultivated were yanked from their roots and torpedoed into the sky like kites in a whirlwind. Two women and three small boys were lost to the elements.

103

After the wind dropped, they emerged from hiding, singly at first, and then in pairs and groups. Arms folded and heads hanging low, they wandered among the debris. No one spoke. What was there to say? When their spirits had recovered sufficiently, they started rebuilding their lives. Thatch was gathered from what remained of the palm trees, and makeshift huts soon appeared. Gardens were cleared and new crops planted in anticipation of the lean times ahead. Ominous signs in the heavens were recalled and gradually a system of predicting impending disaster was devised.

By the fourth year, prosperity had returned, though memories had not forgotten a world in smithereens. How could the fury of the winds be bound? Many meetings were called by the high chief, and solutions debated. Their conclusion: a higher being ruled the powerful forces of nature, a being that blesses and punishes. How else could they explain their joys as well as their sorrows, their helplessness in the face of fury? This higher being needed to find its rightful place in their lives. The high chief's orator stood up to summarize the new order.

"There must be a higher being who rules the earth, for we are not in total control of our lives or the heavens. Let us call this being God. God is invisible, but we can see evidence of both happiness and anger. This God can work either for us, or against us. How can we persuade God to be on our side? By following God's wishes. How do we know what God wants? By identifying what we enjoy in this life—food, fun, laughter, dancing, sex, children. So, we want these things, and God wants them too. But God has access to these things of the good life—after all, God is almighty. There's nothing really that we can give God. How can we reach such a being? [*pause*] Perhaps by giving up what we like best, and denying certain pleasures when we need to seek favors. "

The orator paused, looked at his chief deferentially, and continued: "Soon, we shall have cause for celebration. One of my daughters will be marrying, one moon from now, when my yams will be mature. A wedding joins man and woman so that they might produce children so our numbers will always grow. Is a wedding a time to celebrate or a time to ask for favors? Both. We celebrate by thanking God for the way we have been blessed. Let us have the biggest wedding ever, not because it is my daughter's wedding, but because we are prosperous again.

Let us display for God's benefit all that is of value to us: fine mats, taro, yams, pigs, fish—anything that is dear to our hearts. A wedding is a time of happiness, not mourning. We have been sad for too long. Now it's time to laugh. But what will make us laugh? Who can make us laugh?"

He looked around, then answered his own question. "God can make us laugh. God is laughter, and anger too. We should ask God. Impossible, you say? I know. God lives in the sky, and we live on earth. What we need then is someone who can represent God, to mediate between God and us. Yes. This person will have to be strong, because God is strong. And this person will have to amuse us, for God knows how to have fun. That hurricane. That was God having fun! Mocking us. Reminding us we are just playthings . . . if we cause displeasure."

Another chief who had been listening responded, "Yes, I agree. We can institute this new custom at your daughter's wedding. But who shall it be? A man or a woman?"

The orator answered, "Let's look at man. Can a man be funny? We're all men. Are we funny? Can we make our womenfolk laugh? I have an idea. Let us require him to behave like a woman."

The youngest chief, who was becoming irritated by the orator's monologue, spoke up. "Why is that funny? A man behaving like a woman? And bossing us around? Why not have a woman bossing *you* around?"

At this, everyone laughed, though for what reason wasn't clear. The orator was known to be henpecked at home, and this could have been the reason. Nonetheless, the very idea, the audacity! The orator, who surprised his colleagues by laughing the loudest, raised his hand for silence and continued. "A woman then, bossing men around. [*pause*] Yes, and why not? But remember, all of us will have to obey her. Let a woman be in charge of my daughter's wedding, then. Let a woman play God."

A close relative of the orator asked, "But from the bride's or the groom's side?"

The orator responded, "Does it matter? Maybe she should come from the bride's side, the woman's side. Since it's my idea, let me take the trouble of finding a woman who can play God. I know someone who could play that role to the hilt."

A cock crowed as everyone laughed. The orator had spoken

for too long, and some of the chiefs were already thinking of their wives. The orator concluded: "When God is with us, we must ensure that we do everything the right way. Let God reign supreme, rule over us, and maybe grant us favors. On this occasion, maybe my daughter will be blessed with big healthy children, for it is time I had a grandson. Maybe our crops too will be blessed and special skills bestowed upon us that our women may weave even better mats. And we men can reap a bigger and better harvest next year. At the end of the wedding, we must thank God. We must offer up our best foods and fine mats.

From that time, whenever there was a wedding, God came down, through the chosen representative, and played games with the Islanders. She presided over the ceremonies, and the people did everything her way, according to their custom. She was a God of laughter who must always be obeyed.

One day a ship appeared on the horizon, and a white man carrying a little black book arrived. He told the Islanders that his god was the true god, and theirs was false. God is serious, not frivolous, a god of truth and justice, who doesn't play games like little children. No, god behaves like an adult. God works, six days a week and rests only on Sunday. This god created the earth—and created them.

And the white man stayed. He taught them the new ways. He told them that the new god loathed their evil practices at weddings: cutting their foreheads with stone axes and lying naked in the sea. The high chief and his orator believed. Soon everyone believed. One day, on the orders of their chief, the islanders gathered together all their stone and wooden gods, made a huge bonfire on the beach, and severed their ties with their old religion, forever.

Except for their old God, personified. They didn't tell the missionary who she really was. Because she seemed to be just making people laugh, the missionary didn't query her identity; he was too busy laughing himself. She was funny, a welcome distraction from his serious endeavors to convert the Islanders. Secretly, he envied her.

The missionary has left; but his Bible stays. The Islanders still read it and try their best to follow its teachings. Most of the old ways are gone now. The thatched huts that used to grace the trees by the beach have disappeared. Now, there is illumination, electricity. Lots of cars and motorbikes. Zooming around on the narrow strip of sandy road that circles the island, they rake up dust that disappears into louver-windowed houses made of steel and concrete. The young people too—they're gone now, most of them, looking for education and jobs overseas. The old people remain, waiting . . . for children to send them money, or to return and kiss them happiness at Christmas.

Last year, one of them returned, to ask the people about their gods before the white man came. But none of the old ones knew what he was asking. He tried explaining; when the oldest of them—a toothless eighty-year-old grandmother of twelve—realized what the young man was looking for, she suggested that he attend her granddaughter's wedding the following day.

They say he went looking for God at a wedding, and found a clown.

*   *   *

After writing this story, I become aware that I have allowed my intuitions and my subconscious to influence my creation. The result is a narrative that has the feel of fiction, embodying important threads worthy of further inquiry. First, the clown is an impersonation of a god or ancestral spirit. Second, the chiefs are instrumental in the instigation of this institution. And, third, the original purpose of this custom was to propitiate supernatural forces.

These three points suggest that inquiry into the Rotuman view of the supernatural world and the role of chiefs in the formation of the institution of clowning is essential. Again, I turn to mythology for guidance and discover three clues. I place my bets! I decide to play again, to see where it takes me.

Origin of the *Hàn Mane'àk Su*

The first clue is buried in Churchward's collection in a myth titled *'Äeatos* (1938b); the second is the word *sa'aitu*, which translates as "a wandering band of ghosts consisting of the souls of uncircumcised men"; and the third was manifested in the institution known as *sa'a*—no longer practiced—which refers to the collective weaving of fine mats by women and the associated rituals. The narrative *'Äeatos,* the term *sa'aitu,* and the *sa'a* are the three spotlights I shall focus on the *hån mane'åk su,* who stands center stage, waiting to be fully illuminated.

According to Churchward, the myth of *'Äeatos* is the most imaginative of all Rotuman myths, one that he suggests is "scientifically worthless, yet for sheer charm and entertainment, not to say literary merit, it must surely be accorded a position of especial honor among the myths and legends of the South Pacific" (1938b, 109). There is more to this myth than literary merit. I believe it carries an essential clue that for me, elucidates the Rotuman view of *'atua,* and the role of ritual and play in keeping ghosts away.

This myth is long; I shall summarize, except when direct quotation would be more helpful.

> Two sisters married two brothers who were fishermen. Their husbands told them never to cut down two banana plants near their homes, but did not explain that the plants were their grandparents. One day, while the brothers were away fishing, the two girls were overcome with hunger; they cut down the banana trees and helped themselves. As the two sisters sat down to eat, they wished out loud for some meat or fish to go with their bananas, only to be frightened out of their wits when a voice from under a rock said, "Yes! if only one could be given a torn pad of *lepa* leaves to eat!"[2]
>
> The two sisters rushed back to their homes in fear, chased by their husbands' grandparents. The ghosts of the grandparents entered the elder sister's house and devoured her and her son, in retaliation for cutting the banana trees and for the elder sister's failure to deliver fish to them when she was supposed to. The younger sister, on the other hand, was spared because she had faithfully delivered fish to her husband's grandparents.

Rotumans believed that the spirit of a dead person, *'atua,* could make its home in animals and birds such as dogs, cats, owls, or chickens.[3] Sometimes an *'atua* inhabited a human being and made its wishes known by speaking through its medium. When possessed by an *'atua,* the person was said to be a *tu'ura* 'god's messenger to people'.[4] Birds and animals were also possible mediums. The hooting of an owl, or a rooster crowing in front of one's house, for example, was interpreted as communicating messages of one kind or another.[5]

When an *'atua* became manifest in a bird, plant, or animal, those for whom the *'atua* was a family god were forbidden to eat or harm it, as illustrated in this narrative. An *'atua* 'ghost' therefore can become an *'aitu* 'god or creature regarded as the habitat of the god'[6] once it has been constrained in a physical form.[7] Once an *'atua* is physicalized, it is no longer as wild or malicious, for it has been domesticated or constrained. Each village had its own *'aitu,* which it propitiated: the shark, the sandpiper, the lizard, or the gecko were *'aitu* who acted in the interests of the community.

Although *'atua* that are physicalized may become *'aitu* and there-fore worshiped, an *'atua* can appear in physical form and not be an *'aitu*—for example, in the form of various anomalous creatures. What makes an *'atua* into an *'aitu* is bringing it into the Rotuman moral order and making it susceptible to control through worship and reciprocity. The critical constraint is, I believe, metaphorical constraint by human agency rather than physical constraint.

Once *'atua* have been constrained, people may *'ait'aki* 'worship' their habitats, in the hope of harnessing their powers. These village totems were sacred and could not be killed; should a village *'aitu* be killed, the offender had to make a big feast and cut off his hair and bury it, in much the same way as a man would be buried (Gardiner 1898, 467). To keep *'aitu* happy, they were offered food or sacrifices. An *'aitu* could, should it be displeased or offended, become malevo-lent at any time and behave like an *'atua*. Thus the younger sister in the narrative was spared, and the older one not.

Ghosts of dead ancestors who were not physicalized could also be solicited, with good or evil intent.[8] If certain favors from *'atua* were needed, appropriate rituals were performed. For example, offering first-fruits to a chief was a way of remaining in the *'atua*'s favor. If a person felt unfairly persecuted, a *koua* 'food offering that always included a pig' was prepared, relatives called, and the *'atua* invoked to bring about justice. In pursuit of this goal, the *'atua* of a prema-turely born child was thought particularly trustworthy (Churchward 1939b, 470). Advice, on the other hand, might be sought from a *tupu'a* 'rock or stone' that was reputed to be a person or spirit petri-fied. To continue the narrative:

> When the two brothers returned from fishing, the husband of the elder sister was devoured by his grandparents. The younger sister and her husband fled instead to live somewhere else. As time went by, the husband of the younger woman went fishing again, only to have his canoe capsized by a huge fish.

The fish ate the man but spared one of his knees which managed to make its way back to its owner's home. The wife, whose
name was Sinetearoia, had by this time given birth to two children and had named them after her sister and her sister's son,
Rakitefurusia and 'Aeatos respectively. Sinetearoia turned
around from her daily chores to find her husband's knee rolling on the floor next to her before it jumped into a mat. In her
fear, she fled and left her two children behind. Finally she
arrived at a place called Lulu, a favourite haunt for ghosts.
There were ten ghosts, the first with one head, the second with
two, and so on. As the ghosts were about to eat Sinetearoia, she
begged them to spare her but to go and eat her two children
whom she had left behind.

Although the "unseen region" or *'oroi ta* where human beings
went when they die was believed to be under the sea (off Losa, at the
western end of the island), there were favorite haunts on land that
were feared and avoided, such as Lulu, in the west. Ghosts of ancestors who wandered about were thought to be particularly dangerous
and arbitrary, with an insatiable appetite for human souls (Howard
1979, 248). Rather than try to eradicate the ghosts from their
haunts, Rotumans avoided them, preferring to leave them alone. As
long as *'atua* were confined to their haunts, Rotumans were quite
happy to coexist. Ghosts were only a problem if they wandered at
random.[9]

Such a problem was posed by a group of ghosts known as *sa'aitu*
that traveled around the island. Consisting only of uncircumcised
men, they were powerful and were believed to assist the winning
side in any battle. The word *sa'aitu*—and this is an important clue to
the mystery—is a composite of *sa'* 'to weave' and *'aitu* 'gods'. This
group of wandering *'atua* then may be glossed as "woven gods"
(Churchward 1939b, 470). According to my interpretation, these
ghosts that wandered about should have been called *sa'atua,* 'woven
ghosts' for they were not physicalized. But the answer to this paradox will be presented shortly.

In *'Äeatos,* the narrative focuses on ghosts that leave their haunts
in order to devour human beings, in this instance, two children.[10]
The narrative continues:

The two children continued playing, not realising that their
mother had fled, and that she had offered them to the *'atua* of

Lulu. A kind man who learnt about the impending disaster told the two children how to destroy the knee which was still inside the mat.

To get rid of it, he told the children what to do. They carried the mat to the end of the cliff and uttered the words "Lift it, support it, hurl it!" before they threw it into the sea, thus getting rid of their father's *'atua.*

Relevant to this inquiry is the use of a mat to contain the *'atua* and the ritualized chanting that accompanied its destruction. On the whole, the myths present *'atua* as malevolent beings who were preoccupied with harming humans. Even family *'atua* that had been transformed into *'aitu* were potentially dangerous, if they were offended.

Further on in the narrative, the two children became separated, and 'Aeatos, the brother, was taken to the sky "by three men" to live there. Unlike *'atua,* these three men—whom I interpret to be symbolic of the Rotuman conception of *'Aitu* as 'deified culture heroes'—were relatively kind. Unlike *'aitu* as 'family gods', who are objects of worship (such as the shark or stingray), they were culture 'gods' who were not constrained in physical form. Instead, they resided above land, in the sky. According to the field notes of Jacobson (n.d.), Rotumans had many gods called *'Aitu.* He lists two—Tagroa [Tagaroa][11] and Ravaka. Gardiner is more explicit, claiming that Tagaroa Siria was a great deity over and above all the *'atua.*

> Among his attributes are the giving of the fruits of the earth and the forecasting and the directing of the lives of men. He was prayed to for food, to make the trees fruitful, for rain, or in any great enterprise in which all were taking a part. He could avert a hurricane or any other great calamity, but all his attributes are great; he does not concern himself with the doings of the *'atua.*[12]

In *'Äeatos,* the plants on Rotuma—on the offshore island of Uea particularly—originated from the sky where the three men lived ('Aeatos threw them back to earth), thus supporting an interpretation that the three men were *'Aitu,* and Gardiner's observation that *'Aitu* were prayed to for abundance in crops. *'Aitu* were also believed to be in control of powerful forces in nature. Feasts and dances were directed to Tagaroa for he was the *'Aitu* of the *saṛu* and the *mua;*

Students on Rotuma reenact the myth of *'Äeatos,* 1992. *(A. Buckley)*

prayers to Tagaroa for fruitfulness of the crops and trees were performed by the old people at midday in brilliant sunshine. As Tagaroa was believed to dwell above the earth rather than below the sea,
he saw everything (Gardiner 1898, 467). Thus *'Aitu* of the kings and
therefore of the whole island were more powerful than *'atua* or *'aitu*
that were family gods.

Another distinction between *'atua* and *'Aitu* (including *'aitu*) is
that *'atua* tended to be malevolent while *'Aitu* were, in the main,
benevolent. Unlike *'Aitu,* who were not portrayed in *'Aeatos* as cannibalistic, the *'atua* of Lulu earnestly desired to devour 'Aeatos and his
sister. The narrative continues:

> But the two children, with the help of a kind man, managed to
> scare all ten *'atua* who arrived in turn to eat them. When each
> of the *'atua* arrived and asked them what they were doing, they
> said, "We are *weaving* [my italics] a net to catch the one-headed
> [the right number of heads] *'atua* from Lulu." "If that is the
> case, all right!" replied the *'atua.* "But you wait for me, and
> then you will get it!"
>
> But immediately the two children beat their drums, and rat-
> tled the sinkers of their net, and blew their conch-shells, and

the two hens [which they had captured] cackled as loudly as ever they could. And as soon as the *'atua* heard the noise of the children's things, he was scared out of his wits, and with a terrible whirr he flew back to *Lulu* (Churchward 1938b, 111–126).

This segment of the myth is important for its description of what was done to frighten the *'atua*. It reflects the Rotuman belief that ghosts are frightened of loud chaotic noises. Prior to the arrival of the *'atua*, the kind man instructed the two children how to scare ghosts: first, they were to weave a net; second, they were to assemble all the props necessary for the production of chaotic noise. By following his instructions, the children managed to frighten the *'atua*. The second *'atua*, according to the narrative, was less fortunate than the first: "he dashed as hard as he could into the house, but became entangled in the net in the doorway." He managed to free himself and fled back to his haunt, scared by the noise. When the second *'atua* returned scared out of his wits by the two children, the narrative tells us that "the one-headed *'atua* burst out laughing" (Churchward 1938b, 122–123).

Weaving and noise were the two essential ingredients in the children's performance that made the ghosts retreat. The juxtaposition of order (weaving) and disorder (chaotic noise), or work (weaving) and play (noise), comprises two essential components that complete an act of communication with the *'atua*. Rather than dominate the *'atua*, however, the intention was to send them back to their abode.

The first Catholic fathers in Rotuma noted that "each burial ground has a house for play; that all they do is to laugh, sing, jump, and dance" (cited in Gardiner 1898, 401). As Rotuman ghosts were dead ancestors, a plausible explanation is that playing near the burial grounds was intended to keep the ghosts away. That ghosts were scared of noise is supported by the *'Äeatos* narrative. Chaotic noise, in my view, symbolized life and dominance, in contrast to death and subjugation. Play (in the form of chaotic noise), as revealed in the myth *'Äeatos*, and the presence of the playhouse at the burial ground, were therefore part of rituals associated with keeping *'atua* away.[13] There is further evidence. In a *sa'a*, the same conjunction of weaving and chaotic noise occurred.

A *sa'a* was an occasion when women gathered together to weave fine mats for an important future event. Within this setting, certain taboos were broken, and certain rituals performed. As in a traditional wedding, ritual clowning accompanied the weaving of the fine mats. A brief look at the kinds of fine mats that were woven in the past and the rituals associated with the weaving process will serve to illustrate the importance of clowning on these occasions.

Nine years before the first missionaries arrived, Bennett (1831) reported that four kinds of mats were woven on Rotuma: *'epa* 'ordinary mats' and three grades of fine mats. The lowest was *apei sala* made from pandanus, next was *apei niau* made from hibiscus bark, and finer still was the *armea* [*arumea*], made from the bark of the paper mulberry tree. Further, Bennett commented that the weaving of a fine mat was such a tedious process that it took six months or more to complete.[14] As fine mats served no utilitarian purpose, why should so much time, energy, and food be spent on their production? This is perhaps translatable into the terms of Bentham's idea of "deep play," cited in Geertz as "play in which the stakes are so high that it is, from [a] utilitarian standpoint, irrational for men [or women] to engage in it at all" (Geertz 1973a, 432). Unless of course the act was believed essential for constraining *'atua* that could wreak havoc indiscriminately. A *sa'a*, therefore, is a text[15]—in the same way that the narrative of *'Äeatos* is a text—although a metaphorical one that needs interpretation. The *sa'a*, like the wedding, was a symbolic medium, a concrete situation in which meanings, emotions, conceptions, and attitudes were organized (see Geertz 1973a, 448–449).

Before a *sa'a*, a pig was killed to consecrate the event. The pig was a sacrificial gift to *'aitu* to solicit their powers. As a *sa'a* disrupted the everyday lives of the community, so did the clowning that accompanied the weaving. MacGregor's unpublished field notes contain the following entry:

> Women of district called to make a mat—a *sa'a*—a special fine white mat for some purpose. They have a *manea* [play][16] who calls on people for anything she likes or workers like. Dancers, food, etc. She has powers to demand anything of anybody. When the workers are tired or hungry, they call the manea and ask for food or men to dance for them. Any person passing by that this clown catches, must do her bidding. When it is known that a district had called each hoag [village] to supply their best weavers to work on a saa, . . . all Rotuma will attempt to avoid this place, because of the Manea. During the work each hoag will take a day at feeding the workers. (1932, no. 25)

The narrative of *'Äeatos* suggests that the chaotic laughter the women instigated, and the weaving, were attempts to keep the spirits at bay, away from the boundary of human interaction.[17] As with the net weaving of the two children, mat weaving may be construed as a *sa'a* to catch the *sa'aitu,* who were not confined to their haunts but roamed around.

*   *   *

This interpretation sounds plausible so far. However, I am faced with another problem. If an *'atua* (malevolent spirit) has been captured in a mat, then logically, such a mat will have negative rather than positive associations. Yet, mats have positive connotations. How do I explain this?

For many days I agonize over this problem and work late into the early hours of the morning. Since my small bedroom is also my office, and I rarely go out to socialize during this time, one might say that I breathed little else but my research. A habit of mine during this time is to sleep with pen and paper under my pillow. During the night, if I am lucky and a thought occurs to me, I wake up and write it down. This time, the explanation to my problem appears in a dream. I wake up with the following explanation.

*   *   *

Since the term *sa'aitu* refers to a group of uncircumcised male *'atua* who wandered freely, and the weavers were an assembly of a considerable number of women, it is likely that the weaving was, symbolically, believed to be constraining the *sa'aitu,* in much the same way that ritual cooking constrained and domesticated the giant in *Kirkirsasa.* Both needed to be integrated into the culture. Weaving an *'atua* into a mat was the same as transforming it into an *'aitu:* a potentially malevolent *'atua* could be physicalized and made benevolent or harmless. By being physicalized in the form of a mat, *'atua* were brought into the moral order, making it possible for human beings to exercise control over their disposition. Rotuman fine mats, from this standpoint, are a supreme symbol of domestication, more specifically, of domesticated *mana* 'potency'.

*   *   *

From this point on, I am able to move forward, to complete the rest of this chapter.

The act of scaring the *'atua* and weaving it into a mat symbolically encapsulated the ambivalence inherent in ghost–human interaction; the *sa'aitu,* for example, were believed to be potentially dangerous, yet at the same time assisted in victorious undertakings.[18] As

Shore has written of Polynesian thinking, "relations between humans and gods are both ambiguous and ambivalent" (1989, 164). This explains the anomaly in the term *sa'aitu:* it refers to wandering ghosts that could be woven, "captured" in a fine mat, and turned into *'aitu.* Among other uses, fine mats were worn for protection when going to battle.

> The war mats are of the same texture as the Apē [sic] Sala, but of smaller size; four of these are worn together, fastened round the waist, when going to meet their enemies; they placed vandykes decorated with red feathers on the edge of each, except the upper one, which has two oblong strips ornamented in a similar manner.[19]

The belief that wandering ghosts could be transformed into benevolent or harmless gods resolved fears that malicious ghosts posed to the community. As well, it was a way to harness the *mana* of the ghosts. Life would be unbearable if the *sa'aitu* could not be physicalized, even if only in a symbolic way. Today, the *sa'a* is no longer a part of fine-mat weaving—perhaps because this link between weaving and the *'atua* has been severed—and only the least important of the three grades of *apei* is still being produced. However, *apei* are "sensed" by Rotumans to be sacred, although they are unable to explain why.[20] And fine mats continue to be essential for weddings, funerals, births, welcoming ceremonies, and headstone unveilings[21]—in fact, any ritual of importance.

What made a fine mat sacred? There is evidence to suggest that a fine mat was not sacred (set apart and not to be used for ordinary purposes) until a *hȧn mane'ȧk* "played" it. The word *mane'ȧk* is a transitive verb and used, for instance, when someone asks another to desecrate a sacred place. It has strong connotations of movement or motion, different from the word *mane'a* 'play', which is a noun. Thus, the clown in a *sa'a*, selected from among the weavers, was properly called a *hȧn mane'ȧk* 'the woman who plays'—in this case, the woman who plays the mats.

Similarly, though I have glossed *hȧn mane'ȧk su* thus far as "woman who plays at the wedding," a more accurate literal translation, in the light of this explanation, is "the woman who plays the wedding." The meaning changes slightly, but is more accurate. It captures the idea that the clown activates certain forces. Her role is not passive or ineffectual (as in an intransitive verb).

As in the wedding context, the *hȧn mane'ȧk sa'a* was given complete license during a *sa'a.* She could order people about and strike

Fine mats *(apei)* are brought to wedding two, 1989. They are the most highly valued items at weddings and all important rituals or ceremonies. *(Jan Rensel)*

anyone, even the chiefs, with impunity. She carried a stick, wore flowers in her hair, blackened her face with charcoal, or was masked. Men might be forced to dance or sing for the pleasure of the weavers (Howard 1960). If a chief should pass by on the road, he was abused by the women, who called him *fa ta* 'a man' instead of *gagaj* 'chief' (Hocart 1913, nos 596, 597). If the chief became angry and abused the women, they could hold him to ransom until his people paid with a pig. Ordinary men were also susceptible to the pranks of the women, who grabbed them and demanded green coconuts, pigs, fowls, and other foods. Should the men fail to meet the women's demands, they could be held for ransom and forced to sing all day. Hocart reported a man who ended up urinating in his trousers (1913, no. 4597). Sometimes old women without teeth chewed food and administered mouthfuls to the men as though they were babies, reminding them of a time when they were helpless and dependent on women.

My most recent account of a *sa'a* is from Harieta Katafono who taught in Rotuma in the early 1960s, around the time when this institution disappeared. In a letter to me dated 26 March 1991, she told of a man who was "captured by the *hàn mane'àk sa'a* and forced to clown for the women for some time before he was allowed to go on his way," as well as "truck drivers who were having a hard time trying to avoid having to pass the house where the *sa'a* was being held, or trying to drive past without being stopped."

Hocart's field notes suggest that in the *sa'a*, the women were inclined to violence in their treatment of the men. There is also the strong implication that the women were engaged in a *te fakgagaj* 'chiefly custom' and hence vital to the community. When, in one instance they became angry with the "Commissioner" who supposedly had said he would put them in jail if they took things from the shop without paying, they threatened to stop their weaving. Sometimes the men had to "sweet talk" the women to keep working. The women had the men running in rings trying to please them: "They [the women] said they would not eat it [*fekei* 'pudding']. They would have pig. He brought (a) pig and they said, they would have fish, so they got fish" (Hocart 1913, no. 5073). Men were verbally abused; two examples of expressions noted by Hocart are *ö' al* 'dead parents' and *tauat* [*tau'uat*] 'fuck your head'.[22] But not everything was told to Hocart, who wrote: "There are many dirty practices formerly connected with sa'a which M won't tell. e.g. woman will (as far as I understand) rub her arse upon the man" (1913, no. 4597).

It is not clear from Hocart's account whether there was much laughter, though given all the unbridled activity, including the mock insults and the dancing, it is hard to imagine how it could have been possible for those watching, including villagers living close by, not to laugh. Hocart stated that two women sat at either end of the mat being woven and claimed to be *sau* 'king', and that the only way for the men they had waylaid to be let off was through either paying a ransom or making one of the weavers laugh. When this happened, the man appealed to the two women, who abused the woman who laughed, and let the man off (1913, nos 4596, 4597). Although Hocart does not explain why the weavers were not supposed to laugh too readily, this restriction was probably only in response to a man's funny antics.

Why should the chiefs and the men be the butt of the women's mock attacks and insults? Why was the weaving of fine mats an occasion for license? Why was the structural order of society inverted? The tensions inherent in male–female and chief–commoner relations are relevant here, although this specific context creates further tensions. At a pragmatic level, the weaving of fine mats was hard work, and clowning supposedly helped to make it lighter. After all, it was common for Pacific Islanders who worked in groups, either in the gardens or fishing in the lagoon, to indulge in play. Work and play (in the form of humorous banter or dancing) were not mutually exclusive in Rotuman thought.[23]

However, the inspirational thrust for the women's behavior during a *sa'a* probably stemmed from conflicting forces. A *sa'a* was imposed by the chiefs, who were men, yet women had to provide the labor. Only women knew how to weave fine mats; it was their monopoly. Like giving birth, it was something that women could do and men could not. The production of fine mats was time-consuming, tedious, and disruptive of normal life. A *sa'a,* as a context for privileged expression, allowed the women to force the men to "pay" for their demands. Women's ambivalence and tensions became sublimated into play.[24] This partly explains their tendency toward violent behavior, a strong inversion to compensate for their labor. This pattern of reciprocity is customary in social relations. For example, Vafoóu asserted that one reason why ritual clowns at weddings today are not violent, is that custom dictates that at the end of the wedding, a fine mat must be presented to "pay" any victim who has been humiliated, and relatives of the bride are often reluctant to part with their precious mats because they are now scarce, even on the island. As well, the ritual clown has to be compensated for making a fool of herself in public.

As in the traditional wedding, the *sa'a* inverted the normal social order. However, the rationale was not just pragmatic, but symbolic. Writing in 1960, Howard claimed that clowning did not occur until the mat was almost finished. This meant that clowning occurred when the red feathers—symbolic of the spirit world—were being woven into the mat. And since the *hàn mane'àk* blackened her face,[25] she must have assumed the dramatis persona of an *'atua,* a physical manifestation of the ghosts imagined as being woven into the mat. It makes sense therefore that the secular rulers in normal life, in the period of liminality, should submit to the *hàn mane'àk* clown who is an *'atua* personified. A fine mat that has been "processed" in this manner, one that has been played by an *'atua* clown, is thus charged with generative potency.

A big wedding could amass fifty or more fine mats.[26] The production of fine mats took weeks, if not months, to complete and caused a marked disjunction in the flow of everyday life. But to own a fine mat is to own a symbol that encapsulates the Rotuman world view, one that has been played, and made sacred. Further, a fine mat is a work of art. Although the fine mats of today are only third grade, the quality of the first grade can still be imagined in the best that still exists. Forbes, writing in 1875, was sufficiently impressed with Rotuman fine mats to write: "Compared to Rotuman mats, the finest Batique mats from Fiji are coarse and ugly; while the mats of Samoa and Tonga do not deserve to be mentioned in the same breath."[27]

Thus I find common threads among these three clues. In the past, when women wove fine mats, chaotic laughter accompanied the process. The laughter of the *hån mane'åk* at the *sa'a* was like the laughter of the *'atua* in *'Äeatos*. Furthermore, the weaving that appears in the narrative *'Äeatos* finds a corollary in mat weaving. The term *sa'aitu* 'woven gods', the weaving and chaotic noise in the myth *'Äeatos* in order to entangle the *'atua*, and the conjunction of the same in the weaving of fine mats during a *sa'a*, constitute evidence in support of this interpretation. The *hån mane'åk su* institution has its origins in beliefs related to *'atua*, and the ritual clown was originally an actor who personified *'atua*.

Wedding Rituals

How did Rotumans view marriage? I begin with the premise that the most important reason for marriage prior to missionization was the new alliances that would result from the marriage union. The second important factor was the propagation of the Rotuman people. The first premise implies communication with other human beings. The second premise—that of propagation—implies communication with *'atua* and *'aitu*, who could ruin a happy marriage, and with *'Aitu*, who bestowed fertility. The two premises are not mutually exclusive, but are present in each wedding to varying degrees. The ritual clown's behavior was influenced by both premises; the ultimate goal of a wedding in the past was the attainment of harmony between conflicting and contradictory forces in society and in nature. A traditional wedding was a microcosm of Rotuman culture in all its wholeness and complexity, an enactment of what it meant to be Rotuman, in a social drama whose star actor was the *'atua* clown.

The ritual clown's behavior cannot be completely understood without an analysis of the wedding rituals against which that behavior was juxtaposed.[28] The rituals performed during wedding one (excluding the Christian ceremony) included the *paag ri* 'screening of the temporary shelter', the *'öf sope* 'symbolic cutting of hair', the *fit'äk te* 'display of fine mats', and the *fau ta* 'covering of the couple in fine mats'. All these rituals occurred within the period of liminality in which the clown featured.

The *paag ri* 'screening of the temporary shelter' happened soon after the groom's procession had been granted permission to proceed to where the bride was seated. The women who carried yards of colorful fabric quickly adorned the temporary shelter and started dancing. Malo interpreted the screening as symbolically creating a sacred atmosphere, a transformation into a holy place for the marriage rituals.[29] Vafoóu claimed that fine mats were used in earlier days, and were an ostentatious display by the groom's mother of her skills and talents. This display was directed to the general public, but particularly to the bride—a way of communicating the value of hard work, as symbolized in the making of an *apei*. Today, the cotton fabric used for this ritual may be cut up as "curtains" to provide some privacy for the bridal couple after the wedding, or distributed as gifts to thank relatives of the bride.

This *paag ri* ritual marks the beginning of "liminality . . . the suspension of daily reality." However, although it heralds the beginning of the period when "taboos are lifted, fantasies are enacted, the low are exalted and the mighty abased," there are still some controls, as

Seated on fine mats, the bride awaits the arrival of the groom's party. Wedding three, 1989.

certain acts—rape and murder, for example—are not permissible. Because the groom's side performs the *paag ri* ritual, they demonstrate tacit agreement to sanction the mock antagonism that follows. The screening is therefore a visual manifestation of the play setting, which Turner defined as "the metaphorical borders within which the facts of experience can be viewed, reflected upon, and evaluated" (1984, 21–22). Since the rituals are markers of the journey of transition from one phase to another, this ritual may be viewed as communicating to the couple, "You are now on your way." It is akin to the launching of a canoe.

The '*öf sope* 'symbolic cutting of hair' is performed by the two *sigoa* 'namesakes' of the bride and groom in turn. Each *sigoa* procession arrives (in the wedding of 1987, one *sigoa* procession danced their way into the arena carrying pink and blue fabric, while the other held a fine mat) with the *sigoa* at the front carrying a pair of scissors.[30] The couple are then invited to sit on a pile of mats that has been prepared by women relatives of the *sigoa* (prior to the *sigoa*'s arrival).[31] The *sigoa* or a substitute then symbolically snips above the head of the namesake.[32]

Being seated on mats symbolizes respect for the couple, and moral support from each *sigoa*. As Rotumans regard the namesake as the equivalent of a third parent, this ritual symbolically severs the parent-child relationship (one that is marked by the child's dependence on the parent). It also signifies the change in status for the couple, from *haharagi* 'youth' to *mamfua* 'adulthood'. The bride and groom are now separated from their childhood past and further along on their way to being incorporated into another phase of life.

In the past, a tuft of hair at the side of the head was left uncut until marriage (see Gardiner 1898, 479). Its symbolic removal at contemporary weddings signifies that the couple are now expected to be mature, productive adults in the community. They have control over their affairs, and in the future may be called upon by their namesakes to render services in one form or another (see also Malo 1975, 23). The mats that are spread out in front of the couple— before they sit on them—are exchanged between the two older namesakes, symbolizing the forging of a new relationship through marriage. Considering that there has been mock antagonism between the kin groups, this act is part of what Turner called the "remedial processes" necessary to reconcile conflicting parties (1984, 24).

As is usual in important rituals, the couple are also garlanded with sweet-smelling flowers, what Rotumans call *tefui*. The garlands of flowers mark the couple as special and set apart from others. They are also expressions of the love that each *sigoa* has for the bride and groom.

The *fit'ak te* ritual of displaying mats by the relatives of the bride and groom provides an opportunity for the community to view and evaluate the quantity and quality of fine mats which are the *mosega* 'beds' for the couple. This ritual is called *fit'ak te* 'to open up or reveal'; while it is happening, the women in particular pay attention, and may even count (silently) the number of mats provided by each kin group. *Mosega* do not just evoke connotations of conjugal sexuality, but signify the very essence of kinship. Since these mats will be distributed again among kin after the wedding, and passed down from one generation to another, they symbolize continuity in social relations, from dead ancestors to future offspring.[33] The exchanges in fine mats between the two kin groups also symbolize new obligations and new alliances being forged or consolidated. Usually, both kin groups will find themselves more involved with each other in future life-crisis ceremonies. Also, the mats publicly acknowledge the different *sal hapa* 'family units within a *kainaga* (clan)' that have contributed to the pool of mats, and symbolize the support system that is now available to bride and groom. Even though the journey ahead may be rough, relatives are there to provide support when needed. Because fine mats are consecrated, the amount of mats displayed is perhaps interpreted as commensurate with the amount of *mana* that is generated in honor of the couple and their future well-being. In practice, however, the mats are given away at the end of the wedding; the couple is usually left with just a few for their own use. The redistribution again expresses gratitude to those who have contributed, as it consolidates social and familial ties, and ensures that the mats are kept in circulation rather than hoarded by an individual.

The *fau ta* ritual, whereby the couple are wrapped in fine mats and carried from the bride's side to the groom's side, was traditionally performed on the day of the *naag 'inoso* 'sending the couple'. This happens several days after the wedding, when the bride and groom are taken to the groom's house for the first time. Before entering the groom's village, relatives of the bride dress the couple, who enter in a chiefly fashion, chiefs being the ones who wore fine mats in the past.[34] Being bound by fine mats symbolizes the channeling of the couple's sexuality, now that they are married to each other. According to Werbner, South Asians hold a similar belief, that "the powers of human sexuality, while essential for human reproduction, lead—uncontrolled—to infertility" (1986, 229–230). But the word *fau* does not just mean to cover; it also means to suppress evil (see Churchward 1940a, 196). This ritual is significant for the many different meanings it symbolizes.[35]

A groom who has been married before is usually not wrapped in fine mats, a strong suggestion that the binding in mats primarily symbolizes the exclusiveness of husband–wife sexuality. The confinement of the sexual act to husband–wife relations is particularly significant for the male who, prior to marriage, has had considerable freedom to roam and to indulge in sexual experimentation. Being bound in mats is similar to the Rotuman practice of tying a coconut frond around a tree to indicate that it is forbidden to others.[36] Shore stated that in Polynesian conception ritual binding is associated with "potency in the interest of social and cosmic generation" (1989, 166). This ritual fortified the Rotuman view of adultery. If caught, the guilty man was tied to a canoe and set adrift; the

The *fau ta* ritual, when the bride and groom are wrapped in fine mats. The woman at left is placing the *'at fara* basket on the mat. Rotuma, 1960. *(Alan Howard)*

The *fau ta* ritual. Wedding two, 1989. (*Jan Rensel*)

woman was customarily clubbed to death (Eason 1951, 13). Further, being bound in fine mats symbolically means being enveloped in the protective *mana* of *'aitu,* in the same way that warriors wore fine mats when preparing for battle. It can also signify virginity, particularly for the bride.

Having been wrapped in fine mats, the bride is then lifted on high by young men who are close relatives of the groom and the groom by young men who are close relatives of the bride. They are then carried to the side of the shelter where the groom's kin are seated. The elevation of bride and groom symbolizes respect and support for the value of virginity, particularly by the young men who are least likely to respect its sanctity. Having young men of one kin group carry the spouse of the opposite group is significant because it symbolizes new links and new relationships being forged across kin lines. If there have been previous animosities concerning the union—for example, if brothers of the bride have been antagonistic toward the groom prior to marriage—then this display of support symbolizes that all is well again, that the past has been forgotten, though this may or may not be so in practice. The couple being taken to the groom's side is indicative of the the practice of former times, when this ritual was performed before entry into the groom's village.[37] At a pragmatic level, strong young men are the most appropriate for a ritual requiring physical strength.

These are the important rituals still performed today, at least for wedding one.[38] They are rituals dominated by women and fine mats. The equation of women with fine mats is significant, as though to communicate that in the world of the sacred (or in liminality), women and fine mats are paramount. Once this period ended, men regained control. The emphasis shifted to their gifts of root crops, fruits, and meat, those of the mundane, ordinary world. The normal world was reinstated, the chiefs resumed their previous positions in the social hierarchy, the *sik fono* or food distribution was performed,[39] and women served the chiefs, and other important guests, their food.[40]

The Clown as Liminal Being

Why does the ritual clown deliberately provoke laughter in the midst of serious rituals? The juxtaposition of the serious (ritual) and play (clowning) frequently occurs in the myths and is significant in situations where communication with powerful forces is important, as exemplified in the myths of *Kirkirsasa* and *'Äeatos.* This duality is reflected most powerfully in the *sa'a,* weaving of fine mats. That the same should occur at weddings suggests that both order and disorder, or work (ritual) and play (clowning), are essential for effective communication with *'atua* and *'aitu.* When the orderly nature of ritual is juxtaposed with the antistructural behavior of the clown, tension mounts; spectators are reminded that when the powerful forces of nature strike, in hurricanes for example, human institutions and attempts to order life may be brought to naught. At the personal level, the pull between restraint and impulsive behavior is mirrored in the conjunction of ritual and play.

Ritual—characterized by prescribed procedures—is not complete without the disorderly behavior that complements it. Though Kirkirsasa is not involved in the "cooking" ritual (in terms of administering the hot stones), her role is just as important, if not more so. Ritual (order) and laughter (disorder) are two sides of the same coin, different but complementary. Ritual may be identified with humans and the norms of society, play with the world of the *'atua* and their chaotic nature. Both symbolic manifestations form an essential unity: they complement, contradict, mirror, enhance, and stimulate each other even as they communicate.[41]

One of the first things the clown must do when chosen is seek the permission of her chief. Sanction by the chief implies transference of his *mana* to the clown.[42] Hocart's account of the *sa'a* depicts two women sitting on a fine mat being woven and claiming to be king of the island, in contrast to the *hàn mane'àk,* who indulges in chaotic behavior. The picture is one of two passive figures who are "kings" juxtaposed against a clown "chief" who is their alter ego. This pattern is similar to the wedding scene, where bride and groom are elevated to a god-like status while the ritual clown prances around. Again, the juxtaposition of order and disorder, stasis and movement, the god-like and the human is evident. In the liminal period, both rule, theoretically, for they symbolize two parts of a whole. This partly explains why the bride and the groom are outside the clown's sphere of influence. They are like the two "kings" who sit on the fine mat as it is being woven. Not only are they male and female in real life, they also symbolize the two complementary roles in Rotuman kingship, that of the *mua* (female) and the *sau* (male). These two complementary roles are played out by the clown. In fact, the clown, as both male and female, is the alter ego for male and female qualities that are manifest in discrete and separate forms in life: in the *mua* and the *sạu,* in male and female, and in bride and groom. In the clown, they all fuse. The word *su* does not just mean wedding, it also means to soak in, or to dissolve, such as when water soaks into the ground, or when sugar dissolves completely in water (Churchward 1940a, 315). This is what the term *hàn mane'àk su* implies: the woman who fuses (plays) both maleness and femaleness, as in the act of copulation.

But the clown does not just fuse the sexes in her persona. Though human, she assumes the persona of an *'atua.* As an *'atua,* she is a liminal being, with "the ghost mediating between the actor as person and the actor as stage persona, distancing one from accountability of the actions of the other" (Shore 1977, 365). As Shore has pointed out in relation to the Samoan *fale aitu,* the continual tension between actor as person, actor as ghost, and actor as persona provides the energy for the clown's performance. "The ambiguities inherent in the relationship between the speaker and the social context . . . make the figure of the ghost such an apt organ for the expression of conflict" (Shore 1977, 366). The potency inherent in ambiguity was best summed up by Turner, who explained that dramatic genres like theater and ritual provide a context in which

> [a]mbiguity reigns: people and public policies may be judged skeptically in relation to deep values; the vices, follies, stupidities, and abuses of contemporary holders of high political, economic, or religious status may be satirized, ridiculed or condemned in terms of axiomatic values, or these personages may be rebuked for gross failures in common sense. (1982b, 22)

As an *'atua* clown, the *hàn mane'àk su* wields a stick whose symbolic meaning is multiplex. It is not just a useful prop for pointing and threatening the chiefs, for it also reminds spectators of the stick that men use to plant taro and cassava in their gardens. It may also symbolize supreme authority, that of the *sạu* of the island. The stick further evokes the object of oppression. Oppression by whom? The powerful forces of nature? The chiefs? Culture with its rules and obligations? Men who view women as sexual objects, primarily for procreation? Or all of those things? As symbol, the clown's stick is charged with cultural and cosmic import. It draws attention to the *hàn mane'àk su*'s lack of a penis as well as the excessive size of the stick. Its primary referent, however, is the male phallus, its procreative function in human propagation as well as its "believed" role in cosmic regeneration.

The stick the clown carries and the mats that dominate the rituals are not just "condensation symbols" or symbols that embody many different meanings;[43] they are also oppositional and complementary symbols; mats can be representative of females and the stick of males. Used together, they represent the human race. In conjunction with the *'atua* clown, the unity of the cosmos is fully represented, and the "stage" is set for play in which many things about the social and moral order, and many things about the natural and physical order can be "said," simultaneously (see Turner 1982b, 20).

Rotuma's famous clown Ioane, who was popular in the 1960s and 1970s, used to blacken her face to make herself look like an *'atua*. Was she, as *hån mane'åk su*, a physical manifestation of *hanit te ma'us*, the "spirit-woman," who prevented conflicting forces from destroying the island? Was the stick that she carried intended to represent Raho's stick, which he used to alter the geographical features of the land? In a similar way, the clown in a wedding uses her stick to alter the social structure of society. Moreover, the digging stick that Raho used to destroy the land is the same that men use to dig the soil and to plant taro. In the wedding context, the stick is therefore a symbol of fertility of both the land and the people. Because *'Aitu* were responsible for bestowing abundance in nature and in humankind, the clown's whole performance may be viewed as a communication to deified culture heroes, an acknowledgment that although human beings may be subjugated to the *'atua*—as symbolized in the inverted hierarchical order with the *'atua* clown as chief— *'Aitu* was over and above all.

According to Gardiner, the name Tangaroa Siria (the word *siria* means bigger than anything else) had the attribute of acting "wickedly," and among his responsibilities were the giving of the fruits of the earth and the forecasting and directing of the lives of human beings.[44] He was the god of the *sau* and his name was called out as soon as a boy was born, in the hope that he would direct the life of that boy. On the occasion of a birth, old men and women walked around carrying a stick called *poki*, which was held over the head with both hands and moved rhythmically to and fro with the singing. The word *poki* is not in use today; in Samoa, where this term probably originated, it means penis, supporting the interpretation that the stick was a phallic symbol.[45] Gardiner also described a prayer offering for a fruitful season.

The wedding is another arena in which fertility in human beings is paramount. It is therefore imperative that the *poki* (symbolic of the male phallus) carried by the female clown, who is a medium for the *'atua*, should again be played to *'aitu* to induce regeneration of both land and people. As an embodiment of the human and the divine, with both male and female characteristics, the *hàn mane'àk su* is empowered with all the essential ingredients for fertility; her preoccupation with sexual banter and innuendo is therefore a simu- lated communication about humankind and the cosmos reproduc- ing themselves.[46] Clowning was not just a passive affirmation of the status quo, but an active agent in stimulating regeneration. It was not just recreation, it was re-creation.

As recreation and re-creation, laughter is not inappropriate or diabolical in sacred or contemplative moments in the old Rotuman religion, in which the play house was built at the cemetery. For Rotu- mans, religion was much more than singing hymns, reciting prayers, and putting on pious faces; it was a marriage of complementary, contradictory, and conflicting forces that mirrored, enhanced, and contradicted each other in liminal space. Within the sacred context of the wedding, the Rotuman worldview and ethos, in its wholeness and complexity, was synthesized, producing multiple exposures that simulated and stimulated the total sociocultural system.

7 Woven Gods

> We are what we remember, so the historian and his
> [sic] art of remembering are of paramount impor-
> tance to all societies. They are especially important in
> our societies which are modernising madly.
> ALBERT WENDT, Novelists and Historians
> and the Art of Remembering

The ritual clown in Rotuma is an agent of the power structure as
well as a potential catalyst for change. She exists to reinforce the
status quo, with powers that are constrained within clearly defined
boundaries. She is an older woman, past childbearing age, and non-
threatening outside the boundary of privileged license. Her status
in everyday life is lower than that of chiefs and most men. When all
the festivities are over, she returns to being an ordinary housewife,
while the chief from whom she had temporarily "borrowed" her
powers resumes his position of authority. Moreover, chiefs who have
been humiliated by the clown need compensation in the way of
foods and fine mats. Beliefs that a *hàn mane'àk su* who oversteps her
powers will be punished by the spirits further ensure that the threat
to the authority of men and chiefs is contained. This study supports
the theory that ritual clowning, despite its subversive appearance,
reminds us of the rules and the rulers in real life.

Ambiguity is the hallmark of the ritual clown's communication,
which is multivocal and inverted. She is a paradox in that she inverts
values that are the cornerstones of Rotuman culture—humility,
restraint, respect—while affirming them by drawing attention to
the norm in real life. The destructive and chaotic world that she
"screens" is the antithesis of harmony, testimony to the impracti-
cality of a world in which folly reigns.

Because the ritual clown stands at the interface between original-
ity and conformity, between the individual and society, she is always
potentially dangerous and destabilizing. This interface between

131

ritual and play becomes a site for innovation; clowning need not be just a reinforcement of the status quo, but also a potential creator of its successor. At its most liminal, ritual clowning is exploratory, creative, and progressive; it may be viewed as a "site of actual and symbolic struggle" (Stallybrass and White 1986, 14).

For the bride and groom, change at the personal level, as well as in the social order where they will reside, is inevitable. The status quo in these two realms cannot remain the same, because the bride and groom have been transformed into adults. Whereas they were *haharagi* 'youthful' until the day of the marriage, they become *mamfua* 'adults' as soon as they are married. Not only do they lose their virginity (particularly in the case of the bride) and therefore symbolically lose their youth, but their new statuses, as well as those of their kin, mean a realignment in the ranking of individuals in relation to one another.

Chiefs and men who have been subjected to the clown's destructive and authoritarian behavior at the wedding will have been invigorated by a view of the world where the women reign. Possibly such "shock therapy" (Babcock 1984, 103) will challenge and perhaps modify their chauvinistic attitudes toward women. Clowns who have been particularly successful in the role also rise in status in the eyes of the community, as was the case with Ioane, who is reputed to be the best *hån mane'åk su* Rotuma has ever had. She was a household name when she was alive, and famous for her fearlessness in much the same way that Marilyn Monroe was famous for her beauty. Further, clowns who are poor actors do not usually get asked again, those who draw attention to themselves are labeled "show-offs" and ridiculed, and those who overstep the boundaries of license get ostracized, as was the case with the *hån mane'åk su* of the second wedding, who was not thanked in the traditional manner. Although the chiefs resume their privileged positions at the end of the day, they do so much humbled and aware of the chaos that ensues when authority goes haywire; everyone is emotionally affected in one way or another.

Although in Rotuma the ritual clown is always played by a woman, this is not always the case elsewhere. On the larger volcanic islands such as Samoa and Tahiti, male clowns were the norm, particularly during canoe expeditions between islands. Because performances in which ritual clowns featured often took place within the context of boating expeditions, it is not surprising that young males played the role of lead comedians. They were more mobile than mothers and wives, whose services were needed at home. Besides, in real life, these young untitled men were among the least threatening to the power structure; their ridicule of the chiefs could be entertained without rancor. Further, their being away from home provides a diversion that channels their energy in the pursuit of pleasures that appear to be in their interest, although, as this study has shown, they may ultimately be in the service of maintaining stability.

As designated ruler of the wedding, the *hàn mane'àk su* embodies female and male, human and divine. She fuses ritual and play, stasis and movement, order and disorder—indeed, the forces in society and nature that are essential for life and its regeneration. Her dramatis persona oscillates between these various states, making her particularly suitable as an agent for the expression and mediation of conflict. Her ambiguity and oscillation between the actor as person and the actor as stage persona or ghost make her communications multiplex.

Her functions are many: entertainer and catalyst, mistress of ceremonies, and cultural symbol. She is the ideal mediator between chiefs and commoners, males and females, and kin groups. She draws her repertoire from elements in secular clowning and develops them, carries them further, in the safe arena of play. As a wedding is the most complex and elaborate of transition rites in Rotuman culture, her actions are charged with symbolic significance. For instance, the *hàn mane'àk su*'s preoccupation with sexual innuendo is no different from action that was intended to invoke supernatural forces to produce abundance in crops, or the sexual orgies that accompanied Dionysian worship. It is analogous to the Hopi acts of mock copulation to make the corn grow,[1] to the love-making of the *arioi* society that was dedicated to the gods,[2] to Fijian women's sexual antics when the chief's firstborn is a son,[3] and to Scottish sexual orgies in the fields to invoke the god Shony to send abundant seaweed.[4]

Spirits were believed responsible for the fertility of the land and the people; first-fruit festivals, births, weddings, and other events associated with fertility were contexts in which taboos on sexual license were lifted, and feasting, singing, dancing, and dramatic performances occurred. Clowning was very much a part of the rituals of fertility, suggesting that clowns were either physical manifestations of the spirits—as in Rotuma, Samoa, and Fiji—or believed to have been possessed, as in Tahiti. This link with the supernatural partly explains their flaunting of societal conventions and the submission of everyone, particularly the chiefs, to the temporary but potent authority of the ritual clown.

Ritual clowning is much more than a "cultural steamvalve," or a means of "catharsis and control, palliative remedies, substitute gratifications, or therapeutic reprieves from the oppressions of culture" (Babcock 1984, 107, 113). Nor is it just the communication of social and cultural messages of import. In pre-missionary Rotuma, clowning was a communication with the world of dead ancestors who lived on in the form of *'atua* and *'aitu*. The overturning of the cultural hierarchy was a symbolic submission to the *'atua*, who could wreak havoc in the lives of humans, an inversion that was essential to placate malevolent forces in nature. The ritual clown wielding the symbolic male phallus, and her preoccupation with sexual innuendo, were suggestive communications directed to causing the *'Aitu* to act—to bless the land and the people, and particularly on the occasion of the wedding, to bless the married couple with healthy children to propagate the Rotuman people. During the liminal period of the wedding, complementary, contradictory, and conflicting forces in nature and society were synthesized and played, by the liminal *hån mane'åk su*, into a tune of harmony, in theory, if not in practice.

It is probable that ritual clowning in Rotuma originated in ritual performances addressed to supernatural powers who were supposedly in control of the elements and the lives of human beings. Evidence suggests that the institution of *hån mane'åk su* probably had its roots in ritual dance, performed to harness supernatural powers for human purposes. For example, during wedding one, a comic sketch between the ritual clown and a white Australian man developed spontaneously from dance, supporting the most popular theory of theater origins.[5]

There is one noteworthy difference. Rotumans believed that the act of weaving fine mats symbolized the weaving into the mats of malevolent ghosts. In this way, ghosts could be constrained and transformed into benevolent gods whose *mana* could then be harnessed in the service of prosperity and fertility—of the land and the people. Similarly, the ritual clown who pranced around during the liminal period of fine-mat weaving, and her counterpart at traditional weddings in which fine mats became the central focus, were conduits through which the contradictions of social and divine power were manifest.

In contemporary Rotuma, ritual clowns seem afraid to play their role to the hilt. Perhaps this is because the need to challenge the power structure is less relevant today, when chiefs have less power than ever before. Not only do Rotuman women have more say in Rotuman society today, they also have more control over their lives. Further, Christianity has eradicated many of the old beliefs, so that the institution of ritual clowning is no longer sacrosanct. Besides, I have not met a single Rotuman who is aware of the religious origins or the multiple roles of the *hàn mane'àk su,* as explicated here. Without this understanding, it is easy to take the institution for granted, to take offense when ridiculed, or to view the *hàn mane'àk su* as nothing more than a ridiculous clown. Indeed, this is how most Rotumans view the *hàn mane'àk su* today. She finds herself having to perform in a context that is becoming increasingly westernized, as evidenced by the clothing of the bridal party, the ritual of the wedding cake, and the likelihood that ceremonies will be interrupted

This vehicle was used to take the bride and groom to the church for the Christian ceremony and back again to the wedding site. Wedding one, 1987. *(Aren Baoa)*

A wedding cake that is usually baked in Fiji and flown into Rotuma is now an integral part of many weddings. Wedding two, 1989. *(Jan Rensel)*

The couple with the best man and bridesmaid. Wedding three, 1989. *(Aren Baoa)*

when the bridal party takes off in a decorated pickup truck to receive the blessing of a Christian god.

What of the future?

The underlying social and emotional factors that inspired clowning are changing, and the demise of the clown seems imminent. For the clown to keep pace, she has to find new meanings that will justify her existence. To be an entertainer, custom dictates that she turn the world upside down; however, modern clowns, and Fiji Rotumans, may not regard such behavior as appropriate. The Rotuman sacred clown has become an anomaly, jostling for a slot amid shifting values and rapid changes. Possibly her curtain call will come within the next decade or so, and the *hàn mane'àk su* will have to take her bow; after all, her counterpart, the *hàn mane'àk sa'a* who pranced around during fine-mat weaving, has already made her exit, thanks to Christianity, modernization, colonialism, western ideas of theater, and other forms of play.

Two other possibilities exist. Entertainment at weddings could be left completely in the hands of the "funny women," with no woman designated as the official *hàn mane'àk su*. The religious element will be eradicated completely, and clowning at Rotuman weddings will be no different to clowning in other social contexts. Another possibility is for improvised ritual clowning to evolve in the direction of theatrical clowning—that is, clowning within a comic sketch guided by a plot. Such a convergence between secular and ritual clowning need not be seen as loss in potency; it could turn out to be an ideal site for commentary on important social, cultural, and political concerns of the day.

Should this happen, a new type of theater will emerge, similar to contemporary *fale aitu* that is now seen on television in American Samoa, or as part of the annual comedy competition during Independence Day festivities in Western Samoa. In Samoa—as in other parts of the Pacific—the rich theatrical heritage of the past informs modern performances that are not averse to exploiting the tools and technology of contemporary western theater. Similarly, when the time comes for the Rotuman *hàn mane'àk su* to exit into the realm of history, I hope that—through this book—her reign in the arena of Rotuman culture will not be forgotten. I hope also that this record of Rotuma's *hàn mane'àk su* will be an inspiration and catalyst, assisting young Pacific scholars and artists as they navigate the uncharted waters that beckon—within, and without.

8 Epilogue: Being Rotuman

Our Way

your way
objective
analytic
always doubting
the truth
until proof comes
slowly
quietly
and it hurts

my way
subjective
gut-feeling like
always sure
of the truth
the proof
is there
waiting
and it hurts

Konai Thaman, *Hingano*

The initial process of writing this book was more akin to a voyage of exploration than to the explication of a thesis. However, for the sake of clarity and focus for the reader, I decided to include my thesis in the preface and to make clearer where the journey will end. As a creative writer, I prefer traveling to arrival. Not knowing how a story is going to end is exciting; it makes the exploration full of promise and hope. You are open and sensitive to clues that suggest all kinds of possibilities; you are not closed, locked into a straight and narrow path. This study has a bit of both: at the moment when you think the path is linear, a signpost appears, telling you to return to the center where the ritual clown awaits with instructions; from there you take another path. A dead end awaits you and you return to the center again; instructions tell you to take another path. Such is the structure of this work: paths that are not always straight are enclosed within an elastic membrane called Rotuman culture.

For me, the most significant discovery in this playful exercise was the vindication of my intuitions regarding the sacredness of Rotuman fine mats. If these fine mats were regarded as woven gods imbued with *mana*, was this true of Samoan and Tongan fine mats too? Oral history and the published literature provide supporting evidence,[1] although someone else will have to do in-depth studies for these two societies. In islands where *tapa* substituted for fine mats, did *tapa* hold a similar position in the old religion? During the creation of these religious or ceremonial works of art, were there performative acts that were regarded as essential for the efficacy of the process? For example, what rituals were integral to this process in Samoa or Tonga? Was there chanting or ritual dancing? Were there pig sacrifices offered to the spirits or religious beliefs associated with the process of weaving? Was weaving (very close or fine weaving) associated with the act of capturing or snaring during the period Islanders refer to today as the "time of darkness"?[2]

What if mats were woven gods? Who cares? My Rotuman self cares, for this new knowledge empowers it, and lights up dark corners of experience. My fiction self feels validated in that its expertise and strengths have been fully exercised. And my interpretive self is humbled by this experience of having to share power, of being destabilized for a while but now better centered, positioned in its proper place, in balance with the rest of me.

More important than the resolution to my identity struggles is the ability to see beyond the past, to the future. After all, what is important is not a return to ancestral beliefs but the desire to domesticate foreign tools and tropes to meet the needs and demands of the day. It is possible, contrary to certain postmodern arguments, to acquire some measure of certainty about the nature of the cultural order and distinctive traits and tendencies in people who share the same cultural milieu (see also Sahlins 1993). Hybridity, fragmentation, juxtaposition, and other tools of modern scholarship should illuminate rather than obfuscate. There should always be an element of playfulness, and a readiness to probe, question, modify, and acknowledge when necessary that as long as we are dealing with humans and not objects, we cannot afford to be dogmatic about our predictions regarding human behavior. We can afford, however, to pay attention to changes in the present.

For instance, it would be instructive to examine the ways in which fine mats—for Rotumans, Samoans, and Tongans—are being used in the present, in church or in the marketplace. Fine mats, once symbols of ancestral religions, are now being used in Christian worship in some parts of the Pacific (e.g., see Aiavao n.d., 10). Increasingly, they may be acquired from a pawn shop in Suva, or bought at a handicraft store for several thousands of dollars. Even as I write this book, a weaving exhibition at the East-West Center in Honolulu features a quality Rotuman fine mat as its centerpiece, accompanied by a label claiming this specimen was Fijian in origin.[3] Times have certainly changed.

It is time for Pacific Islanders to infuse western scholarship with their own ways of being and doing. Shunning the benefits of world systems is no longer an option; domesticating them is a much more attractive alternative. Whenever the oppressive face of a dominant culture rears its ugly head to subjugate, in whatever guise or form, Islanders should subvert and resist, preferably through laughter.[4]

They were all sitting around a bowl of *kava* telling stories when I arrived, the men of my village Mea, and a few others from the neighboring villages of Salvak and Mälsa'a. Stories of myself as a professor had been circulating before and during my arrival, and the men were all eager and seemingly pleased to have me join them in this social and macho activity for the first time. "Tell us a Professor story!" the leader of the group asked. All eyes turned to stare at me, in anticipation. I pretended I hadn't heard, and looked at the floor. But they would not let me off the hook, and after two others had repeated the same question, I realized that I had to tell them a "Professor story." My mind raced for something to say.

I pontificated on the findings of this study. I assumed they would be interested, because I was telling them something about their culture (and mine) that they did not know. I thought I would have their full attention. But as I summarized my conclusions for them, in Rotuman, their eyes started to wander, to look away, to lose interest. A few started to close, lulled, no doubt, by the drone of the now-I'm-beginning-to-get-bored-as-well sound of my voice. This was the first time I had tried to explain anything academic in Rotuman. And I was putting them to sleep. Disappointed, I quickly ended my "Professor story." The closed eyes opened. They looked at me. The silence was painful. "Okay," piped the leader, "tell us, how many women did you screw in Hawai'i?" Laughter erupted all around me, as it dawned on me what kind of "Professor story" they really wanted to hear.

Am I to think that these men did not care about fine mats or the *hån mane'åk su?* Perhaps the setting was not right. Perhaps I should have told the women instead. Maybe they would have cared. But then, it wasn't the women who wanted a "Professor story"! As I thought about my misreading of the situation, I realized what the problem was.

Until I could make an emotional connection with these men, my abstract theorizing was of little consequence. I was too serious and earnest. I needed to relax, to laugh together with these men, to be connected to them at an emotional level. Better still, I needed to tell a good Rotuman story, a narrative that speaks to the heart, engaging and entertaining. This is more important to Rotumans—how could I forget?—than intellectual gymnastics. In this instance, I was privileging my interpretive "anthropological" self, and thereby failing to connect with other Rotumans. But thanks to them, they would not allow me to dictate the tenor of our encounter, and subverted my attempts to play the intellectual. Besides, who was I to presume that I had a moral right to represent Rotuman culture to them, they who had lived and tilled the Rotuman soil while I marked time in a university in a foreign city?

My academic training had taught me that emotion and fiction have no place in western scholarship. What my interpretive "anthropological" self (and my fear of breaking the conventions of western scholarship) wants is a privileging of itself, and a denial of other parts of my identity. These Rotuman men, however, taught me an important lesson: my need to acknowledge my fictional and Rotuman selves, both of which are essential components of the *I* that I am. Reconciliation of my many selves in this monograph, however, is like clowning in a Rotuman wedding: a sanctioned performance by the *hån mane'åk su* that is potentially subversive of the status quo.

You ask: Why then are you publishing your thoughts and interpretations in a monograph, bound and hidden between covers, labeled number twelve in a series? Is it because, like the Rotuman *hån mane'åk su*, your playful, subversive ethnography has been co-opted by the power structure?

*   *   *

Do I hear a clown laughing somewhere?

Appendix: Comparisons of Theory and Practice

> The clown is passionately opinionated about the human condition and, via parody and burlesque, breaks the frames of proper behavior to instruct, criticize and transform.
>
> WILLIAM MITCHELL,
> *Clowning as Critical Practice in Oceania*

Clowning may be categorized into secular and ritual clowning, a distinction I have only hinted at so far. In this appendix, I discuss clowning under these categories, highlighting the prevalence of this phenomenon throughout the Pacific, but also drawing attention to the dispensability of comparative and theoretical analysis that is usually a core requirement of academic scholarship.

Secular Clowning

Secular clowning is informal, spontaneous, and intended primarily to entertain others. It is a universal and omnipresent human practice that exists in every culture and manifests itself whenever individuals who like to act silly or horse around come together. The performance of antics that cause laughter may occur among individuals sitting around having a few beers, in a social gathering, or during celebrations involving hundreds of individuals. Clowning in this context may be verbal, physical, or a combination of both. It may be a rehearsed comic sketch guided by a plot, or it may be improvised on the spot, with no specific story to propel the action forward. It may last only a few seconds, or it may last many minutes.

In the Pacific, clowning tends to occur whenever individuals gather for celebrations of one kind or another. Those who are sufficiently excited may suddenly jump up and, with gay abandon, dance in a ludicrous manner—wagging hips, parodying someone, flirting with another, rolling on the floor, or generally behaving in a manner intended to cause laughter. On such occasions the clown provides a "service" to the community, for laughter is viewed as intrinsically pleasurable and an indicator of the community's well-being. Since dancing is the most popular form of entertainment in Polynesia, clowning is often part of dance, although it may occur independently.

Samoan dancing usually involves certain acts of license. In the *siva*, the dignified female dancer at the center is accompanied by male dancers who may roll on the ground, jump and shout, slap their thighs, or do anything that appears disorderly. As a member of the University of the South Pacific's dance troupe in the mid-1970s, I was often surprised by the antics of the male dancers accompanying the female dancer at the center. Those of us who were non-Samoans became quite anxious, as we could never tell what would happen. For example, during an evening performance, a male dancer was sufficiently fired up to grab the stage curtain and, like Tarzan, try to swing to the other side, only to end up unceremoniously on the floor with the curtain draped over him. But "Tarzan"— and the female dancer at center stage—was oblivious to the dismayed reaction of the audience. The *siva* continued as if everything was proceeding normally, which indeed it was, in the context of the *siva*.

Shore explained that in the *siva* the complementarity between restraint and impulsive expression is of supreme importance. The dance exemplifies the maintenance and elaboration of a code-distinction that is ubiquitous in Samoa. Licensed behavior at the periphery is seen as respect for the dancer, or dancers, at the center. "The wilder and more disordered the periphery, the more graceful and ordered the center appears by contrast. The code-distinction is clarified and reinforced" (Shore 1977, 453). (The same code-distinction is also seen in the Tongan equivalent of the same dance called the *tau'olunga*.)

Arno wrote of a wedding feast on Moce island in Fiji, in which old women from the bride's side awakened the villagers on the second day by "shouting, laughing, and banging pots, pans, and empty biscuit tins as they escorted the mother of the bride home from the newlyweds' house" (1992, 43). He also mentioned old Fijian women performing an Indian *meke* for the audience's amusement.

> The women wrapped themselves in white bed sheets, covered their faces with flour, and balanced buckets and pots on their heads. Each wore an exaggerated, fixed grin on her face . . . and they danced

before a woman seated on a large chair, who represented a fierce looking "sultan" attended by two guards with warclubs on their shoulders. (Arno 1992, 44)

During the performance of this dance, members of the audience dashed out with scented talcum powder and showered the dancers with sweets, cigarettes, and paper money.[1] Some young men stripped off their shirts and draped them around the dancers.

Perhaps most revealing of the pervasiveness of clowning in the Pacific is Arno's account of how, when he sat down to join some old men who were drinking *yaqona* 'kava', he was dismayed to discover that they, though carrying on as usual, were dressed as women. To show their happiness and appreciation, they had put on the "gifts" that women of the groom's side had given them to take to their wives (Arno 1992, 45). This apparent readiness to dress in attire of the opposite sex is an important aspect of ritual clowning in the Pacific; it underlines the symbolic significance of role-reversal, a point that will be explored later on.

During the celebration of the one-hundred-fiftieth anniversary of the arrival of the first missionaries in Rotuma—held in December 1989—the Fiji Police Band was invited to entertain at the festivities on the island. During a traditional dance, several Fijian males from among the band members stood up and imitated the female dancers, employing exaggerated arm and hip movements and prancing around. One used a branch to sweep the ground; all these antics were much appreciated by the Rotuman audience.

Clowning lightens a heavy burden. It may occur among men working in a community garden, or be employed to relieve tension during a seemingly hopeless situation. Macintyre (1992) described an impromptu jest at her expense by Tubetube women as they were digging and planting yams; Hau'ofa told of a Tongan family who took shelter in their low kitchen after their house had been leveled by hurricane winds. As family members hung on to the roof of their kitchen to prevent it from being blown away, they laughed and joked for hours while the hurricane did its best to destroy them. Indeed, it is not unusual for Pacific Islanders to laugh and cry simultaneously (Hau'ofa 1989, 38, 40).

In Hawai'i, the *oli* 'chants' were used "for the songful expression of joy and affection" and as "the vehicle of humorous or sarcastic narrative in the entertainment of their comrades" (Emerson 1965, 254). The *oli* was a favorite form of amusement, even for Hawaiians who ended up as sailors. Richard Dana reported the use of ridicule and mimicry in a song by a Mr. Manini to entertain the Kanakas at the expense of Americans and Englishmen (1959, 117). Emerson also reported that the *oli* was sometimes used to poke fun at foreigners who did not know the Hawaiian language (1965, 254).

The pervasive comic sketch is another domain in which clowning may be seen. The sketch may develop spontaneously from dance, or it may exist in its own right as a rehearsed dramatic piece. Referring to secular clowning in Tonga, Hauʻofa stated that satirical and ribald comic sketches are the most popular items in variety concerts. He described a comic sketch performed by a Wesleyan group that was fundraising for their new church; the plot was about an "over-sexed clergyman who was regularly conducting a private and ungodly session between himself and a parishioner's wife on a pew inside the sacred house" (Hauʻofa 1988). It is hard to imagine another context when such criticism—from the bottom up, so to speak—can be aired without causing conflict.

In the early days of colonialism, the white man was a favorite target.[2] In Samoa, mimicry was a favorite way of burlesquing foreign behavior, as evident in this account:

> Two or three of them jumped up and began to act with immense spirit, great contortion of face, and an enjoyment so keen that it could not fail to communicate itself to onlookers. One series of gesticulations was supposed to represent "German fashion"; the imitation of walk and countenance was hardly complimentary to the supporters of the late Tamasese. (Jersey 1893, 257)

Agricultural celebrations in Samoa included pageants, full-length plays based on mythology, and reenactment of legends (Sloan 1941, 106–112). Sloan's account of a legend being enacted mentions a chorus of about fifty people who sat off to one side and sang throughout the whole performance. This legend was about the first arrival of "Fijian cannibals" and the way they sexually assaulted Samoa's beautiful women (including the beautiful Sina) until the gods of Samoa, led by Tangaloa, arrived and clubbed the "black warriors from Fiji." But the gods had arrived too late to prevent penetration of Sina, who gave birth soon afterward to a child who jumped up from behind her and cried out aloud, "I am a rat." This was how Samoans explained the presence of rats on their islands. Fijians, according to Sloan, played the role of villain in Manuʻan legends and, at the end of the reenactment just mentioned, other women who had been sexually molested by the Fijians gave birth to thornbushes, nettles, and obnoxious weeds that grow in Samoa. The performance lasted for an hour or more, and a hundred people took part. The dialogue was chanted by the chorus while the actors mimed their parts, except for the clowns who "occasionally dashed in with a robust line of chatter to liven things up a bit" (Sloan 1941, 107).

Cook Islanders also enacted historical events as well as myths and legends called *nuku*. Te Rangi Hiroa recorded a chorus that sang songs to provide the narrative for a performance, as well as village humorists who indulged in exaggerated actions that aroused much laughter among the audience (Hiroa 1932, 198–203). These included mimicry, sticking out the tongue, and placing the thumb to the nose and spreading out the fingers. In a performance seen at Rakahanga, the clown's costume included a turban made from a piece of fishing net; whiskers, beard, and mustache made from coconut husk fiber; and eyelashes caked with dry mud. The male clown in this instance was naked except for a loincloth, his entire body plastered with gray mud.

Thorogood's account of a *nuku* mentions hundreds of children singing and acting in biblical dramas. Dressed in colorful costumes, they march around with their banners, singing marching songs. Pageants that have been rehearsed in advance are then presented; it takes a full day to see them all. Adults take the larger parts, though the center of attention is usually the younger children, who sing and act as though drama comes naturally. Thorogood described a scene of Naboth's vineyard made up of small children wearing green and trailing long green creepers. These children marched and wheeled, creating a "Rarotongan version of Birnam wood marching to Dunsinane." He also mentioned the ingenious use of natural raw materials to create beards (gray trailing moss), helmets (coconut husks), and trumpets (conch shells). Thorogood asserted that the activities associated with the celebrations are "often the greatest communal tie within a village" (1960, 16–17). My reading of these performances at the Festival of Pacific Arts in 1992 is that the sketches entertain through exaggeration and other humorous antics as well as impart important historical information about the early missionaries and their reception (or otherwise) by the Islanders.

Although the *nuku* began as historical enactments (and it is unclear whether or not it was linked with religious beliefs), it has now become synonymous with biblical pageants, with the clowning that was once an integral part still being practiced. It has, however, been embraced and encouraged by the church, to the extent that the *nuku* is now a big annual event that involves old and young alike. Other Pacific Islanders, from groups such as Tonga, Samoa, and Rotuma, also perform biblical dramas, usually on what is known as Children's Sunday, but on a much smaller scale.

Similarly, inhabitants of Santa Isabel in the Solomon Islands perform *thukma* or *bina boli* sketches that reconstruct historical events, including (but not confined to) the Christian encounter. Performed mainly at feasts and similar occasions, these plays employ parody, exaggeration, and caricature for humorous effect. Since most of the actors are Christian converts, the plays tend to portray ancestors as heathens who were ignorant and aggressive toward the European missionaries. As in the Cook Islands *nuku,* these plays inform as well as help explore ambivalent feelings about the coming of Christianity (G. White 1991, 139–144, 220–222).

In Tokelau, women clowns—wives and mothers in middle age or older—usually perform comic sketches at social gatherings, though briefly. Wearing "European shirts, ties, coats, trousers and shoes, garments crumpled and filthy, trouser flies gaping open and shoes odd and ill-fitting," women reenact a scene from "blackbirding" days, or parody a medical scene—using a "stethoscope" made from a piece of rope, checking out each other's orifices, and exclaiming in amazement, envy, or disgust (Huntsman and Hooper 1975, 415). They may wrestle with each other, sometimes ending up in a pile on the floor, cursing as they do. In about thirty minutes the show is over. The women retire to change into their usual clothes, while the children mimic all that they have seen.

Tokelauan women also act as mediators between quarreling men by clowning to diffuse tension. They provide entertainment during work parties and divert attention from tasks that are otherwise tedious. Sometimes women separate themselves from the menfolk, moving away to a secluded area where the comedy "escalates from one plateau to the next in an unplanned manner—each episode becoming more obscene, the general hilarity inspiring even greater licence" (Huntsman and Hooper 1975, 428).

As in ritual clowning in Rotuma, the men are the targets of the women's antics during contests or undertakings. In the political domain in Tokelau, "it is always men who have authority, and display it; it is men who sit in council, orate, judge and decide, while the women sit on the sidelines or are absent altogether" (Huntsman and Hooper 1975, 416). In clowning performances, the roles are reversed, and the men become "things of no account." In this context of "games" or "play," Tokelauans enact a world in which women are the ones who rule.

In highly stratified social structures, it is common for jesters to be part of the royal or chiefly entourage;[3] Tonga and Samoa are no exceptions. Gifford noted that in Tonga, "certain individuals, termed *fakaaluma* or *fakatakataka,* who were considered particularly witty, would take it upon themselves to amuse the chiefs" (1929, 126). Further, a "jester" called Kaho from Vava'u made fun of people and indulged in witty remarks to amuse a landed royal navigator called Akauola (Gifford 1929, 126). The same jester, on one hilarious occasion, was carried to a feast tied up like a pig. Writing in 1861, George Turner mentioned a Samoan chief attending a ceremonial gathering who had "in his train, one or more Merry Andrews who by oddity of dress, gait, gesture or by lascivious jokes, would try to excite laughter" (1861, 211).

The humor that exists in western literature was sometimes co-opted by Islanders. Shakespeare, for example, seems to have been a favorite of Samoans in the past. Writing about a Samoan adaptation of *The Winter's Tale,* Lady Fergusson praised the way Shakespeare was adapted into the Samoan language and the ingenuity of the actors in their use of local materials. She noted that the Samoans "have a strong sense of humor, and roars of laughter greeted each touch of comedy" (1928, 370). The performance of scripted plays also occurs in most schools—and sometimes among youth groups—throughout the Pacific.

The popularity of the comic sketch may be caused by several factors: it objectifies the issue being lampooned, allowing for reflexivity; it distances the real persons being ridiculed from feeling they are being singled out; and it uses laughter to "punish" the transgressors. In an attempt to cover up their embarrassment, it is conceivable that the persons being lampooned may be the ones laughing the loudest. In societies where social harmony is valued, yet few avenues exist for criticism of authority figures, the comic sketch is particularly valuable as an arena in which a society can inspect and comment on itself.

Clowning, whether it be spontaneous, or within a dramatic sketch, provides a diversion that adds excitement to the predictable routines of everyday life. Sometimes it offers more than entertainment by imparting important historical or religious information; at other times, it offers commentary on social, cultural, or political issues; and at still other times it alleviates the burden of work or stress. Even when individuals are being lampooned in a comic sketch, the overall goal is to bring into line those who threaten community unity. All of these functions, if that is what they can be called, ultimately draw attention to the norm in society.

The comic sketch seems to have evolved from dance. Pacific dance, which encourages audience participation, lends itself well to improvisation and on-the-spot creation of a sketch. The arrival of Christianity and formal education probably consolidated, and, in most islands, appropriated indigenous forms for the propagation of their gospel. One would be hard-put to find an island in the Pacific where biblical dramas are not enacted. Schools also encourage the production of scripted plays, and no doubt there is a spillover into the larger community.

In secular clowning, either gender might participate. However, in Tonga and Samoa, the jesters who were part of a chief's retinue seem to have been invariably males of low rank. Their attachment to chiefs of high status, reminiscent of the court jesters of Europe in the Middle Ages, suggests a political connection that needs further investigation. The reasons for the clown's immunity from retaliation also need to be examined in more detail. The answer probably lies in beliefs about the role and nature of clowns, as well as the beneficial value of humor within a context of privileged license.

Ritual Clowning

Ritual clowning is customary and has a religious significance that transcends existing circumstances. Whereas secular clowning is impulsive, ritual clowning is programmed by society, although it employs many of the performative techniques as well as the form and structure of secular clowning. However, the juxtaposition of humor with serious ritual, as well as beliefs in the supernatural, transform these performances into symbolic communications.[4]

The literature on ritual clowning suggests that humor used by sacred clowns is characterized by role reversal, parody, sexual innuendo, and simulation of bodily functions such as urination or defecation (Apte 1983, 190). Clowning in these sacred contexts is juxtaposed with ritual that has a formal set of procedures with symbolic significance, particularly for the performers (Firth 1967, 12). Reversal, which may occur in ritual or clowning, may be specific (e.g., behaving like a member of the opposite sex), or general. When it is general, all rules of normal behavior are suspended, and "sexual licence, obscenity, insults, derision, assault or mock assault, flouting of authority, and the destruction of property might be permitted or encouraged" (Norbeck 1979, 55–56). These rites of reversal existed among the American Indians, the European carnival of former times, the saturnalias of Greece and Rome, the Wape (Papua New Guinea) *niyel* 'curing' carnival (Mitchell 1992b), and in the Pacific Islands, particularly during celebrations or festivals. Irrespective of their location, these sacred rites of reversal appear to have a divine origin.

The Origin of Ritual Clowning

Ritual clowning, which falls under the larger rubric of theater or performance, may have begun as rituals addressed to supernatural powers who were supposedly in control of the elements and of human lives.[5] Rites were enacted to cause the rain to fall, to make the crops grow, to ensure success in battle, to increase human fertility and thereby to prolong the family line. These rites employed elements that are important to successful theater—dance, costume, masks, make-up, music, performers, and performing space. This theory of divine origin is supported by ritual clowns who cite a supernatural aspect to their art as well. "To us the clown is somebody sacred, funny, powerful, ridiculous, holy, shameful, visionary. . . . Fooling around, a clown is really performing a spiritual ceremony. He has a power. It comes from the thunder beings."[6] A Pueblo medicine man provided a similar perspective: "The purpose of our ceremonies is not entertainment but attainment; the attainment of the Good Life. Our dramas, dances, songs are not performed for fun; no, they are more than that: *they are the very essence of our lives;* they are sacred" (quoted in Laski 1958, 2).

These two statements support my findings regarding the origins of the Rotuman *hån mane'åk su.* Further, I have heard Rotumans suggest that the death of a famous clown in the 1970s was caused by spirits. The reason given was that in her role as ritual clown, she did not fear the chiefs—whom Rotumans believe to have spiritual sanction—and had overstepped the boundaries of license. As a result, she had to suffer retributive consequences for her wrongdoing. This notion is supported by another ritual clown's response when asked why she did not hit any of the wedding guests on the head (as some of her predecessors were reputed to have done). She replied that if she overstepped her powers, the ancestral spirits would punish her (see the interview with Ta in chapter 4.)

The well-documented *arioi* society of Tahiti originated in rituals associated with the spirits.[7] This institution consisted of young men and women who traveled from island to island performing dances and comic sketches. Prior to their departure, sacrifices of pigs and large quantities of fruits were made to the god 'Oro (Angas 1866, 296–297). Oliver, whose information on the *arioi* in the context of Tahitian society is illuminating, lists twelve different descriptions for the *arioi*, ranging from "a society of comedians," to "human harpies . . . in whose character and habits all that is most loathsome—earthly, sensual, devilish—was combined."[8] Descriptions of *arioi* performances suggest that the comic sketches lampooned those in positions of authority as well as nonconformists.[9] A focus on the genitalia and the lower bodily functions was a common feature.[10]

According to Henry, preparations for a tour (reminiscent of the Samoan *malaga*) took many days, and the *arioi* god 'Oro was invoked by their chief *arioi* before their departure.[11] On their canoes the *arioi* had platforms on which their leaders sat or their dancers performed. A member of the company would be anointed with oil and highly perfumed and dressed up to represent the god of paradise, Roma-tane, who was then invoked to accompany them on their travels. On arrival they were welcomed before further invocations to 'Oro were performed, followed by feasting and exchanges of gifts with the high chief.

Ridgeway claimed that the *arioi* society of Tahiti originated in funerary rites. He provided as supporting evidence that membership included both the living and the dead; performances celebrated the mysteries of 'Oro, their founder and protector; and some of the *maraes*—that served as places of sepulchre and for human sacrifices—were occupied by *arioi*.[12] Opoa, on Raiatea, was believed to have been the birthplace of 'Oro. Here, a great *marae* called Taputa-puatea was built. As the center of 'Oro worship, it served as an arena for the practice of offering human sacrifices as well as a shrine for members of the *arioi* society.[13]

Andersen (1969) reported that societies similar to the *arioi* existed in the Caroline Islands, New Zealand, Mangareva, and the Tuamotu Archipelago. Angas mentioned that the Jesuit missionaries found a similar institution to the *arioi* in the Caroline and Ladrone

(Mariana) Islands (1866, 296). Webster wrote of remarkable parallels in the Caroline and Marianne [sic] Islands, New Zealand, the Cook Islands (Rarotonga), and Hawai'i (1968, 164–170).

In *The Lost Caravel*, Robert Langdon claimed that before the arrival of Wallis, Bougainville, and Cook, "a party of light-skinned immigrants [Spaniards] settled on Opoa on the south-eastern side of Raiatea" (1975, 154). From there Opoa colonists spread to the rest of the Society Islands, to Rarotonga in the Cook Islands, and to New Zealand (Langdon 1975, 154). Was the *arioi* institution introduced by the Spaniards? Langdon argued that evidence in several published sources indicates that European settlers and their descendants had "left their mark on the political, social and cultural life of the region" (1975, 153). Although it is tempting to infer from these statements (and from Langdon's studies on Spanish influences in the Pacific as a whole) that the *arioi* society was a Spanish introduction, there is no overt statement by Langdon to this effect. During a conversation in 1990, he said he would not go so far as to agree that the Spaniards had introduced the *arioi* institution; available evidence supports an origin in rituals associated with supernatural beliefs.

The contexts in which ritual clowning occurs support the theory of a divine origin. According to Apte, ritual humor occurs during performances at calendrical ceremonies to mark a change of season, such as harvesting activities, or anniversaries of prophets and saints; and at rituals performed to mark important transitions in an individual's life—birth, initiation, puberty, and marriage (1983, 190). When clowns appear at seasonal calendrical rites, they are usually linked to ideas of fertility, renewal, and regeneration (Handelman 1981, 364).

In Fiji, for example, ritual clowning occurred during festivals associated with agricultural fertility (Clunie and Ligairi 1983, 57). At such festivals, first fruits were offered to the gods and to the chiefs—who were the gods' representatives on earth. The yam was regarded as the most important crop, and when yams grew abundantly their harvest signaled a season of plenty. Webster described how yam festivals were held at the *Nanga* enclosure, where Fijian initiation rites were held. The first fruits of the yam harvest were presented to the ancestors of the tribe (Webster 1968, 164). In parts of Fiji where yams did not grow well, other crops superseded the yam in importance.

During the months building up to the harvest, certain prohibitions were placed on crops, fish, and other livestock. Dances were rehearsed and artifacts produced for exchanges between hosts and visitors. People looked forward with great enthusiasm to witnessing the performances of the masquers, who "on this day could mock earthly authority with a licence normally undreamt of" (Clunie and Ligairi 1983, 57).

Clunie and Ligairi concluded that the "masquers were representatives of ancestral spirits called *veli* 'a species of rustic and contrary gnome that still haunts the Fiji bush'."[14] Their conclusion was based on accounts in the published literature and the following evidence: on Vanua Levu, the masquers were drawn from a priestly class; the masquers represented named spirits associated with agricultural productivity; they were cared for by the priests of the host tribe following the first fruits presentations; and they showed contempt for strictly human social institutions (1983, 70).

The Samoan *fale aitu* also has its origins in rituals associated with the spirits. According to the late John Kneubuhl, *fale aitu* originally referred to the spirit house in each village in which the *aitu* 'spirit' in the form of some object was kept (1993, 101). The comic sketches were usually performed in a spirit house, and usually during *poula* 'teasing nights' that were part of a *malaga*. The *poula* began with old people gathering at dusk to sing and dance for each other. After it became dark and these old people (who were naked, according to Kneubuhl) had left, young men and women who were fully dressed would enter and sit at opposite ends of the *fale aitu*. Singing and dancing began slowly and built up in tempo as the young people became increasingly ribald and erotic, culminating in their being embroiled in a wild sexual frenzy. At this point, someone shouted: "I see the ghost, he is coming!" and everyone rushed out into the darkness. The ghost referred to in this instance was the "ghost of complete libidinous license, the uncontrolled unconscious" (Kneubuhl 1993, 104). After the sexual act, the young men and women returned to the *fale aitu* for the performance of comic sketches.

Sexuality was also a major theme in Hawaiian dances and chants, particularly during contexts when uninhibited expression was the norm: mourning after the death of an important chief or during the annual harvest festival—*makahiki*—which lasted three or four months. During *makahiki* celebrations to honor Lono, one of the gods of fertility, "solemn ceremonies were followed by feasts, sports, games, dancing, and other entertainment" (Luomala 1984, 76).

The *arioi* society of Tahiti, the *poula* nights of Samoa, the Fijian skits related to agricultural fertility, and the ritual clowning in Rotuman weddings all appear to have been linked with fertility, of the land and the people. This suggests that the rituals, through dance or clowning, were acts directed toward the spirits, to bless the land and the people as well as the assembled company. The communications were multivocal, with many different messages communicated simultaneously. Ritual clowning (which also includes dance) seems particularly suitable for the expression and exploration of the gamut of complex human emotions. From dance, the comic sketch evolved.

Luomala reasoned that in Hawai'i, the name *hula ki'i* suggests a later development from the *hula* or dance. In the Hawaiian *hula ki'i*, ancient Hawaiians used puppets dressed up to represent human beings. The puppets, which were about one-third life size, were held by a performer (or performers) who stood behind a screen.[15] The performer manipulated the movements of the puppet from under its clothing so that its actions were appropriate and in time with the action of the play, while at the same time reciting the words that were apparently being uttered by the puppet. Sometimes human dancers imitated the puppets (Luomala 1984, 5). The use of puppets in a comic sketch that was often satirical and critical of members of the general public provided a distancing that made the barbs of ridicule and criticism more palatable. For sound, the human voice, the double-gourd drum, or both, were used. If there were human dancers, they would join with the drummer-chanters in all or part of a song; or sometimes they merely mouthed the words silently. In a dialogue between the puppets and the spectators, the puppeteer spoke. An experienced *hula* master—male or female— "gives the beat, explains the song or story to the audience, and acts as interlocutor for the puppets' pantomime or talk" (Luomala 1984, 82). Emerson took into account the migration of peoples and the possibility that the *hula ki'i* could have been introduced from outside. However, he believed that the structure and content of the *hula ki'i* bear convincing evidence of a Hawaiian antiquity (1965, 91).

Victoria Kneubuhl (1987) stated that during the *poula,* it was the custom to have two dancers who mimicked the actions of the best dancers, causing merriment among the audience; from mimicry evolved the *fale aitu* form. As evidence, Kneubuhl cited George Turner's observation that a chief of importance would always have one or two "Merry Andrews" to excite laughter (Turner 1861, 211).

In chapter 3, I have described how a comic sketch developed spontaneously from ritual dance during a Rotuman wedding—further support for this proposition.

Ritual clowning also occurs during funerary rites, as Mosko observed among the North Mekeo peoples of Papua New Guinea. According to him, members of the host clan, who are still in grief and supposed to cry and wail rather than laugh, watch the physical discomfort of their overeating spouses who continue to call out for more and more food until they end up laughing—and happy again (Mosko 1992). Similarly, Barlow recorded that among the Murik people of Papua New Guinea, clowning performances during death and end-of-mourning deflect attention from loss and disruption by emphasizing the reorganized relations and obligations among the living (1992). Stair also recorded accounts of funeral clowning that included buffoonery (1983, 183–184); Ritchie has reported that Maori try to outdo each other in comic stories on the night before burial, particularly if the deceased is of high status (pers. comm. 1990). Ritual clowning therefore affirms life, of which fertility is an integral part. These studies imply that in some societies, and certainly in the Pacific, comedy and tragedy are not necessarily discrete phenomena, and may occur at a funeral or a wedding.

Two accounts of ritual clowning at weddings have reported that the women take on these roles, and for purposes other than mere entertainment. David and Dorothy Counts described old women clowns in Lusi-Kaliai who dress as warriors carrying fighting clubs or spears. During the distribution of bride-wealth, these women clowns rush and leap about, threatening the men, who are expected to flee.[16] As in Rotuman weddings, the men from the groom's side are harassed by the women from the bride's. According to the Counts, clowning mediates tensions and potential conflict between the bride's and groom's parties. Writing about Pakistani migrants' weddings, Werbner noted that when young girls present their gifts to the bride (which, in one instance, included a baby doll, a bra, and a pair of panties), it is customary for a young girl or woman to dress as an old man and to mock-attack others who are present (1986, 240). Like the warrior clowns of the Lusi-Kaliai, this "old man" clown indulges in behavior that is normally forbidden. But for what purpose? Werbner concluded that this behavior is an attempt "to harness the potentially dangerous and disorderly powers of sex and nature for the sake of human fertility" (1986, 246). One wonders if the Counts would have reached the same conclusion had they had more data on the Lusi-Kaliai. For instance, why does the clowning occur during the distribution of wealth?

Apte has raised a problem that has not been resolved in the debate on humor in religious contexts. He asks why a religious context is chosen for the application of humor that supposedly serves cathartic and social control functions (1983, 206). Studies by Honigman (1942) and Spicer (1954) have suggested that humor reduces the seriousness of ritual, and that many sacred rituals are counterbalanced by humor. However, this answer, seems inadequate; it does not take seriously the spiritual element that is an integral part of ritual clowning, as evidenced by my analysis of the Rotuman material.

As so-called western civilization spread its influence throughout the world, and as Christianity or other religions penetrated indigenous cultures, beliefs in the ancient religions began to disappear, along with the role of the ritual clown, whose performance has lost its spiritual potency (Elliot 1960, 330). This evolution is universal, and not even the Pacific is spared.

Liminality and the Ritual Clown

Important questions that need answers now include: Why is it that during ritual clowning, chiefs and those in positions of authority are mocked and ridiculed? Why is the normal order inverted? And why does the ritual clown take on an ambiguous dramatis persona? Let me venture some theses.

Ritual clowning is an exploration of other ways of being, a process in which individuals play at being someone or something else. Norbeck defined play as voluntary pleasurable behavior that is separated in time from other activities and that has a quality of make-believe (1971, 48; see also Schwartzman 1980). Celebrations associated with social disjunctures that mark important transitions in life—birth, death, and marriage, for example—are institutionalized forms of play. As discussed earlier in this chapter, social disjunctions of this type are usually marked by excessive license and the breaking of taboos. However, the message "This is play" allows for communication at multiple levels of abstraction (Bateson 1972, 193). Csikszentmihalyi and Bennet (1971) asserted that play is necessary to relieve boredom and the worries of life. During play, the players lose self-consciousness, a view also held by Norbeck, who claimed that transcendence or alteration of consciousness is an essential part of play (1969, 43–55).

Following the reasoning of the evolutionists and finding a corollary in dreams, Parman concluded that play is most vivid and demarcated in societies characterized by a state of relative deprivation (1979, 34). Human beings prefer changing environmental conditions, for change and variety are necessary in order to function effectively. Although the demands of day-to-day living are often sufficient to provide variety, we all need dreams during the night and play during the day "to prevent epilepsy, internal time-locking, madness, or other maladaptive aspects of synchrony" (Parman 1979, 30).

Parman's theory implies that society, individually and collectively, needs different kinds and amounts of play. Further, play requirements change as members of a specific society adapt to their geographical, biological, and cultural environment. Differing needs and environmental adaptations explain why some individuals employ humor (or seem to need to play) more than others. Each society organizes itself—unconsciously—in such a way that its well-being is ensured. From Parman's perspective, the so-called frivolous amusements of the Polynesians take on a special significance; the clowning and the accompanying laughter are essential for their well-being.

The context in which the process called play occurs is a liminal state or condition, one that Turnbull called holy, "a timeless state of grace" (1990, 80). Within its parameters, individuals, and society in general, explore another way of being, that which they have chosen not to be. Through the liminal clown that embodies ambiguity and contradiction in all its various manifestations, individuals can see the part of themselves that they suppress in everyday life, and can be made to feel complete again. A brief foray into the attributes of the ritual clown should clarify this point.

Handelman described the ritual clown as a symbolic type: one that is clumsily integrated, but with strong connotations of movement, motion, and fertility (1981). Internally, this symbolic type is composed of sets of contradictory attributes, among which it oscillates without stabilizing itself, which it is dissolving continuously. So long as this figure is true to type, it evokes inconsistencies and ambiguities of meaning. The type is a mechanism of reflexivity, which exists in an ongoing state of self-transformation. It is a powerful solvent and a representation of "process." At the center of this process is the ambiguous persona of the ritual clown.

The lead comedian in a *fale aitu* sketch is usually an untitled male who adopts the persona of an *aitu,* spirit associated with chaos, wilderness, danger, and darkness.[17] Rather than maintain an illusion of being an *aitu* while in role, the lead comedian continually breaks out of role to remind the audience of his real identity. Is he a ghost masked as transvestite, or is he just a man? Is it Petelo (a famous Samoan comedian) the infallible ghost speaking, or is it the fallible human being? This constant shifting in and out of character led Shore to assert that "comic virtuosity makes the clown at once admirable, dangerous, and funny." The clown is therefore a caricature or parody of himself, and since his ability to slip into multiple characters is undercut by the inappropriateness of the context in which he performs, the clown's behavior is viewed by Samoans as displaying aspects of either social tragedy or dramatic comedy. The context of the *fale aitu* therefore, according to Shore, is a metaphor for the expression of what it means to be Samoan; it is where the language of actors, roles, playing, and the wearing of masks in social relationships find their proper expression (Shore 1977, 333, 334, 365).

Because the lead comedian is a male transvestite assuming the persona of a ghost, these dual roles reinforce the marginal position of the comedian on stage, distance him—the roles serve the same function as masks—and free him from taking responsibility for what happens within the comic setting (Shore 1977, 333). Moreover, through the clown's persona, we recognize our potential for being someone else; despite our physiological limitations, we have something of the other gender. We also recognize that the clown's antisocial behavior is dysfunctional, even though we may briefly enjoy its manifestation. These other parts of ourselves that we suppress for the sake of group harmony are real and need expression every now and then.

John Kneubuhl (1993) provided an explanation for the ambiguous sexuality of the lead comedian. He said Samoans believed that the spirit *tuiatua* was capable of switching gender when necessary. It could manifest itself as a handsome young man or gorgeous young woman. Should sexual intercourse occur between *tuiatua* and a human being of the opposite sex, death would result. A male comedian who was sexually ambivalent and capable of switching gender was therefore protected from seduction by *tuiatua*. Kneubuhl added that the humor in the comic sketches was usually verbal rather than physical, and that the sketches focused primarily on sexual encounters that might involve seduction. This was the surface explanation for the ambiguous nature of the ritual clown's persona.

Emerson gave some information on the dramatis personae of the puppet actors in a *hula ki'i*. He mentioned four of the puppet actors in the context of discussing a play that presumably used only dialogue and gestures: *Maka-ku*—a famous warrior; *Puapua-kea*—a small, brave, active man; *Maile-lau-lii*—a young woman who marries the warrior; and *Maile-Pakaha*—the younger sister of the warrior's wife (Emerson 1965, 92). Variations influenced the plot of the stories told (Luomala [1984] contains a survey of Hawaiian puppets in museums around the world).

According to Luomala, the illusion that the puppets were real human beings was maintained sometimes by the puppeteers speaking directly with the spectators (1984, 98). However, the separation between audience and actors preserved their mysterious aloofness. A member of the audience who was lured onto the stage usually ended up looking ridiculous in a setting where to behave and look normal is to be out of place.[18] As is typical of the *fale aitu* sketches, a certain amount of improvisation ensured that the acting and dialogue were relevant and dynamic.

Apart from Hawai'i, there is evidence that marionettes were used in New Zealand, and that a type combining strings and rods was used in Mangaia. There are also theories that Easter Island had a sacred puppet theater, though Luomala has convincingly dismissed these speculations.[19] Nonetheless, the use of puppets, as in gender shifting, created ambiguity in the persona of the actor.

According to Angas, and supported by Oliver and other sources cited here, members of the *arioi* were drawn from both sexes, with a ratio of about five males to one female. In Fiji, the ritual clowns in the agricultural rites were males; in Rotuma, the designated ritual clown is always female. How does one explain the gender differences in these societies?

For Tokelauans, the female is an ambiguous being who is vulnerable to the wiles of the spirits and at the same time capable of harnessing their powers. The ambiguous relationship that women have with the spirits, according to Huntsman and Hooper (1975), explains their appropriateness as clowns. However, since they imply that the Tokelauan *fale aitu* is a borrowing from Samoa, this hypothesis raises an important question: Since the Samoan lead comedian is invariably male, are they implying that males in Samoan society are more susceptible to the influence of the spirits? John Kneubuhl's explanation of gender shifting perhaps holds a clue. Another possible explanation could be that in Samoa, as in Tahiti, young men were more readily available for boating expeditions. However, the truth is more likely to be embedded in the structure of Samoan society, and its views of young men and their place in the sociocultural system, as well as their relationship with the spirit world.

The Clown's Functions

Studies by Shore, Victoria Kneubuhl, and Sinavaiana concur that the *fale aitu* acts as an agent for social control in Samoa. Victoria Kneubuhl (1987) wrote about the release of tension through laughter, and relief from the constraints of regimented daily routine; Shore mentioned the value of the *aitu* in dealing with conflict that is impossible or difficult to resolve through direct confrontation (1978, 178). Possible conflict in relations of complementarity that overtly deny the possibility of conflict—such as between chiefs and their subjects or between the sexes—are dealt with covertly in the safe arena of the comic sketch (Shore 1978, 197–198). Sinavaiana (1992a) emphasized the value of *fale aitu* as an indigenous critique of the "west," thereby "de-mystifying and defusing that which is potentially threatening to social/cultural equilibrium."

According to Norbeck, religious beliefs pervade every sphere of traditional life. They validate and regulate play, particularly if the outcome is potentially threatening to group cohesion (Norbeck 1976). Mead suggested that in "traditional" societies, organized play is an integral feature of religious displays, and as such, it functions as a means of interpreting ritual (1934). As a ritual form, play allows participants to mimic the behavior and actions of deities and culture heroes, so learning broader social actions and ideals.

Don Handelman wrote that play had the potential for commenting speedily on ongoing events, while ritual commented on the "truth" of the whole structure (1980, 67). Fox, on the other hand, argued that play and ritual serve a similar function in many cultural contexts: both enhance group solidarity as well as release personal and collective aggression, thereby reducing conflict (1980, 56). As a whole, studies of humor in religious contexts have emphasized the psychological benefits of humor: cathartic release of tension and of antisocial feelings, and vicarious gratification of repressed sexual urges and other infantile desires (Apte 1983, 205).

Luomala identified entertainment as the primary function of the *hula ki'i*.[20] Laughter was achieved through the selection and exaggeration of certain traits of character by the nonhuman bodies of the puppets. Such distortion of villainy or heroism, for example, made the trait being lampooned appear comical. Occasionally a *hula ki'i* praised a person's body by alluding to the landscape or weather, or another referred to deeds and the divine origin of ancestors. Juxtaposition with the "lively but stilted motions or a human being's imitations" undercut the nobility of the sentiments expressed, and probably caused much mirth among the audience (Luomala 1984, 72). As the puppets had limited flexibility, verbal devices that contained "hidden ribald, critical, or hostile meanings" were the main resource, rather than clothing or properties. In this sense, the subtext in verbal utterances in the comic sketch, and its use to maintain social control even as it entertained, is reminiscent of the Samoan *fale aitu*.

Andersen's *Myths and Legends of the Polynesians* (1969, 435–451), unlike Ellis's accounts, tried to explain the *arioi* institution from the Tahitian point of view. The author furnished detailed information regarding the religious beliefs of the society, and provided evidence to suggest that the gods 'Oro and Mahoui,[21] whom the *arioi* worshipped, were the gods of sun and fertility. Oliver differed in that 'Oro is referred to by eyewitness accounts as the "war god," or "the most powerful god," or even *the* God (1974, 912). As an explanation for all the "licentiousness" Andersen posited that this was "the representation of fertility of nature, to which representation was due the indulgence in excesses" (1969, 435).

Moerenhout provided a similar rationale for preoccupation with the sexual act, asserting that the uninhibited representation of sexuality and love-making is only shocking to European eyes; also, that *arioi* performances are "nothing more or less than the living portrayal (in lieu of inanimate symbols) of the natural principle of sexual generation—no different from that symbolized by the Ancient Egyptian's *phallus* or the East Indian's *lingam*" (cited in Oliver 1974, 923–924).

Several accounts emphasized the role of the *arioi* as warriors, claiming that members were renowned for their "prowess, valour, and activity in battle" and that infanticide was necessary because of this warrior role (Surgeon William Ellis 1782, 160). Oliver, however, believed the main reason for infanticide among the *arioi* was their concern to perpetuate their "youthfulness" in all its gratifying aspects (1974, 942–944).

Although the functions of ritual clowning vary in detail from one society to another, the literature suggests that ritual clowning helps in the maintenance of social equilibrium, although it is potentially a subversive and destabilizing force.

Clowning and the Status Quo

In the context of ritual clowning, role reversal and status reversal are usually the norm, including the mocking of those in positions of authority. This is true of the comic sketches of the *arioi* society, the *fale aitu* of Samoa, the Fijian skits associated with agricultural fertility, and the improvised clowning of the Rotuman *hàn mane'àk su*. Is clowning—or the transgression of society's norms—conservative or progressive? Does it really subvert the powers that be, or does it merely reinforce the status quo?

Victor Turner stated that absurdity and paradox underline regularity, and that although extravagant or illicit behavior satisfies temporarily, we are merely reminded that such behavior is not the way things ought to be. By making the high low and the low high, rituals of status reversal merely reaffirm the hierarchical principle.[22] Bakhtin also noted (1968, 106) that carnival laughter in European traditions rarely challenges the ruling elite, who allow themselves to be mocked, knowing full well that come the following morning, they will be "more firmly entrenched" in their privileged positions. Similarly, Eco argued that clowning and comedy "remind us of the existence of the rule."[23] On the other hand, Voegelin (1938) reported that among the Tübatalabal, a chief who is severely criticized by a clown is replaced by a new leader.

Huntsman and Hooper's study of Tokelauan clowning viewed the combination of female lack of control and male authority and strength, resulting in unbridled license, as unacceptable because the result is chaos. The elderly women's performances do not really challenge the normal structure of society; instead, they confirm the view that men should be in control (Huntsman and Hooper 1975, 428). Most essays in a recent book from the Association for Social Anthropology in Oceania titled *Clowning as Critical Practice: Performance Humor in the South Pacific,* have tended to support the same view—that is, that clowning is more culturally conservative than subversive—although its editor has argued that clowning "may be a social harbinger of creative change." However, he has acknowledged that clowning on its own does not cause revolutions in the social order; rather, he asserted, "its power is in mockingly chipping away at the culture, acting as a political accessory to temporal social transformation" (Mitchell 1992a, 25).

In his study of Rabelais, Bakhtin stated that "carnivalesque" is a temporary liberation from the oppressive nature of the established order. This inversion of hierarchies was not just a festive critique of "high culture," but the true "feast of becoming, change and renewal" (Bakhtin 1968, 109). Allon White (1982) and Kristeva (1980), among others, agreed that the act of transgression inverts or subverts the socially valued norm, rule, structure, or contract and is therefore intrinsically radical and aesthetically progressive (see also Stallybrass and White 1986). Closer to home, Subramani supported this view when he wrote that Epeli Hauʻofa's *Kisses in the Nederends* (1987) "expresses a new kind of freedom . . . a liberation from a narrow-minded seriousness that typifies the early literature" (Hauʻofa 1989, 50).

There is no conclusive evidence that literature that flouts convention leads to a liberation resulting in more writers being outspoken. The list of writers who have been exiled from their own countries or in hiding because of their apparent disregard for tradition—Salman Rushdie being the most obvious example—suggests that radicalism in literature does not necessarily lead to more freedom of expression, but less. Writers who do not practice self-censorship often find that outside forces can either co-opt them, or ban the sale or distribution of their work altogether. Besides, as Eagleton has pointed out about carnival, a *licensed* affair is a permissible critique of hegemony, "a popular blow-off as disturbing and relatively ineffectual as a revolutionary work of art" (1981, 148). However, there may be a few individuals who find that writing such as Hauʻofa's in *Kisses* strengthens their resolve and frees them from their own inhibitions and restraint.

In her dissertation on the *fale aitu,* Sinavaiana theorized that because information that is communicated in the comic sketch is usually critical of those in power, they provide "at least the opportunity for constructive change" (1992a, 295). However, until there is more concrete evidence of social, cultural, or political change being caused by comedic performances in Samoa (or in other parts of the Pacific), Sinavaiana's notion must remain in the realm of possibility.[24] The likelihood of *fale aitu* becoming a catalyst for change increases as Samoa (and the rest of the Pacific) "navigates the fragile bridge 'betwixt and between' cultural epochs of ancient Polynesia and the modern West" (Sinavaiana 1992b, 212). Identifying or measuring change, however, is difficult to research, because a transformation that occurs internally may not lead to an immediate overt change in attitude or action. On the other hand, there is ample evidence in Sinavaiana's research to support Shore's earlier assertion that *fale aitu* functions as an informal avenue for resolving conflict and therefore is an agent in the maintenance of social equilibrium (Sinavaiana 1992a; Shore 1978).

Victor Turner suggested that within the liminal phase that features reversal, behavior may be likened to comedy (1969, 201). Susanne Langer explained that when human beings gather to celebrate life, comedy provides an image of human vitality at work to restore a lost balance and to anticipate a new future. She added that as individuals shake off the shackles that bind them, and vent instincts hitherto repressed, they express the sheer vitality that is theirs as well as belonging to society. This briefly manifested vitality in individuals adds to the collective total, imbuing the atmosphere with a performance "in-process" as it straddles the world that is, and the one that is about to be. "The essential comic feeling is the sentient aspect of organic unity, growth, and self-preservation" (Langer 1965, 140).

Langer elaborated on comedy. Because all creatures love life, they continually seek it in the world, which is promising and alluring and at the same time dangerous and opposed. The world becomes the real antagonist whose services we seek to harness in our favor. In comedy—and by implication in rites of reversal—the human battle is played out, in a seemingly trivial make-believe performance. Its dangers are therefore not real, the only real effects being embarrassment and loss of face (Langer 1965, 139). The fool wins in comedy, if only temporarily: symbolically, the people triumph over the powerful forces of nature. Within the frame of transition rites, therefore, comedy may be viewed as an analogy for the ambivalence that human beings feel toward nature.

The type of sacred clown that instigates comedy cannot be drawn as wholly, or simply, comic, otherwise it is no longer reflexive. Because of its ambiguity and oscillation in its internal organization, as well as its juxtaposition with contextual phenomena, there are continual shifts in the meaning of the clown's behavior (Handelman 1981, 364). Such shifts may be a major locus for the generation of humor and laughter, as well as for the creation of ambiguity. Implicit meanings conflate to create a multivocal communication that is powerful because it is experienced rather than thought about.

Whether the Apaches resort to their wit and humor in order to make some sense of the "white man's" attitude toward them,[25] or the Samoans parody German fashion, or the Tokelauans reenact scenes

of blackbirding days, or the possessed figure of a Songhay burlesques a European, the motivation is the same. According to Parman, these are attempts to "sort out and make sense of a wide range
of sensory input" (1979, 29). Parman's theory finds a kindred spirit
in Vine Deloria who concurred that the ability to laugh at ourselves
and others, as well as maintain a strong center that prevents anyone
else from driving us to extremes, is essential for our very survival
(1969, 48).

Is clowning a conservative or a progressive agent? An either-or
response would be counterproductive; is it not possible for clowning
to be both? The Rotuman material supports the view that clowning
may be a catalyst for change as well as an agent for hegemony.

Conclusion

Fools (or secular clowns) either were attached to powerful poten-
tates or performed voluntarily at social gatherings: sacred (or ritual)
clowns were woven into the ancient religious fabric of society. With
the spread of Christianity worldwide, including into the Pacific, the
old beliefs in spirits disappeared, and so began the demise of the
sacred clown. Although in some parts of Polynesia sacred clowning
is still evident, its performance has lost its *mana*[26] and socioreligious
import. Papua New Guinea, where colonization was late to pene-
trate, has been more successful in preserving its sacred ritual performances. Accounts of the Iatmul mothers' brothers' *naven* clowning,[27] the fertility ceremony of the Umeda villagers in the Sandaun
Province (Gell 1975), and the *niyel* 'curing' carnival among the
Wape (Mitchell 1992b) include characteristics—such as the wearing
of masks, elaborate costumes, and explicit sexual displays—that did
not survive the nineteenth century in Polynesia.

Although the religious significance of sacred clowning has been
severely eroded, the urge to amuse others, to satirize the behavior of
the stranger or the pompous, or to tell a story in a humorous way
cannot be suppressed by westernization or by Christianity. In the
Pacific, clowning in non-sacred but socially significant occasions is
pervasive. As practiced today, the functions of both secular and ritual clowning are similar insofar as both entertain, instruct, criticize,
and transform. Ritual clowning, however, as explicated in the body
of this book, has a supernatural role that transcends everyday reality.

Notes

1 Prologue: Homeward Bound

1   For social changes on the island since 1960, see Rensel 1991.

2   When I was a student at Rotuma High School, I was taught to spell in Rotuman according to the way the word is pronounced, in which case, *hän mane'äk su* is an acceptable alternative.

3   Two sources that explore related issues are Rosaldo 1989 and Clifford and Marcus 1986.

4   Three very prominent academics and fiction writers whose work I hold in high regard are Albert Wendt, Konai Thaman, and Epeli Hau'ofa (see References).

5   Issues related to marginality and resistance to Euro-American hegemony are explored in more depth by West 1990; hooks 1990a; 1990b; Anzaldúa 1987; Sinavaiana 1992a.

2 Homemade Entertainment

1   As most people are related, or acquainted with one another, each death affected the whole island, not just the village or district where it occurred.

2   This is the *rot haharagi* 'young church people' who consisted of girls and boys from about ten to unmarried adults of about forty. Seven married adults who were part of the group on this occasion included the catechist and his wife, the man in charge of Sunday school, the Rotuman lady and her Australian husband, a woman who simply turned up to rehearsals, and myself.

3   This was unusually late for this young man to be circumcised. Usually, boys are circumcised around seven or eight. I was surprised at the teasing the young man had to endure—all in good humor—and the catechist's incessant joking, often alluding to sexual matters.

4   Everywhere we danced we were given tins of biscuits, bags of rice, and pineapples to take with us.

5   The house belonged to a retired principal of the high school on the island. His daughter, one of the main leaders in the youth group, helped me to teach the songs and dances.

6   I learned later that this woman has a reputation for being generous with her sexual favors. Her eagerness to carry out any requests that came her way was very amusing to the players.

7   This card game was a favorite when I was growing up. I cannot remember anyone asking to confiscate someone else's property during the game, and was surprised when the request was made because it was not at all funny. I put it down to the player who made the request being part-Fijian and perhaps not familiar with the purpose of the game.

8   Only after I got back to Fiji did I realize that the card playing was relevant to my study.

9   At about four thirty in the morning breakfast was served outside, with everyone sitting in a straight line on either side of a cloth on which cups of tea, biscuits, and pancakes were spread. Afterward the singing, dancing, and card playing continued until six, when the group dispersed.

10   See Hereniko 1991 for a description and analysis of Rotuman dance forms.

11   This does not happen if the *tautoga* is in a formal context. Sometimes during the third segment of the dance, the *tiap furau*, one or two dancers may stand up before the others, yelp, and perform some funny antics before the others stand up to perform (see Hereniko 1991, 120–142).

12   I witnessed only part of the ceremonies. Some of the specific examples are from Howard's field notes of 1989.

13   Similarly, at a performance by Samoan students at the University of the South Pacific in Suva, Fiji, to celebrate independence day in 1989, I noticed a dancer acting like a clown. His exaggerated body contortions, weird facial expressions, and actions slightly out of rhythm with the others made me think he was drunk. I was told later by a Samoan student that the dancer thought their item was too long and that clowning would make it seem shorter.

14   There are no clowning societies in Rotuma, nor is there any formal training. Theoretically, any woman could be a *hän mane'äk su*, although certain constraints (age, availability, relationship to the bride, etc.) mean that certain individuals are more likely to be asked by the bride's kin than others.

15   My information for this wedding is from the field notes of Alan Howard and Janet Rensel who were on Rotuma at the time.

16   The doctor is closely related to the bride's family, his wife being the bride's *sigoa* 'namesake'.

17   This is a traditional custom, but the clowning that follows is not obligatory.

18   The implication was that sexual ardor would cool; in fact, this is what Rotumans do to copulating dogs that are stuck together.

19   Other factors that were probably influential in the bride's parents' attitude to the clown are inappropriate to divulge here. Such incidents are sometimes symptomatic of a more complex problem among relatives.

20   Sometimes, a schism between the kin groups is evident during the period of feasting. Ideally, and this was probably the custom in the olden days, the relatives of the bride and groom feast as one at the end of the wedding. Today, it is more common for each of the two kin groups to feast on the food they have brought rather than share it with the other group. The excuse is that it simplifies matters; the symbolic import of joined feasting as a visible manifestation of unity—in contrast to the oppositional arrangement during the wedding proper—is lost.

21   The clown admitted in an interview that she was indeed unsuitable for the part. She was chosen because she was closely related, and her behavior predictable. The couple who were wed live in Fiji but went specially to the island to get married. How much their being from "overseas" had anything to do with this clown's mild manner is uncertain.

22   When interviewed, she said she was wary of the Oinafa chiefs. Both clowns for weddings three and four are from Itu'muta, the westernmost part of the island that is associated with commoners, in contrast to the Oinafa chiefs from the east. Perhaps this partly explains why both clowns who featured in weddings involving Oinafa chiefs were restrained, in contrast to the first clown who lives in Lopta, which is part of Oinafa.

23   They were originally invited by the people of Oinafa to entertain at their celebrations of the one-hundred-fiftieth anniversary of the arrival of missionaries on Rotuma.

24   At this wedding I was surprised to see the use of garlands with hanging dollar bills (instead of sweet-smelling flowers as was formerly the custom). As a wedding cake is now part of Rotuman weddings (all weddings discussed here had them imported from Fiji), its associated ritual, and the singing of "For He's a Jolly Good Fellow," is another potential area of discord. The only people who know this song have been exposed to the custom overseas; even then, Rotumans on the island are following a custom whose meaning is not known to most of them.

25   Oinafa is also the district where the wharf is located, and where signs of European goods, modern houses, and electric appliances are most evident. Because of historical circumstances and signs of material wealth, the Oinafa chiefs seem to be regarded with more respect than the chiefs from the western (and poorer) districts.

4 Mythologizing Humor and Clowning

1   Presented here are my translations of the Rotuman versions of the interviews, which are in my possession. The real names of the *hàn mane'àk su* have not been used.

2   See Howard (1985, particularly 45–47), for a detailed description of

Howard's assumptions, which are very much influenced by Marshall Sahlins's perspective that Hawaiian history often repeats itself, appearing first as myth and then as an event (see Sahlins 1981, 9, 14). Believing Sahlins to be correct, Howard asserted that "the study of myth in Polynesian societies can be viewed as an important means of *organising* and *interpreting* history rather than *chronicling* it" (italics in original).

3   I am not aware of other versions of this story. See also Churchward (1940b), where all the myths and legends referred to in this study may be found.

4   Allen (1895, no. 5). Gardiner (1898, 414–415) described the patterns for men's designs: flowers, stars, circles, crosses, and other geometrical designs. See also Thompson (1915, 138–139) and Lucatt (1851, 178–179).

5   "The common class is called *haf ne koua* [stones of the earthen oven]." See MacGregor 1932.

6   The name Hänfakiu is a composite of the words *hän* 'woman', *fa* 'man', and *kiu* 'one thousand'. Another possible interpretation is that the name *Hänfakiu* means a woman who transforms herself; in this case, into an *'atua*. For this interpretation, *fak* means pertaining to, and *iu* means to change or transform. As *fak* is a prefix and *iu* is a transitive verb rather than a noun, this interpretation seems forced.

7   This myth includes a claim that at the end of the battle, the custom of choosing the king from each district in turn was instituted.

8   See Churchward (1938b, 109–116) for the story of Raho, which appears under the title *"Haoag ne Rotuam 'I"* ("The Planting of This Rotuma") in the Rotuman version and "The Founding of Rotuma" in the English version. See also Howard (1985, 39–77) for an analysis of this myth and others.

9   Rotuman manuscript at Sumi Mission Station; cited in Howard (1985, 41).

10   Gardiner (1898, 467) wrote: "The mua's feast and dance . . . was a prayer to him [Tagaloa] for fruitfulness for the crops and trees."

11   Täväke is a tropic bird.

12   Tinrau is known as Tinilau or Tinirau in other parts of Polynesia. Because the place of residence changes in the case of kings or chiefs, the bride lives at the home of the king or chief. See also Malo (1975, 28).

5 Woman on Top: Why Not?

1   See also Hereniko (1992) for a description and analysis of the wedding described in detail in this chapter.

2   There are no initiation rites; though first births and deaths are important transitions, marriage celebrations are the most complex and elaborate.

3   For detailed information on kinship, see Irava 1977b; Howard 1963, 1970b.

4   There are few employment opportunities for women, although there are some women teachers, bankers, and nurses.

5   It is possible of course that some European practices, over the years, may become traditional once they become established. However, whether a European custom has become established or not is difficult to tell, for weddings on Rotuma vary in terms of their European content. There does not seem to be a hard and fast rule regarding ceremonies (such as that surrounding a wedding cake) that are European in origin.

6   The video crew was present at my request to make a visual record of the wedding.

7   The word *fao* means to cook overnight for use the following day.

8   These mats were woven by women relatives of the bride. There are at least four categories of mats of varying degrees of value, with the fine mats of greatest importance.

9   This was just an ordinary stick (softwood). In the past, it was probably made of hardwood and specially carved.

10   The meeting together of the two kin groups on this day is called *su soko*, which implies that the two separate sides are now one. This initial joining together is regarded as particularly sacred and is marked by solemnity and a profound display of mutual respect between the two kin sides. It heralds the frame of licensed behavior, but is outside it. At a wedding observed in 1989 (wedding three) an elder stood up and reminded the spectators that the dancing and merrymaking were not to begin until the groom's side had taken their seats and the welcome speeches (from both sides) had been delivered. At the 1987 wedding (wedding one), the dancing began as soon as the temporary shelter had been screened.

11   She is called a *mafua*, a "man [or woman] appointed to act as the spokesman of a district chief, to announce the kava" (see Churchward 1940a, 255).

12   Both district chiefs of the bridal couple choose an *'asu* to represent them in places of honor close to the couple's seat of mats. Usually this person is related to the chief.

13   See Malo (1975, 21). Churchward (1940a, 341) defined *utu* as "staple food (yams, etc.) brought straight in from one's garden." In the wedding context, the food has been cooked, in readiness for the wedding feast.

14   I use the word "screened" since this was the original intention when fine mats were used. With the use of fabric, the word *decorated* would be more appropriate.

15   The Christian ceremony *(a'lel ta)* usually happens some time after the *paag ri* ritual.

16   According to some elders, it was the custom for the groom's side to have their own clown as well, to entertain the crowd on this occasion and on the day before the wedding. However, this was an informal arrangement and subject to the availability of a funny woman on the day itself. On this

occasion, the funny man was from the groom's side and voluntarily took it upon himself to provide some entertainment. Though his services were appreciated, he had no formal powers. Unlike the "woman who plays at the wedding," he was not thanked with gifts of food and mats at the end of the festivities.

17   These chiefs were not dancing, but playing cards, which seemed to irritate the clown. Moreover, the funny woman who called out the suggestion was upstaging the clown by her boisterous behavior, and at the time it seemed as if the clown were reasserting her authority.

18   The clown called herself Princess Sakura to make her name sound exotic. Her real name is similar in pronunciation and spelling; this play on words was part of the humor.

19   See Werbner (1986, 242) for a similar interpretation in relation to Pakistani weddings.

20   To me throwing sand and hitting someone on the head seemed close to overstepping the boundaries of license; it appeared as if they were intended to hurt. In contrast to the others, this funny woman's behavior seemed more aggressive. It transpired that she was originally going to be the *hàn mane'àk su* but her children objected, saying she might do something that would embarrass them.

21   A karate expert was very much in the news earlier in the year for claiming to be the king of Rotuma, although he lived in New Zealand. That the funny woman was parodying the "king" is a possible reading of her actions.

22   This man exemplified the contemporary image of the stereotypical young male at social gatherings. In this instance, his drunken behavior was of the kind that the clown sometimes burlesques. (For example, I saw him rubbing his thighs sexily against the body of a female dancer.) The clown's act of ordering the drunken male to leave (being drunk posed a threat to the make-believe world of the clown's performance, which is dependent on the audience accepting the frame "This is play") seemed to me at the time to border on the breaking of illusion. For example, was she acting as any old woman would toward a drunken man in real life, or was she exercising her powers as the sacred clown, or both?

23   This verbal exchange is atypical, particularly between young men and mature women. The young men were stretching the boundaries of license, and so was the clown. Both the band boys and the clown showed a lack of restraint.

24   Earlier she had told the crowd she was afraid to force the white man to dance. Though she did not explain, it was probably because she was not sure whether he would obey her or not.

25   Gardiner (1898, 478) lent weight to this interpretation. Eason (1951, 12) supported Gardiner; on the other hand, Malo (1975, 14) claimed that the initial move was made by the boy's parents to the girl's.

Malo is correct insofar as present practice is concerned. According to MacGregor's informants, it was also the practice in the 1930s.

26   See Geertz (1973b) for an analysis of a similar funerary rite that went wrong.

27   The clown never attends the church service. Perhaps the clown of today feels instinctively that her domain is confined to the non-Christian rituals that take place at the arena in front of the temporary shelter.

28   When I was growing up, I used to perform in a club dance called *kạlo'a*—similar to the Tongan *kai lao*—in which a *mạnmạn heta* always featured.

29   According to the clown, she stayed behind in this instance because she is a close relative of the bride and not because of her role as clown.

30   Rotumans are like Samoans in that situations rather than principles tend to guide their behavior, which may appear to outsiders to be inconsistent, even contradictory (Shore 1977, 206).

31   The colors red and black are associated with ghosts.

32   This is an abridged version of a long interview that covered many different aspects of Rotuman culture, some of which are not relevant to clowning or to marriage.

6 Fine Mats and Spirits

1   This myth does not parallel actuality in every detail. For example, in this myth, there is reference to only one god, although we know that Polynesians had many gods. Although I have a much better idea of clowning, Polynesians, and Polynesian gods now than when I first started writing this book, to rework the original story is to destroy the unique circumstances that prompted the creation of this myth. I could not have written the myth if I had known the answers before I began. The plot of this story therefore remains in its original form.

2   *Lepa* leaves are taken from the *sa'a* tree and used for covering an earthen oven.

3   See Howard (1979), who summarized the information on *'atua* from various sources. However, he made no reference to *'Aitu* 'Gods'. The unpublished field notes of Hocart and MacGregor (Methodists) have some information on *'atua* and *'Aitu* that is not in the published literature. Catholics (a minority on the island) translate *'atua* as "gods."

4   MacGregor (1932) wrote that *tu'ura* means a shaman or one who can call the gods or a god. The gods enter the shaman's body and use his voice to communicate messages to people who seek his advice. *Ape'aitu* refers to one whom the gods visit only occasionally; for some people, both terms were synonymous. "Ape aitu seems to mean mat of the god"; "When the *tuura* felt the god had entered his body he went to the pile of mats and sat there. Then the family would question through the *tuura*."

5   See Russell (1942, 251). MacGregor also wrote, "If a rooster crowed

in front of one's house while facing it, it signified someone would die in the family. When a bird (*feere* [sic]) appears on the road, someone is about to appear."

6   See Churchward (1940a, 349), in which '*aitu* is defined as "god, object of worship; shark, stingray, or other creature regarded as the habitat of a god; God (*'Aitu)."*

7   See also Brigham (1906, 39–53), in which there is strong evidence to support this interpretation. According to Brigham, in Samoa, "the basket contained a sort of vicarious divinity, for on Hawaii a number of gods (e.g., Kukailimoku) were constructed of wickerwork, either plain or covered with feathers" (39). As well, Brigham wrote that the Samoan war god Ga'e fefe, who was a war god in some of the villages, was seen in a coconut-leaf basket. During a battle between the gods of Samoa and those of Tonga, "the former [Ga'e fefe] crouched about the trunks of the coconut trees; but Ga'e fefe hid in a coconut leaf basket and escaped while many others were killed. Hence the *basket* became a sign of the god, and no one would step on such a thing, supposing the god might be in it" (39–40). As in Rotuma, Samoans treat their fine mats with great reverence. Brigham recorded a legend of the origin of one of these Samoan mats (44–45) that suggests that fine mats were imbued with supernatural powers—"Lightning and thunder and hurricane were the omen of the mat" (45). Brigham also mentioned that on the completion of a fine mat, it was immersed in fresh water and then a feast was "provided by the hostess to celebrate the completion of her mat" (41). Of Hawaiian mats, Brigham implied that there were sacred rites but Christianity had caused their disappearance (53).

8   See Churchward (1939b) for a more detailed description of Rotuman religious beliefs. See also Howard 1979; Gardiner 1898; MacGregor 1932; Hocart 1913.

9   Christianity has lessened the belief in ghosts to some extent, but has not eradicated it completely. For instance, in December 1989, I was told recent stories by devout Methodists who claimed to have heard female ghosts laughing in the night as they went past a certain spot on the road on their motorbikes in the early hours of the morning. Women '*atua* are thought to often manifest themselves through laughter; in this case, laughter is a form of indirect aggression.

10   See also Romilly (1882) who reported how fearful Rotumans were of ghosts. He even described the ghost of a murdered man (Kemueli) that he saw with others. However, though the Rotumans believed the vision was indeed Kemueli's ghost—and Romilly's description suggests that he himself felt the same way—he still wrote: "I am not a believer of ghosts. I believe a natural explanation of the story to exist, but the reader, who has followed me thus far, must find it for himself, as I am unable to supply one" (82). Scribbled in pencil after the quote above (in the copy at Hamilton Library, University of Hawai'i at Mānoa), is the following: "You dum [sic]

English man. It is Kemueli's ghost. There is no need for any scientific explanation—"Seeing is Believing."

11 Known as Tagaloa in some parts of Polynesia.

12 Gardiner (1898, 467). Samoans hold a similar belief.

13 This view is reminiscent of the use of firecrackers by the Chinese.

14 The time taken to weave a fine mat depends on its size and the number of women working.

15 See Geertz (1973a, 448–449), who argued that the notion of a text should be extended beyond written material and cited Nietzsche and Freud in support.

16 *Mane'a* is a generic term for play. It could also mean to have illicit intercourse; it could be used to refer to an unmarried man or woman (literally, playing man or woman); or it could mean picnic, sports, games, or recreation of any kind. In this context, I think Churchward means *hàn mane'a* 'playing woman'.

17 Compare with Victoria Kneubuhl (1987, 171), who wrote that in Samoa *aitu* (the meaning is similar to *'atua* in Rotuma) are associated with chaos, wilderness, danger, and darkness, but are called on to permit the release of social tension.

18 My hypothesis is that male–female symbols, among others, were possibly woven into the patterns, to the accompaniment of chanting. Rotuman mats, like many others in the Pacific, have distinct patterns. Keller (1988) suggested that the patterns of woven West Futunan baskets symbolically represent social life and human continuity, as well as depicting activities such as eating, marriage, and sexual intercourse.

19 Bennett (1831, 476–477). See also Keller (1988); her bafflement about the origin of the word *uol* in West Futuna, referring to the crowning tassels of the baskets, is noteworthy. In Rotuma, the word *'alol* refers to the strands used in weaving; in this narrative *'Aeatos,* the kind man, tells the two children to find the *'alol* strands to weave their fishing net (in the Rotuman version, line 242, page 113). Today, the word is also used for the wool (instead of feathers) that women weave into the edges of their mats.

20 For me as a Rotuman, fine mats symbolize death and life in a vague sense, the former more than the latter. An *apei* is normally hidden when it is not displayed publicly, and is therefore associated with darkness and perhaps dead ancestors. A Rotuman will not carry an *apei* uncovered (unless it is for the specific purpose of publicly displaying it in a ritual context), or treat it in a way that would make it ordinary. For example, in a Fiji Arts Council Craft dinner in 1987, my sister, who brought an *apei* to be exhibited as part of a craft parade (and explanation), refused to put the fine mat on the cement floor, saying it had to be placed on top of another mat. She could not explain why. Also, *apei* on top of *päega* 'seats' are covered with cloth before people sit on them, at least in contemporary practice.

21 The headstone of a dead person is wrapped first in a fine mat and

then unveiled. Though no one seems to know why a fine mat should be used, the custom probably originated from the same idea—wrapping the fine mat around a headstone was akin to constraining a ghost (malevolent being) and transforming it into a benevolent being that does not wander around aimlessly.

22   Churchward (1940a, 327) simply wrote that it is a strong word of abuse.

23   For Rotumans, the opposition is between work and rest, not work and play. I am grateful to Alan Howard and Jan Rensel for this insight from their field notes.

24   Betty Inia, whom I interviewed in 1991, believes that the *apei* is "synonymous with virginity," and the women's behavior toward the men during a *sa'a* is a symbolic expression of their ambivalence toward men from the groom's side "for wanting to steal the virginity of their bride."

25   Rotumans think of ghosts as being either red (*'atua mi'e*) or black (*'atua kele*).

26   At the wedding of the case study, I counted at least twenty fine mats brought by the bride's kin.

27   Forbes (1875, no. 79: 227). Gardiner (1898, no. 462) mentioned a type of fine mat worn by chiefs that was "almost completely covered with the red feathers of the *arumea Myzomela chermesina* [small black bird with red breast]," Rotuma's only endemic species. The oldest and finest *apei* I have seen is owned by Ilisapeti Inia. According to her, this fine mat is more than a hundred years old. The weave is much finer than present-day mats, it is about four times larger, and red feathers are woven around the edges. Despite its age, it is still in excellent condition.

28   The ritual associated with defloration happens a few days after the wedding. In an interview with the groom of one of the weddings I observed in 1989, I was told that his first sexual encounter with the bride did not happen until all the festivities were over, which meant at least four days after the wedding day. His reason was that old women were always lying next to their bed—a pile of mats—at night. As a result, he and his bride were too embarrassed to consummate their marriage. Eason (1951, 13) wrote that "the couple were required to sleep together one or two nights under strict observation to prevent the consummation of the marriage." Was this a way of coercing the couple to learn the value of restraint in relation to extramarital liaisons? Eason's reasoning is unclear.

29   Eason (1951, 12) mentioned that "girls of a lower class usually had a screened room in the father's house," which suggests that the fine mats used for this ritual were perhaps for the purpose of screening off an area for privacy. Because the mats have been "played," they are potent.

30   According to Vafo'ou Jiare (in an interview) a sharp *'ipesi* 'wooden knife' made from *to'a* 'hardwood' was used in the past.

31   Eason (1951, 401) mentioned that a mat—presumably a fine mat— was the king's throne.

32   Ilisapeti Inia wrote in a letter to me in 1991 that in former times, the ritual clown tried her best to find a way to cause blood to be "spilled" from the heads of men belonging to the groom's side, particularly the namesake of the groom. This blood would compensate for the blood soon to be "spilled" during the bride's defloration.

33   See also Kaeppler, who wrote that objects of production in Polynesia are "manifestations of social relations" (1978, 246).

34   Gardiner (1898, 411–412) noted that fine mats of large size were generally worn by chiefs, and that fine mats were the proper dress for marriages, burials, and feasts.

35   Turner (1982b, 18) used the term *polysemous* to refer to symbols that "transmit their messages in a number of sensory codes simultaneously"; however, these messages remain in the realm of the unconscious. Compare Grotjahn (1957, 95–96).

36   See Melville (1876, 252) for the same practice in the Marquesas.

37   This ritual anticipates the virginity tests that were practiced in earlier days.

38   Eason (1951, 13) mentioned a water ceremony in which the bride and groom washed each other, and another in which young men who were related to the groom cut their foreheads with a stone axe until blood came out, perhaps as a way of reciprocating for the bride's blood to be shed during the sexual act. Eason's information on the first ceremony was from an English runaway sailor named William John. See also Bennett (1831, 473–482). For the second ceremony, see also Lucatt (1851, 160); and Allen (1895, 556–559), who reports the same incident.

39   It is important that wedding guests have more than enough to eat and plenty to take home. Rotumans often say that a wedding is good if they *'a ka rava* meaning that they were "defeated" by the food. Shore wrote that "sexual fecundity and agricultural abundance are linked [and that] food and sex are the two media of growth and prosperity" (1989, 141–142).

40   See Malo (1975) for an elaboration.

41   Turner also wrote that both structure and antistructure acted, in opposition or conjunction, "to enhance the understanding a society had of its own essential nature, its plural reflexivity" (1982b, 24).

42   Churchward defined *mana* as "supernatural, miraculous, possessed of or manifesting superhuman power of extraordinary efficacy" (1940a, 259).

43   Edward Sapir, cited in Turner (1982b, 24).

44   From the words of the song that Gardiner provided (1898, 465), a god called *Naragosou* (another name for Tagaroa Siria, who is believed to be the god of the winds, rain, and sun) was entreated to bring about a fruit-

ful season. See also Williamson (1924, 336), who reported that during annual rituals of increase, a libation of *kava* was dedicated to the dead *sạu* 'king'; the living *sạu* was required to eat of all the grasses on top of the hill where the dead kings of the island were buried, a symbolic act of submission before the dead ancestors.

45   The proper Samoan term is *poti*, which was a swear word in Rotuman when I was growing up. *Poki* is slang for penis today in Samoa.

46   See Muensterberger (1951, 381–382), who wrote that the aboriginals of the northern territory of Australia used sacred, life-giving sticks, which were in the custody of female ancestors only. These sticks "signified the sexual act, pregnancy and birth."

7 Woven Gods

1   Don C. Talayesva, cited in Simmons (1942, 190).
2   Moerenhout cited in Oliver (1974, 923–924).
3   Henry Rutz, personal communication, 1990.
4   Martin Martin, cited in Parman (1979, 31).
5   This is also supported by the evidence from Samoa and Hawai'i. See Appendix.

8 Epilogue: Being Rotuman

1   Anthropologists Jeannette Mageo (Samoa) and Kerry James (Tonga), in conversations with me, confirm my belief that fine mats in their respective fields of study were imbued with *mana* and were symbols of the gods. Also see Field (1991, 22), who writes "Queen Salote, in Kenneth Bain's 1967 book *The Friendly Islanders,* said the mat [Tongan *ta'ovala*] was first worshiped as "a symbol of the ancient gods." Helpful references in the published literature are sketchy: see Keller 1988; Brigham 1906.

2   For an overview of the way Pacific islanders divide history, see Hereniko 1994b.

3   This exhibition was held at the East-West Center from 14 December 1992 to 19 February 1993.

4   See Hereniko (1994a) for a paper on clowning as an indigenous form for critiquing the power structure in Polynesia. See also Sinavaiana 1992a, 1992b.

Appendix: Comparisons of Theory and Practice

1   This practice is called *fakawela*. Rotumans also shower dancers with talcum powder and douse them with perfume to show their appreciation.

2   Europeans and their practices are still satirized even today. See Sinavaiana 1992a, 1992b; Mageo 1992; Shore 1991. Also compare with Basso 1979; Lips 1966.

3   For court fools of Europe, see Billington 1984; Welsford 1966; Zijderveld 1982.

4   The literature on ritual clowning is vast. For reviews of this literature, see Mitchell 1992a; Sinavaiana 1992a; Hereniko 1992; Apte 1985. For practice and theory, see Handelman 1981; Hieb 1972; Makarius 1970; Leach 1966.

5   For examples, see Brockett 1979; Hartnoll 1968.

6   Erdoes and Fire (1971, 236). See also Cameron (1981, 89), where the granny in the story says, "our clowns were with us all the time, as important to the village as the chief, or the shaman, or the dancers, or the poets."

7   See Ellis 1834; Henry 1928; Oliver 1974.

8   See Oliver (1974, 913–914) for a summary.

9   For example, see Andersen (1969, 438); Henry (1928, 237–241).

10   For example, see Bligh (1792, 35), who described three male dancers who distorted the penis and testicles. Compare with Mitchell (1992b, 149), who reported carnival clowning in Wape society in which a Niyel initiate's wife's parents shame themselves by dancing naked; the father-in-law also "pulls back his penis's foreskin to reveal the glans as he cocks his head to one side." To me such behavior appears to be related to ideas of fertility in nature and among the people, although neither Bligh nor Mitchell interpreted it in this way.

11   See Henry 1893; 1894; 1913; 1928.

12   Ridgeway (1915, 350–352). See also Webster (1968, 168), who cited the Reverend Daniel Tyerman, an early missionary who, having noted that one of the *maraes* was occupied by the *arioi*, stated, "This building is famous for having been the rendezvous of the *Areois*. Here they celebrated their horrid excesses."

13   William Ellis, cited in Langdon (1975, 156).

14   Clunie and Ligairi (1983, 55). See also Luomala (1951) for a comparison with the Hawaiian *menehune*.

15   See Luomala (1984) in which she identifies seven kinds of *hula ki'i*, one of which does not use a screen or wooden puppets.

16   Counts and Counts 1992. They also reported clowning during rituals associated with a firstborn child.

17   Shore (1977, 318); Kneubuhl (1987, 167). Shameem (1978) reported that among Fiji Indians, only men (of low status) play the role of comedian in a dramatic retelling of an ancient myth on the night before a fire-walking ceremony.

18   Usually the defense is to be just as ridiculous as the puppets, and it is possible for the "victim" to turn the tables.

19   See Luomala (1973, 28–46). Luomala concluded that the movable images were strung and worn as necklaces in secular and religious processions and dances, as well as carried in the dancer's hands or arms.

20   See Luomala (1984, 71–138) for a detailed explanation of the functions briefly summarized here.

21   For different versions regarding the origin of 'Oro see Oliver (1974, 890–900). Oliver made no reference to Mahoui.

22   Victor Turner (1969, 176); see also Balandier (1970), who supported this argument.

23   Eco (1984, 6). See also Gluckman (1965, 109), who says that rites of reversal are "intended to preserve and strengthen the established order."

24   For a discussion on the unruly woman and social and political change in pre-nineteenth-century Europe, see Davis 1978. Davis also argued that topsy-turvy play had "much spillover into everyday 'serious' life and the effects there were sometimes disturbing and even novel" (172).

25   See Basso 1979; Jersey (1893, 253); Huntsman and Hooper (1975, 427); Stoller (1984, 180).

26   See Shore (1989) for a review of the literature on *mana* and its various connotations.

27   Bateson 1958. The Oroikava people of North Papua had complex dances in which masks were worn to represent fish and animal characters. Clowns, called *samuna,* often livened up the simple plots of these dances. In modern times, these clowns have tended to wear European trousers and coconut goggles. See Williams 1940; and Bier (1971, vii).

References

For a more comprehensive list of titles on clowning in Polynesia, see my PhD dissertation, Polynesian Clowns and Satirical Comedies, University of the South Pacific, Suva, 1990.

Aiavao, Tunumafono Apelu
    n.d.   Who's Playing Naked Now? Religion and Samoan Culture. *Pacific Perspective* 12(2): 8–10. Suva: South Pacific Social Sciences Association.

Allen, W.
    1895   *Rotuma: Report of Australian Association for Advancement of Science.* Sixth meeting. January.

Andersen, Johannes C.
    1969   *Myths and Legends of the Polynesians.* Rutland, VT: Charles E. Tuttle.

Angas, F. L. S.
    1866   *Polynesia: A Popular Description of the Islands of the Pacific.* London: Society for the Promotion of Christian Knowledge.

Anzaldúa, Gloria
    1987   *Borderlands/La Frontera: The New Mestiza.* San Francisco: spinsters/aunt lute.

Apte, Mahadev
    1983   Humor Research, Methodology, and Theory in Anthropology. In *Handbook on Humor Research,* edited by Paul E. McGhee and Jeffrey Goldstein, 183–212. New York: Springer-Verlag.
    1985   *Humor and Laughter: An Anthropological Approach.* Ithaca: Cornell University Press.

Arno, Andrew
    1992   *The World Is Talk: Conflict and Communication on a Fijian Island.* Norwood, NJ: Ablex.

Babcock, Barbara
1984   Arrange Me into Disorder: Fragments and Reflections on Ritual Clowning. In *Rite, Drama, Festival, Spectacle: Rehearsals toward a Theory of Cultural Performance,* edited by John J. MacAloon, 102–128. Philadelphia: Institute for the Study of Human Issues.

Bakhtin, Mikhail
1968   *Rabelais and His World,* translated by Helene Iswolsky. Cambridge, MA: Harvard University Press.

Balandier, Georges
1970   *Political Anthropology.* London: Allen Lane.

Barlow, Kathleen
1992   Dance When I Die! Context and Role in the Clowning of Murik Women. In Mitchell, ed 1992, 58–87.

Barthes, Roland
1986   *The Rustle of Language,* translated by Richard Howard. New York: Hill & Wang.

Basso, Keith
1979   *Portraits of "The White Man": Linguistics Play and Cultural Symbols among the Western Apache.* Cambridge: Cambridge University Press.

Bateson, Gregory
1958   *Naven: A Survey of the Problems Suggested by a Composite Picture of the Culture of a New Guinea Tribe Drawn from Three Points of View.* 2d ed. Stanford, CA: Stanford University Press.
1972   A Theory of Play and Fantasy. In *Steps to an Ecology of Mind,* 177–193. New York: Ballantine.

Bennett, George
1831   A Recent Visit to Several of the Polynesian Islands. *United Service Journal* 33: 198–202, 473–484.

Bier, Ulli, ed
1971   Introduction to *Five New Guinea Plays,* vii–ix. Port Moresby: Jacaranda Press.

Billington, Sandra
1984   *A Social History of the Fool.* New York: St. Martin's Press.

Bligh, William
1792   *A Voyage to the South Sea, . . . for the Purpose of Conveying the Breadfruit Tree to the West Indies, in [the] Ship Bounty. Including an Account of the Mutiny. . . . * Vol. 2. London: G. Nicol.

Brigham, William
1906   *Mat and Basket Weaving of the Ancient Hawaiians Described and Compared with the Basketry of the Other Islanders, with an Account of Hawaiian Nets and Nettings, by John F. G. Stokes.* Vol. 2.1. Honolulu: Bernice P. Bishop Museum.

Brockett, Oscar G.
1979   *The Theatre: An Introduction.* New York: Holt, Rinehart & Winston. First published 1964.

Cameron, Anne
1981   *Daughters of Copper Woman.* Vancouver: Press Gang Publishers.

Churchward, C. Maxwell
1937   Rotuman Legends. *Oceania* 8(2): 247–255.
1938a   Rotuman Legends. *Oceania* 8(3): 482–497.
1938b   Rotuman Legends. *Oceania* 9(1): 109–126.
1939a   Rotuman Legends. *Oceania* 9(3): 335–339.
1939b   Rotuman Legends. *Oceania* 9(4): 469–473.
1940a   *Rotuman Grammar and Dictionary.* Sydney: Methodist Church of Australasia, Department of Overseas Missions.
1940b   *Tales of a Lonely Island.* Oceania Monographs, 4.

Clifford, James
1988   *The Predicament of Culture: Twentieth Century Ethnography, Literature and Art.* Cambridge, MA: Harvard University Press.

Clifford, James, and George E. Marcus
1986   *Writing Culture: The Poetics and Politics of Ethnography.* Berkeley: University of California Press.

Clunie, Fergus, and Walesi Ligairi
1983   Traditional Fijian Spirit Masks and Spirit Masquers. *Domodomo: Fiji Museum Quarterly* 1: 46–71.

Counts, David, and Dorothy Counts
1992   Exaggeration and Reversal Clowning Among the Lusi Kaliai. In Mitchell, ed 1992, 88–103.

Cox, Harvey
1969   *The Feast of Fools.* New York: Harvard University Press.

Crumrine, N. Ross
1969   Capakoba, the Mayo Easter Ceremonial Impersonator: Explanations of Ritual Clowning. *Journal of the Scientific Study of Religion.* 8:1–22.

Csikszentmihalyi, Mihalyi, and Stith Bennet
1971   An Exploration Model of Play. *American Anthropologist* 73: 45–58.

Dana, Richard
1959   *Two Years Before the Mast.* New York: Bantam Books.

Davis, Natalie Zemon
1978   Women on Top: Symbolic Sexual Inversion and Political Disorder in Early Modern Europe. In *The Reversible World: Symbolic Inversion in Art and Society,* edited by Barbara Babcock, 147–190. Ithaca: Cornell University Press.

Deloria, Vine
1969   *Custer Died for Your Sins.* New York: Macmillan.

Eagleton, T.
1981   *Walter Benjamin: Towards a Revolutionary Criticism.* London: Verso.
Eason, W. J. E.
1951   *A Short History of Rotuma.* Suva: Government Printer.
Eco, Umberto
1984   The Frames of "Comic Freedom." In *Carnival,* edited by Thomas A. Sebeok, 1–9. Berlin: Mouton.
Elliot, R. C.
1960   *The Power of Satire.* Princeton: Princeton University Press.
Ellis, William (Surgeon)
1782   *An Authentic Narrative of a Voyage Performed by Captain Cook and Captain Clerke, . . . 1776 . . . 1780, Including the Unfortunate Death of Captain Cook.* Vol. 1. London: G. Robinson, J. Sewell, & J. Debrett.
Ellis, William
1834   *Polynesian Researches, During a Residence of Nearly Six Years in the South Sea Islands.* 2d ed. London: Fisher, Son & Jackson. First published 1829.
Emerson, Nathaniel
1965   *Unwritten Literature of Hawaii.* Vermont and Tokyo: Charles E. Tuttle.
Erdoes, Richard, and John Fire
1971   *Lame Deer: Seeker of Visions.* New York: Pocket Books.
Fergusson, Lady Alice
1928   Shakespeare amongst the Samoans. *Blackwoods Magazine* 224: 365–370.
Field, Michael
1991   Tradition Survives in Tongan Society. *Fiji Times,* 25 May.
Firth, Raymond
1967   *Tikopia Ritual and Belief.* Boston: Beacon Press.
Forbes, Litton
1875   *Two Years in Fiji.* London: Longmans, Green.
Fox, Steven J.
1980   Theoretical Implications for the Study of Interrelationships Between Ritual and Play. In Schwartzman, 51–57.
Gardiner, J.
1898   The Natives of Rotuma. *Journal of the Royal Anthropological Institute* 27: 396–435, 457–524.
Geertz, Clifford
1973a   Deep Play: Notes on the Balinese Cockfight. In *The Interpretation of Cultures: Selected Essays,* 412–453. New York: Basic Books.
1973b   Ritual and Social Change: A Javanese Example. In *The Interpretation of Cultures,* 142–169. New York: Basic Books.

Gell, Alfred
1975   *Metamorphosis of the Cassowaries: Umeda Society, Language and Ritual.* London: Athlone Press.

Gifford, Edward Winslow
1929   *Tongan Society Bulletin* 61(16): 126.

Gluckman, M.
1965   *Custom and Conflict in Africa.* Oxford: Blackwell.

Grotjahn, Martin
1957   *Beyond Laughter.* New York: McGraw-Hill.

Handelman, Don
1980   Rethinking Naven: Play and Identity. In *Play and Culture,* edited by Helen B. Schwartzman, West Point, NY: Leisure Press..

1981   The Ritual Clown: Attributes and Affinities. *Anthropos* 76: 321–370.

Hartnoll, Phyllis
1968   *A Concise History of the Theatre.* Norwich: Jarrold & Sons.

Hau'ofa, Epeli
1975   Anthropology and Pacific Islanders. *Oceania* 45: 283–289.

1983   *Tales of the Tikongs.* Auckland: Longman Paul.

1986   Interview. *Pacific Woman,* July–August, 18.

1987   *Kisses in the Nederends.* Auckland: Penguin.

1988   Oral Traditions and Writing. Paper presented at Pacific Writers' Conference, Commonwealth Institute, London, 28–31 October. Copy in University of the South Pacific library.

1989   Interviewed by Subramani. *Landfall* 43(1): 35–51.

Henry, Teuira
1893   A Raiatean Ceremony. *Journal of the Polynesian Society* 2: 105–108.

1894   The Birth of New Lands. *Journal of the Polynesian Society* 3: 136–139.

1913   The Oldest Great Tahitian Maraes and the Last One Built in Tahiti. *Journal of the Polynesian Society* 22: 25–27.

1928   *Ancient Tahiti.* Bulletin 48. Honolulu: Bernice P. Bishop Museum.

Hereniko, Vilsoni
1990a   The Clown's Story. In *After Narrative: The Pursuit of Reality and Fiction,* edited by Subramani, 223–229. Suva: University of the South Pacific.

1990b   Polynesian Clowns and Satirical Comedies. PhD dissertation, University of the South Pacific, Suva.

1991   Dance as a Reflection of Rotuman Culture. In *Rotuma: Split Island,* edited by Chris Plant, 120–142. Suva: South Pacific Social Sciences Association and Institute of Pacific Studies. First published 1977.

1992   When She Reigns Supreme: Clowning and Culture in Rotuman Weddings. In Mitchell, ed 1992, 167–191.

1994a   Clowning as Political Commentary: Polynesia, Then and Now. *The Contemporary Pacific: A Journal of Island Affairs* 6(1): 1–28.

1994b   Representations of Cultural Identities. In *Tides of History: The Pacific Islands in the Twentieth Century,* edited by K. R. Howe, Robert C. Kiste, and Brij V. Lal. Sydney: Allen & Unwin.

Hieb, Louis Albert

1972   *The Hopi Ritual Clown: Life As It Should Not Be.* Ann Arbor: University Microfilms.

Hiroa, Te Rangi (Peter H. Buck)

1932   *Ethnography of Manihiki and Rakahanga.* Bulletin 99. Honolulu: Bernice P. Bishop Museum.

Hocart, A. M.

1913   Field notes on Rotuma. In Turnbull Library, Wellington.

Honigman, J. J.

1942   An Interpretation of the Social-Psychological Functions of the Ritual Clown. *Character and Personality* 10: 220–226.

hooks, bell

1990a   Marginality as Site of Resistance. In *Out There: Marginalization and Contemporary Cultures,* edited by Russell Ferguson, Martha Gever, Trinh T. Minh-ha, and Cornel West, 337–340. New York: Museum of Contemporary Art and Massachusetts Institute of Technology.

1990b   Talking Back. In *Out There,* 341–343.

Howard, Alan

1960   Field notes in Howard's possession.

1963   Land, Activity Systems and Decision-Making Models in Rotuma. *Ethnology* 2: 407–440.

1970a   *Learning to Be Rotuman.* New York: Columbia Teachers College Press.

1970b   Some Implications of Dominant Kinship Relationships in Fiji and Rotuma. In *Kinship and Culture,* edited by Francis Hsu, 96–105. Chicago: Aldine.

1979   The Power to Heal in Colonial Rotuma. *Journal of the Polynesian Society* 88(3): 243–275.

1985   History, Myth and Polynesian Chieftainship: The Case of Rotuman Kings. *Transformations of Polynesian Culture* 45: 39–77.

1986   Cannibal Chiefs and the Charter for Rebellion in Rotuman Myth. *Pacific Studies* 10: 1–27.

1989   Field notes in Howard's possession.

1990   Dispute Management in Rotuma. *Journal of Anthropological Research* 4: 263–292.

1992   Symbols of Power and the Politics of Impotence. *Pacific Studies* 15(4): 83–116.

n.d.   Youth in Rotuma: Then and Now. Manuscript.

Huntsman, Judith, and Antony Hooper

1975   Male and Female in Tokelau Culture. *Journal of the Polynesian Society* 84(4): 415–430.

Irava, Ieli

1977a   History, Superstition and Religion. In *Rotuma: Split Island,* edited by Chris Plant, 7–15. Suva: Institute of Pacific Studies, University of the South Pacific. Reprinted 1991 in *Rotuma: Hanuạ Pumue, Rotuma: Precious Land.*

1977b   Kinship, Reciprocity and Society. In *Rotuma: Split Island,* 24–61.

Jacobsen, [initials unknown]

n.d.   Field notes. Copy in library of University of the South Pacific.

Jersey, M. E.

1893   Three Weeks in Samoa. *19th Century Review,* January, 249–254.

Kaeppler, Adrienne

1978   Exchange Patterns in Goods and Spouses: Fiji, Tonga and Samoa. *Mankind* 11: 246–252.

1989   Art and Aesthetics. In *Developments in Polynesian Ethnology,* edited by Alan Howard and Robert Borofsky, 211–240. Honolulu: University of Hawaii Press.

Keller, Janet

1988   Woven World: Neotraditional Symbols of Unity in Vanuatu. *Mankind* 18(1): 1–12.

Kneubuhl, John

1993   Interviewed by Vilsoni Hereniko. *Mānoa* 5(1): 99–105.

Kneubuhl, Victoria

1987   Traditional Performance in Samoan Culture: Two Forms. *Asian Theatre Journal* 4: 166–176.

Kristeva, Julia

1980   *Desire in Language: A Semiotic Approach to Literature and Art.* New York: Columbia University Press.

Langdon, Robert

1975   *The Lost Caravel.* Sydney: Pacific Publications.

Langer, Suzanne

1965   The Comic Rhythm. *Comedy: Meaning and Form.* San Francisco: Chandler.

Laski, Vera

1958   *Seeking Life.* Philadelphia: American Folklore.

Leach, E. R.

1966   Ritualization in Man in Relation to Conceptual and Social Development. *Philosophical Transactions of the Royal Society of London* 251: 403–408.

Levin, Harry
1966   *Refractions: Essays in Comparative Literature.* New York: Oxford University Press.

Lips, J. E.
1966   *The Savage Hits Back,* translated by Vincent Benson. New Hyde Park: University Books.

Lucatt, Edward
1851   *Rovings in the Pacific, 1837–49 . . . by a Merchant Long Resident in Tahiti.* London: Brown, Green & Longmans.

Luomala, Katherine
1951   *The Menehune of Polynesia and Other Mythical Little People of Oceania.* Honolulu: Bernice P. Bishop Museum.
1973   Moving and Movable Images in Easter Island Custom and Myth. *Journal of the Polynesian Society* 82: 28–46.
1984   *Hula Ki'i: Hawaiian Puppetry.* Honolulu: Institute of Polynesian Studies.

MacGregor, Gordon
1932   Field notes on Rotuma. Honolulu: Bernice P. Bishop Museum.

Macintyre, Martha
1992   Reflections of an Anthropologist Who Mistook Her Husband for a Yam: Female Comedy on Tubetube. In Mitchell, ed 1992, 130–144.

Mageo, Jeannette
1992   Continuity and Shape-Shifting in the Cultural Function of Samoan Spirits. Paper presented at meeting of Association of Social Anthropologists in Oceania, New Orleans.

Makarius, Laura
1970   Ritual Clowns and Symbolical Behaviour. *Diogenes* 69: 44–73.

Malo, Tiu
1975   *Rotuman Marriage.* Suva: South Pacific Social Sciences Association.

Mead, George H.
1934   *Mind, Self, and Society.* Chicago: University of Chicago Press.

Melville, Herman
1876   *Typee.* New York: Harper.

Mitchell, William
1992a   Introduction: Mother Folly in the Islands. In Mitchell, ed 1992, 3–57.
1992b   Horrific Humor and Festal Farce: Carnival Clowning in Wape Society. In Mitchell, ed 1992, 145–166.

Mitchell, William, ed
1992   *Clowning as Critical Practice: Performance Humor in the South Pacific.* Pittsburgh: University of Pittsburgh Press.

Mosko, Mark S.
1992   Clowning with Food: Mortuary Humor and Social Reproduction among the North Mekeo. In Mitchell, ed 1992, 104–129.
Muensterberger, Warner
1951   Roots of Primitive Art. In *Psychoanalysis and Culture,* edited by George Wilbur and Warner Muensterberger, 371–389. New York: International University Press.
Nietzsche, Friedrich
1969   *On the Genealogy of Morals and Ecce Homo.* New York: Vintage Books.
Norbeck, Edward
1969   Human Play and Its Cultural Expression. *Humanitas* 5: 43–55.
1971   Man at Play. *Natural History: Special Supplement* (December): 48.
1976   Religion and Human Play. In *The Realm of the Extra Human: Agents and Audiences,* edited by Agehananda Bharati, 95–104. The Hague: Mouton.
1979   Rites of Reversal of North American Indians as Forms of Play. In Norbeck and Farrer, eds 1979, 51–66.
Norbeck, Edward, and C. R. Farrer, eds
1979   *Forms of Play of Native North Americans.* Proceedings of the American Ethnological Society, 1977. St. Paul: West Publishing.
Oliver, Douglas L.
1974   *Ancient Tahitian Society.* 3 vols. Honolulu: University Press of Hawaii.
Parman, Susan
1979   An Evolutionary Theory of Dreaming and Play. In Norbeck and Farrer, eds 1979, 17–34.
Rensel, Janet
1989   Field notes in Rensel's possession.
1991   Housing and Social Relationships on Rotuma. In *Rotuma: Hanua Pumue, Rotuma: Precious Land,* edited by Chris Plant, 185–203. Suva: Institute of Pacific Studies, University of the South Pacific.
Rensel, Janet, and Alan Howard
1993   The Place of Disabled Persons in Rotuman Society. Paper presented at Symposium on Culture and Disability in the Pacific, at meeting of Association for Social Anthropologists in Oceania, Kona, Hawai'i, March.
Ridgeway, William
1915   *Dramas and Dramatic Dances of Non-European Races in Special Reference to the Origin of Greek Tragedy with an Appendix on the Origin of Greek Comedy.* Cambridge: Cambridge University Press.

Romilly, Hugh Hastings
    1882   *A True Story of the Western Pacific in 1879–80*. London: Long-
            mans, Green.
Rosaldo, Renato
    1989   *Culture and Truth: The Remaking of Social Analysis*. Boston: Bea-
            con Press.
Russell, W. E.
    1942   Rotuma: Its History, Traditions, and Customs. *Journal of the
            Polynesian Society* 51: 229–255.
Sahlins, Marshall
    1981   *Historical Metaphors and Mythical Realities*. ASAO Special Publi-
            cation 1. Ann Arbor: University of Michigan Press.
    1993   *University of the South Pacific Bulletin* 26 (6, 16 March): 1–2.
Schwartzman, Helen B., ed
    1980   *Play and Culture*. Proceedings of the Association for the
            Anthropological Study of Play. West Point, NY: Leisure
            Press.
Shameem, Shaista
    1978   The Performance of an Ancient Drama on the Night
            Before the Firewalking Ceremony at the Howell Road
            Temple, Suva. In *Essays on Pacific Literature,* edited by
            Ruth Finnegan and Raymond Pillai, 50–60. Suva: Fiji
            Museum.
Shore, Bradd
    1977   A Samoan Theory of Action: Social Control and Social Order
            in a Polynesian Paradox. PhD dissertation, University of
            Chicago.
    1978   Ghosts and Government: A Structural Analysis of Alterna-
            tive Institutions for Conflict Management in Samoa. *Man* 13:
            175–199.
    1989   Mana and Tapu. In *Developments in Polynesian Ethnology,* edited
            by Alan Howard and Robert Borofsky, 137–173. Honolulu:
            University of Hawai'i Press.
    1991   The Absurd Side of Power in Samoa. Paper presented in
            honor of Sir Raymond Firth on the occasion of his 90th birth-
            day, London, December. Forthcoming.
Shutler, Richard Jr., and Jamie S. Evrard
    1991   Rotuma: A Case of Archaeology Documenting the Rotuman
            Oral Tradition of the First Tongan Landing. *Man and Culture
            in Oceania* 7: 133–137.
Simmons, Leo W., ed
    1942   *Sun Chief: The Autobiography of a Hopi Indian*. London: Institute
            of Human Relations.

Sinavaiana, Caroline
1992a   Traditional Comic Theater in Samoa: A Holographic View. PhD dissertation, University of Hawai'i at Mānoa.
1992b   Where the Spirits Laugh Last: Comic Theatre in Samoa. In Mitchell, ed 1992, 192–218.

Sloan, Donald
1941   *Polynesian Paradise: An Elaborated Travel Journal Based on Ethnological Facts.* London: Robert Hale.

Spicer, E. H.
1954   *Potam, A Yaqui Village in Sonora.* Memoir 77. Menasha, WI: American Anthropological Association.

Stair, John B.
1983   *Old Samoa.* Papakura, NZ: R. McMillan. First published c. 1897.

Stallybrass, Peter, and Allon White
1986   *The Poetics and Politics of Transgression.* London: Methuen.

Stoller, Paul
1984   Horrific Comedy: Cultural Resistance and the Hauka Movement in Niger. *Ethos* 12(2): 180.

Subramani
1985   *South Pacific Literature: From Myth to Fabulation.* Suva: Institute of Pacific Studies in association with Fiji Centre of University of the South Pacific. Revised edition, 1992.

Thaman, Konai
1974   *You, the Choice of My Parents.* Suva: Mana Publications.
1981   *Langakali.* Suva: Mana Publications.
1987   *Hingano.* Suva: Mana Publications.

Thompson, Basil
1915   Voyage of HMS *Pandora.* London: Francis Edwards.

Thorogood, Bernard
1960   *Not Quite Paradise.* London: London Missionary Society.

Turnbull, Colin
1990   Liminality: A Synthesis of Subjective and Objective Experience. In *By Means of Performance: Intercultural Studies of Theatre and Ritual,* edited by Richard Schechner and Willa Appel, 50–81. Cambridge: Cambridge University Press.

Turner, George
1861   *Nineteen Years in Polynesia: Missionary Life, Travels and Researches in the Islands of the Pacific.* London: John Snow.

Turner, Victor
1969   *The Ritual Process: Structure and Anti-Structure.* Chicago: Aldine.
1982a   *From Ritual to Theatre: The Human Seriousness of Play.* New York: Performing Arts Journal Publications.

1982b   Introduction to *Celebration: Studies in Festivity and Ritual,* edited by Victor Turner, Washington, DC: Smithsonian Institution Press.

1984   Liminality and Performance Genres. In *Rite, Drama, Festival, Spectacle: Rehearsals toward a Theory of Cultural Performance,* edited by John J. MacAloon, 19–41. Philadelphia: Institute for the Study of Human Issues.

Voegelin, Erminie
1938   Tübatalabal Ethnography. *Berkeley Anthropological Records* 2(1): 55–56.

Webster, Hutton
1968   *Primitive Secret Societies: A Study in Early Politics and Religion.* 2d ed. First published 1908. New York: Octagon Books.

Welsford, Enid
1966   *The Fool: His Social and Literary History.* Gloucester, MA: Peter Smith.

Wendt, Albert
1976   Towards a New Oceania. *Mana* 1(1): 49–69.
1977   *Pouliuli.* Auckland: Longman Paul.
1979   *Leaves of the Banyan Tree.* Auckland: Longman Paul.
1980   Introduction to *Lali: A Pacific Anthology,* edited by Albert Wendt, xiii–xix. Auckland: Longman Paul.
1987   Novelists and Historians and the Art of Remembering. In *Class and Culture in the South Pacific,* edited by Antony Hooper, Steve Britton, Ron Crocombe, Judith Huntsman, and Cluny Macpherson, 78–91. Suva: Institute of Pacific Studies.

Werbner, Pnina
1986   The Virgin and the Clown: Ritual Elaboration in Pakistani Migrants' Weddings. *Man* 21(2): 227–250.

West, Cornel
1990   The New Cultural Politics of Difference. In *Out There: Marginalization and Contemporary Cultures,* edited by Russell Fergusson, Martha Gever, Trinh T. Minh-ha, and Cornel West, 19–36. New York: New Museum of Contemporary Art and Massachusetts Institute of Technology.

White, Allon
1982   Pigs and Pierrots: The Politics of Transgression in Modern Fiction. *Raritan* 2(2): 51–70.

White, Geoffrey M.
1991   *Identity Through History: Living Stories in a Solomon Islands Society.* Cambridge: Cambridge University Press.

Williams, F. E.
1940   *Drama of Orokolo.* Oxford: Clarendon Press.

Williamson, Robert W.
  1924   *The Social and Political Systems of Central Polynesia.* Vol. 3. Cambridge: Cambridge University Press.
Wood, C. F.
  1875   *A Yachting Cruise.* London: Henry King.
Zijderveld, Anton
  1982   *Reality in a Looking Glass: Rationality Through an Analysis of Traditional Folly.* London: Routledge & Kegan Paul.

Index

About the Author

Vilsoni Hereniko was born on Rotuma but has lived and studied in Fiji, England, and Hawai'i. He is a playwright and scholar who teaches Pacific literature at the University of Hawai'i. The youngest of eleven children, he is also a "gifted clown" and storyteller.

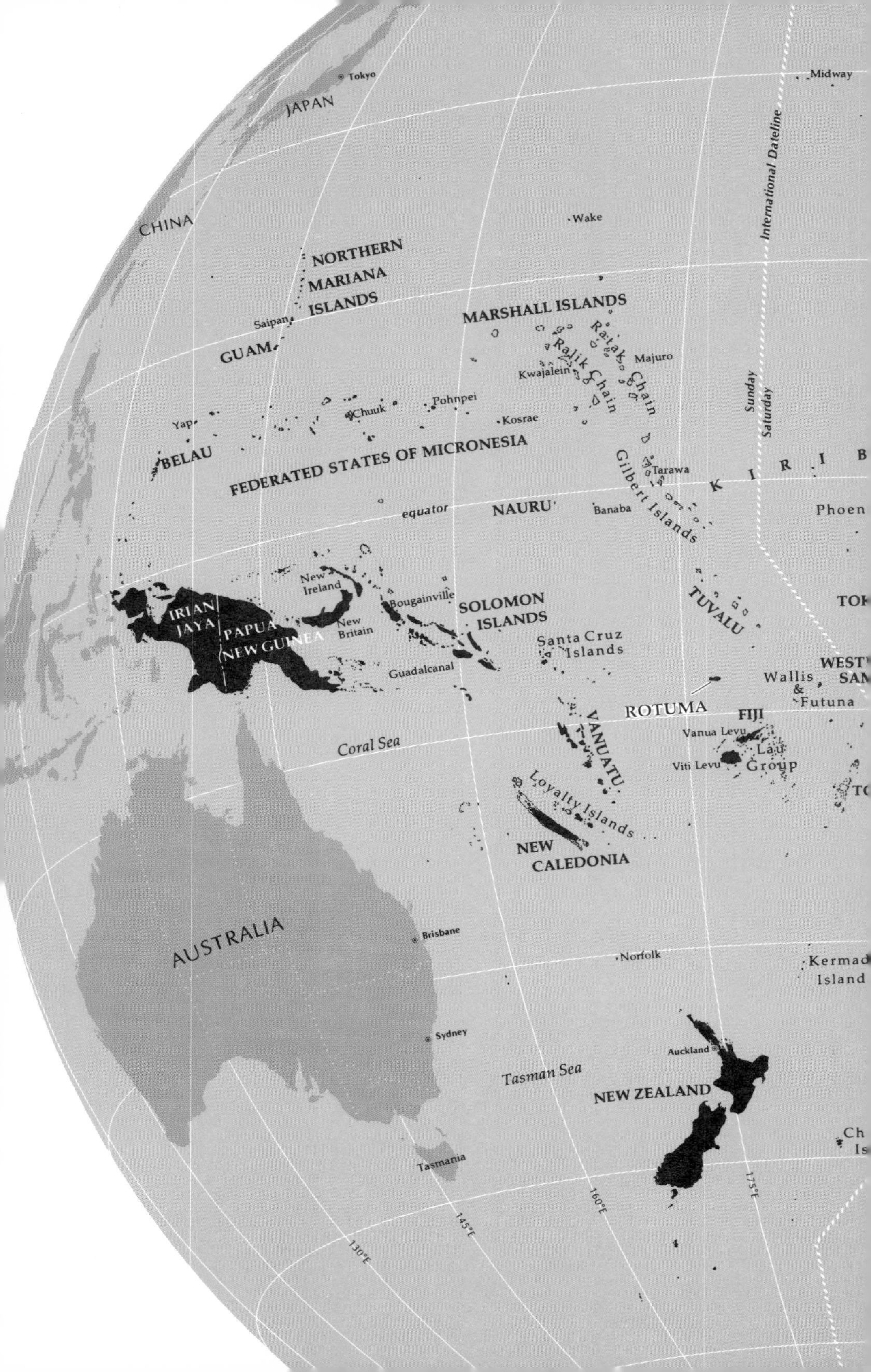
Tokyo
JAPAN
Midway
International Dateline
CHINA
Wake
NORTHERN MARIANA ISLANDS
Saipan
GUAM
MARSHALL ISLANDS
Ratak Chain
Ralik Chain
Majuro
Kwajalein
Yap
Chuuk
Pohnpei
Kosrae
Sunday
Saturday
BELAU
FEDERATED STATES OF MICRONESIA
Gilbert Islands
Tarawa
K I R I B
equator
NAURU
Banaba
Phoen
New Ireland
IRIAN JAYA
PAPUA NEW GUINEA
New Britain
Bougainville
SOLOMON ISLANDS
Guadalcanal
Santa Cruz Islands
TUVALU
TOK
WEST SAM
Wallis & Futuna
ROTUMA
FIJI
Vanua Levu
Viti Levu
Lau Group
Coral Sea
VANUATU
Loyalty Islands
NEW CALEDONIA
AUSTRALIA
Brisbane
Norfolk
Kermad Island
Sydney
Auckland
Tasman Sea
NEW ZEALAND
Tasmania
130°E
145°E
160°E
175°E